LONGING FOR THE GOOD LIFE

T&T Clark Enquiries in Theological Ethics

Series editors
Brian Brock
Susan F. Parsons

LONGING FOR THE GOOD LIFE

Virtue Ethics after Protestantism

Pieter Vos

LONDON • NEW YORK • OXFORD • NEW DELHI • SYDNEY

T&T CLARK
Bloomsbury Publishing Plc
50 Bedford Square, London, WC1B 3DP, UK
1385 Broadway, New York, NY 10018, USA
29 Earlsfort Terrace, Dublin 2, Ireland

BLOOMSBURY, T&T CLARK and the T&T Clark logo are trademarks of
Bloomsbury Publishing Plc

First published in Great Britain 2020
This paperback edition published in 2022

Copyright © Pieter Vos, 2020

Pieter Vos has asserted his right under the Copyright, Designs and Patents Act, 1988,
to be identified as Author of this work.

For legal purposes the Acknowledgments on p. x constitute an extension of
this copyright page.

All rights reserved. No part of this publication may be reproduced or transmitted in
any form or by any means, electronic or mechanical, including photocopying, recording,
or any information storage or retrieval system, without prior permission in writing
from the publishers.

Bloomsbury Publishing Plc does not have any control over, or responsibility for, any third-
party websites referred to or in this book. All internet addresses given in this book were
correct at the time of going to press. The author and publisher regret any inconvenience
caused if addresses have changed or sites have ceased to exist, but can accept no
responsibility for any such changes.

A catalogue record for this book is available from the British Library.

A catalog record for this book is available from the Library of Congress.

ISBN: HB: 978-0-5676-9507-9
PB: 978-0-5676-9683-0
ePDF: 978-0-5676-9508-6
eBook: 978-0-5676-9510-9

Typeset by Deanta Global Publishing Services, Chennai, India

To find out more about our authors and books visit www.bloomsbury.com
and sign up for our newsletters.

For my daughter Emma Vos

CONTENTS

Preface	viii
Acknowledgments	x
List of Abbreviations	xi
INTRODUCTION	1
Chapter 1 SOURCES OF THE GOOD LIFE	19
Chapter 2 CHALLENGING EUDAIMONISM	41
Chapter 3 CALVINISM AND THE BREAKDOWN OF TELEOLOGY	63
Chapter 4 RETRIEVING REFORMED SCHOLASTIC VIRTUE ETHICS	85
Chapter 5 CHARACTER FORMATION AS KIERKEGAARDIAN EDIFICATION	109
Chapter 6 PUTTING ON CHRIST	131
Chapter 7 THE FRAILTY OF HUMAN VIRTUE	151
Chapter 8 THE SANCTIFICATION OF ORDINARY LIFE	171
Bibliography	193
Index	205

PREFACE

This book is the result of research that has been conducted in various contexts and with the support of a number of people and institutions. In a sense, the idea for the project goes back to the chair of moral education (lectorate) that I held until 2012 at VIAA University of Applied Sciences, Zwolle. The aim of this lectorate was primarily educational and pedagogical-philosophical, but, given VIAA's Reformed background, discussions I conducted at the time with colleagues of my multidisciplinary team (*kenniskring*) regularly circled around the status of virtue and the virtues from a Protestant theological perspective. Later, the Protestant Theological University, where I currently work, offered the perfect conditions for delving more deeply into these matters, not only by granting me two sabbaticals, but also by being an excellent community of theological research and education. I am grateful to the members of the research group Beliefs and its leaders over the years—Gerrit de Kruijf, who passed away in 2013 at the age of sixty, Mechteld Jansen, now the university's president, Frits de Lange, and Benno van der Toren—for their support. Meanwhile this project fits well into one of the two new research foci of the Protestant Theological University: Mediating Good Life. I would like to thank the colleagues of the Ethics Colloquium and in particular the Moral Compass Project, to which my project is closely related and which formed the stimulating context of its final stage: Rob Compaijen, Petruschka Schaafsma, Theo Boer, Stef Groenewoud, Klaas-Willem de Jong, Dominique Klamer, and Margriet Zwart, under the inspiring leadership of Maarten Wisse, who shows what it means to be a virtuous leader. Several of them provided me with excellent feedback on earlier versions of my work. I am grateful to my students, who raised good questions about virtue ethics and Protestant theology, and to numerous scholars from all parts of the world for illuminating discussions about aspects of this book during annual meetings of societies of ethics, working groups of theological and philosophical ethics, Kierkegaard seminars, and conferences of the International Reformed Theological Institute.

Parts of this book have been realized thanks to the research grant from the Beacon Project and the Templeton Religion Trust that I received in the academic year of 2016/2017. I would like to thank the project leaders William Fleeson, Michael Furr, and especially Christian Miller and Angela Knobel, as well as all other scholars who participated in this project, for their support and helpful feedback. I am also grateful to several anonymous reviewers for their excellent comments, Anthony Runia for his language editing, Anna Turton and Veerle Van Steenhuyse from Bloomsbury T&T Clark for their publishing work, and Brian Brock and Susan Parsons for accepting this book in the series Enquiries in Theological Ethics.

This book is dedicated to my youngest daughter, Emma. Though as a twelve-year-old Dutch girl she cannot read it, I trust that one day she can (and perhaps will). More importantly, this dedication expresses that this book, though primarily an academic piece of work, is not disconnected from ordinary life, such as that of a family, in which we try, with ups and downs, to cultivate the virtues and to live the good life with and for others. I thank Trijnie, Thomas, Maartje, and Emma for their patience and humor, and for being the loving community that is home. In the awareness that the good life is something we long for, without being able to realize it in its fullness or by our own power alone, I hope that this book will contribute not only to the understanding of the good life, but also to staying open to the gift of its often surprising, graceful flourishing.

ACKNOWLEDGMENTS

Portions of this book are revisions of previously published texts. I am grateful for permission to republish four (reworked) articles.

- Chapter 3 is a reworked and extended version of Pieter Vos, "Breakdown of the Teleological View of Life? Investigating Law, *Telos* and Virtue in Calvinistic Ethics," *Journal of Reformed Theology* 9/2 (2015), 131–47.
- Chapter 5 was previously published as: Pieter Vos, "'A Human Being's Highest Perfection': The Grammar and Vocabulary of Virtue in Kierkegaard's Upbuilding Discourses," *Faith and Philosophy* 33/3 (2016), 311–32.
- Chapter 6 is a slightly reworked version of Pieter Vos, "Neither Hypocrisy Nor Replication: A Protestant Account of Imitating Christ as Moral Exemplar," *International Journal of Systematic Theology* 19/3 (2017), 271–86, copyright Wiley, https://onlinelibrary.wiley.com/doi/abs/10.1111/ijst.12223.
- Parts of Chapter 8 are derived from my article, "Learning from Exemplars: Emulation, Character Formation and the Complexities of Ordinary Life," *Journal of Beliefs and Values* 39/1 (2018), 17–28, copyright Taylor & Francis, available online: https://www.tandfonline.com/doi/abs/10.1080/13617672.2017.1393295.

Parts of this book, in particular Chapters 6, 7, and 8, were made possible through the support of a grant from the Beacon Project at Wake Forest University and the Templeton Religion Trust. The opinions expressed in this book are those of the author and do not necessarily reflect the views of the Beacon Project, Wake Forest University, or the Templeton Religion Trust.

ABBREVIATIONS

CO   *Ioannis Calvini opera quae supersunt omnia*, Guilielmus Baum, August E. Cunitz and Eduard W. E. Reuss (eds.), *Corpus Reformatorum*, vols. 29–87. Halle: Schwetschke, 1863–1900.

CR   *Corpus Reformatorum*. Edited by Karl Gottlieb Bretschneider a.o., 101 vols. Halle: Schwetschke, 1834–1860.

DBW   *Dietrich Bonhoeffer Werke*, 16 vols. Gütersloh: Kaiser, 1987–2005.

EN   Aristotle, *Ethica Nicomachea*. Unless indicated otherwise, quotations are from Loeb Classical Library edition.

Ep.   Augustine, *Epistulae*. Unless indicated otherwise, quotations in English are from the Atkins and Dodaro translation in Augustine, *Political Writings*.

Inst.   John Calvin, *Institutio Christianae religionis* (ed. 1559). Unless indicated otherwise, English quotations are from the McNeill edition.

JN   *Kierkegaard's Journals and Notebooks*. Edited by Bruce H. Kirmmse and K. Brian Söderquist, 11 vols. Princeton: Princeton University Press, 2010–2020.

LW   *Luther's Works*, 55 vols. St. Louis/Minneapolis: Concordia Publishing House/Fortress Press, 1957–1986.

PL   *Patrologiae cursus completus: Series Latina*, 221 vols. Edited by Jacques Paul Migne, Paris, 1844–1855, http://www.documentacatholicaomnia.eu.

SKS   *Søren Kierkegaards Skrifter*, 28 vols. København: G.E.C. Gads Forlag, 1997–2013.

ST   Thomas Aquinas, *Summa Theologica*. References in translation are to the Benziger Bros. edition.

WA   *Martin Luthers Werke*, 120 vols. Weimar: Böhlaus, 1883–1961.

INTRODUCTION

Already in 1947, decades before the revival of virtue ethics in the 1980s, Paul Ramsey made the following challenging statement:

> Distinctively Christian elements in the theories of virtue given by St. Augustine and St. Thomas, when corrected from within and by reference to the New Testament, display surprisingly similarity to the insights of the Reformation. This similarity in turn suggests the possibility and desirability of developing a theory of virtue within Protestant theological ethics.[1]

This book can be seen as an attempt to take up the challenge contained in this statement, albeit in a somewhat different way than Ramsey proposes. My aim is not so much to develop a theory of virtue within a Protestant ethical framework and from a reading of the New Testament, but rather to investigate how Protestantism and Protestant theology relate to the long and multifaceted tradition of virtue ethics and may contribute to the development of a viable contemporary virtue ethics. In fact, one of my aims is to demonstrate that Protestantism has never abandoned virtue ethics at all. Let me start by explaining how I enter this field of inquiry and how my approach is related to others.

Virtue Ethics' Multifaceted Tradition: A Grammatical Approach

In my approach it is presupposed that virtue ethics does not consist of one univocal tradition that was once and for all established by Aristotle and completed by Aquinas

---

1. Paul Ramsey, "A Theory of Virtue According to the Principles of the Reformation," *The Journal of Religion* 27/3 (1947), 178-96, republished in his *Basic Christian Ethics* (Louisville: John Knox Press, [1950] 1993), 191-233, quote from 192-3. In the Netherlands, a similar attempt was made in the 1950s by Gerrit Brillenburg Wurth, *Eerherstel van de deugd* [Rehabilitation of virtue] (Kampen: Kok, 1958), which is inspired by Max Scheler's plea *Zur Rehabilitierung der Tugend* of 1913 (in Max Scheler, *Abhandlungen und Aufsätze*, 2 Bdn (Leipzig: Verlag der weissen Bücher, 1915), Bd. 1, 1-38).

as its prime Christian representative, as has often been assumed.² Throughout history, virtue ethics rather has developed in a wide variety of ways. It may be true that virtue ethics has its inception in ancient Greek philosophy,³ Plato, Aristotle, the Stoics, and the Epicureans in particular, but significant differences remain not only between but also within classical, medieval, modern, and contemporary understandings of virtue ethics. Virtue ethics does not consist of a homogeneous framework of fixed concepts but has developed in various ways throughout time and continuously transforms under historical conditions. Furthermore, neither is virtue ethics just about one deliberative question ('what would the virtuous person do?') nor can it be reduced to just a systematic set of concepts that counts as an alternative to other moral theories, but is an approach that allows to have a variety of ethical thoughts covering a range of moral questions, such as what does it mean to live a good life, which dispositions are virtues, what does it mean to see the world from the perspective of virtue?⁴

Yet, all this does not mean that there are no commonalities between the varied virtue ethical accounts and representatives. Otherwise it would be meaningless to speak of 'virtue ethics' at all. There are at least significant 'family resemblances,' as Ludwig Wittgenstein would say, between the varieties of virtue ethics.⁵ Rather than approaching virtue ethics from a univocal definition that includes all variations, I propose to conceive it in terms of a particular *grammar*, that is, in Wittgensteinian terms, a kind of internal conceptual order that is characteristic of virtue ethical 'language.'

Following this grammatical approach, we can say that the grammar of virtue ethics is defined by the kind of answers that are given to three questions in particular that are generally speaking at stake in ethics and are recognizable as defining questions in the various strands of virtue ethics: What is (the) good? What ought to be done? How do we know the good?⁶ Following the general structure of

---

2. Although Alasdair MacIntyre acknowledges the situatedness of all historical enquiry and his own 'modern' understanding of the tradition of virtue ethics, in his "Prologue" to the third edition of *After Virtue: A Study in Moral Theory* (Notre Dame: University of Notre Dame Press, [1981] 2007), ix–xvi, he regards Aristotle and Aquinas as virtue ethics' most important representatives.

3. One could also think of Eastern philosophy, such as Confucianism, which seemingly contains virtue ethical elements, but I leave this out of consideration.

4. Cf. Timothy Chappell, "Virtue Ethics in the Twentieth Century," in Daniel C. Russell (ed.), *The Cambridge Companion to Virtue Ethics* (Cambridge: Cambridge University Press, 2013), 168–9.

5. See, for example, Ludwig Wittgenstein, *Philosophical Investigations* (London: Blackwell, [1953] 2001), § 67.

6. Paul van Tongeren, *Leven is een kunst: Over morele ervaring, deugdethiek en levenskunst* [Life is an art: On moral experience, virtue ethics and art of living] (Zoetermeer: Klement/Pelckmans, 2012 (trans. *The Art of Living Well: Moral Experience and Virtue Ethics* (London: Bloomsbury, forthcoming)), 101.

these basic questions, we can say that virtue ethics answers the *first* question in terms of *happiness*, blessedness or human flourishing (εὐδαιμονία or *beatitudo*), which is taken as the τέλος of life, that is, the good (τὸ ἀγαθόν or *bonum*) that makes life indeed a good life. Although there is no agreement on what precisely constitutes such a good and flourishing life, whether it be honor, pleasure, the common good, the contemplation of God, or something else, yet the answer is given in such teleological terms. The precise answer depends partly on the ethos of the particular time and culture in which the answer is given. The *second* question is in one way or another answered by defining moral acting as acting from *virtue* (ἀρετή or *virtus*), be it understood as an underlying *habitus*, stable disposition, character trait, or perfection of the soul, either acquired by habituation or received as a (divine) gift. In any case, the question what we ought to do in one way or another is related to the sort of persons we ought to become. The *final* question, about the ground or source of our knowledge of the morally good, is answered from an understanding of *human nature*, whether in terms of potentiality that is to be actualized according to reason or as fundamentally in need of external (divine) revelation. In any case, knowledge of the good is in one way or another rooted in human nature, whether defined as natural law (*lex naturae*) or as reason, whether potentially sufficient for self-realization or as damaged and in need of external divine transformation.

Taking virtue ethics as existing in a wide variety of ways yet sharing these important family resemblances makes it an open question as to which thinkers and currents of thought precisely are part of its multifaceted history. Although the theology of the Reformation may be seen as significantly distinct from and even opposed to late medieval Aristotelianism, this theology may still reveal the basic characteristics of virtue ethics, that is, understanding the good in terms of the good life, taking moral qualities that are regularly seen as virtues as necessary for living the good life and somehow considering human nature, as created and as in need of redemption, as a source of moral knowledge. Especially the final element seems challenging, but is not at all absent in Protestantism, as we will see. In some strands of Protestant thought these characteristics may be more present than in others, since Protestantism cannot be regarded as one homogeneous tradition either.

Moreover, if virtue ethics is not to be understood as one unified tradition with its roots in Antiquity that has undergone some relative modifications in Christianity, neither is the theological aspect necessarily to be considered as just relative to the philosophical, nor is the Christian virtues as only additional to the cardinal virtues. Although it may be right that theological virtue ethics depends on an underlying philosophical framework when it comes to basic virtue ethical concepts, such as understanding virtues as character traits, the role of habituation and exemplarity in acquiring the virtues and a teleological ordering of the good life, this can be doubted when it comes to how these concepts are understood materially. A Christian understanding of the good life as relational, that is, as related and devoted to God and the neighbor, and an inclusive, universalist conception of the good (i.e., as a common good in which all may share), for instance, make a significant difference in determining which virtues are to be attained, which exemplars are to be followed and especially how the good of the good life and the abilities of human nature are to be understood. If the partnership and fusion between Christianity and Antiquity is overemphasized—and Christian thinkers have had and still have good reasons to support the convergence (e.g., Plato's conception of the good that helped Augustine go beyond Manicheism)—the contrast between the Judeo-Christian tradition and ancient pagan philosophy may be lost from view.

On the other hand, neither should the difference between Christianity and Antiquity be overemphasized as if there is no continuity at all. Such a position has been defended both by Christian thinkers (I will come back to that) and by non-Christian thinkers who try to get rid of what they consider deteriorations rooted in Christian understandings of earthly life as just a means to the final end of eternal life. A prominent current of thought that is regularly defined in opposition to Christianity is the so-called philosophy of the art of living (*L'étique du souci de soi, Philosophie der Lebenskunst*) that flourished after Michel Foucault had rediscovered the classical idea of 'care of oneself' (ἐπιμέλεια ἑαυτοῦ, *cura sui*, or *souci de soi*) as a core element of all philosophical schools in Antiquity. According to Foucault, in the Christian way of life the care for the self was defined in terms of renunciation of the desires of the flesh and the denial of any self-interest for the sake of God and the other.[7] This interpretation can be doubted from a different understanding of the relation between the eternal and the present life as well as from a non-competitive understanding of the relationship between care of oneself and care for the other. Yet, even in Foucault's understanding it is evident that in Antiquity the Christian faith was primarily seen as *a way of life* rather than as a matter of adopting the right doctrines and in this sense was understood as an alternative life view among other competing views of the good life. In short, we need to do justice to the contrast between Christianity and ancient thought as well as to their convergence in how the human quest for the good life is addressed.

Something similar holds for the continuity and discontinuity within the Christian tradition. The shifts from premodern classical-medieval thought to modernity as inaugurated by the Reformation are not necessarily greater—probably even smaller—than those from Antiquity to Christianity. Rather the continuities within the Christian tradition are at least of equal importance to the changes within this tradition. As Charles Taylor puts it, original potentialities of the Christian faith that could more or less become neutralized in an amalgam with ancient philosophy are reemphasized and developed in Protestantism.[8] This

---

7. "L'étique du souci de soi comme pratique de liberté," interview by Raúl Fornet-Betancourt, Helmut Becker, and Alfredo Gomez-Müller (January 20, 1984), trans. in Michel Foucault, *Breekbare vrijheid: Teksten en interviews* [Fragile freedom: Texts and interviews] (Amsterdam: Boom/Parrèsia, 1995), 169–207.

8. Charles Taylor, *Sources of the Self: The Making of the Modern Identity* (Cambridge: Harvard University Press, [1989] 2000), 221. Cf. Charles Taylor, *A Secular Age* (Cambridge: Belknap Press of Harvard University Press, 2007), 80–2.

concerns in particular the emphasis on other-centered virtues, the affirmation of ordinary life, and the transformation of life as core elements of the Christian understanding of life. It is these traditional Christian ideas that gained a new—in some respects unprecedented and radicalized—status in the Reformation and afterward. In this sense, Protestantism can be seen as a renewed attempt to become aware of the distinctiveness of the Christian faith and its ethic.

Let us look a little closer at these distinctive elements as they are rooted in three major shifts caused by Christianity. A first shift that Christianity causes in relation to classical thought is the shift from self-centered virtues or virtues that center around the common good of one's own community toward *other-centered virtues* rooted in love of the neighbor, including one's enemy, and as directed to a common good in which *all* may share. Yet, the eudaimonistic framework is maintained, and both the other and the self share in the common good. As we will see, Augustine develops a non-competitive view of the common good, based in the biblical conception of love, which finds its expression in particular virtues. In Protestant views similar emphases can be found, for instance in how the *imitatio Christi* is understood, namely as directed to the good of the neighbor, including one's 'enemy'.

A second shift is the turn to *ordinary life* which, as Taylor argues, is not merely a modern Protestant aspect but in an important sense already given in the Jewish and Christian tradition: because God as creator and redeemer himself affirms life and creation—life in a profession or in a married state could be seen as fully Christian. In the gospel, the spiritual status of the everyday is accredited. Rather than considering Christian thought as just a continuation of Platonism, Aristotelianism, or Stoicism by other means, we should be fully aware of the difference between the Christian valuation of life and Antiquity in this respect. Taylor gives an illuminating example:

> The great difference between Stoic and Christian renunciation is this: for the Stoic, what is renounced is, if rightly renounced, ipso facto not part of the good. For the Christian, what is renounced is thereby affirmed as good—both in the sense that the renunciation would lose its meaning if the thing were indifferent and in the sense that the renunciation is in furtherance of God's will, which precisely affirms the goodness of the kinds of things renounced: health, freedom, life.[9]

A third shift has to do with the emphasis on the *transformation* of orders. In Judaism and Christianity, the sanctification of life is not something that takes place only at the moments of transition in life (birth, marriage, and death) but is a change that penetrates life as a whole and also affects social orders. Ideas of superiority and hierarchy (the hero, the aristocrat) stemming from Antiquity are discredited from the gospel notion that the orders of this world are reversed in the

---

9. Taylor, *Sources of the Self*, 219.

kingdom of God. The Reformation radicalizes this notion in its emphasis on the transformation of life to its full mundane extent.

What I want to demonstrate is that the way Protestantism has articulated other-centered virtues, affirmed ordinary life, and emphasized the need of transformation of this life and its orders is meaningful with regard to developing a contemporary virtue ethics. This presupposes that virtue ethics should be developed and rearticulated under present-day conditions. I think that this is indeed an internal necessity. It belongs to the very nature of virtue ethics itself that it rests on a particular *ethos* as this is formed by and develops under particular conditions of time and place. Virtue ethics has always been a sort of ethics that is highly dependent on the conditions of culture and time, which determine to a significant degree how particular virtues, conceptions of the good life, and human nature are interpreted. The enormous influence of Aristotelian virtue ethics precisely can be explained from its internal flexibility that allows for accommodation in various social conditions.[10] This also means that any account of virtue ethics that is relevant in our times is not just a matter of repeating what has been developed over time, but is in need of being rethought continuously under new conditions, in our case, those of late modernity.

It is precisely in understanding these conditions that Protestantism as a typically modern phenomenon becomes highly relevant, for Protestantism has been a major factor in what Taylor in the subtitle of his *Sources of the Self* calls "the making of the modern identity." This tradition cannot be ignored if we want to develop any virtue ethics that is relevant for our time. It can be regarded as one of the important linking pins between premodern virtue ethics and late modern moral conditions. This concerns several relevant themes related to the universal scope of the common good, the affirmation of ordinary life, and the transformation of social orders, as I will point out. Therefore, the aim of this book is to develop an account of virtue ethics 'after Protestantism,' that is, taking these Protestant features into account in developing a contemporary virtue ethics. For sure, the Protestant perspective that is adopted in this book is intended neither as an exclusivist point of view nor as an antithesis to Catholicism, but as a particular, less explored, and often neglected perspective that may offer innovative contributions to the broad field of virtue ethics.

Challenging the Dominant Narrative

Of course I am not the first to address the relationship between Protestantism and virtue ethics. Since Elizabeth Anscombe, Alasdair MacIntyre, and others initiated a

---

10. Cf. Dorothea Frede, "The Historic Decline of Virtue Ethics," in Daniel C. Russell (ed.), *The Cambridge Companion to Virtue Ethics* (Cambridge: Cambridge University Press, 2013), 128.

revival of virtue ethics in philosophy[11] and Stanley Hauerwas started to think of the Christian moral life in terms of character, community, and narrative,[12] Protestant theologians have shown growing interest in an ethics of virtue. In the first decade after the publication of *After Virtue*, Richard Mouw initiated a profound dialogue between Calvinistic divine command ethics and MacIntyrian virtue ethics,[13] Gilbert Meilaender offered an account of the virtues from a Lutheran perspective in a study of 1984,[14] and Eilert Herms developed a positive account of virtue ethics in response to the critical stance in the Protestant theology of the early twentieth century.[15] These studies corrected the common conviction that Protestants have no place for the virtues at all, but nevertheless hold that either divine command ethics or a dialectic of law and gospel is the main ethical perspective of Protestantism.[16]

Those who adopt a comprehensive virtue ethical perspective too regularly presuppose that their view is contrary to the dominant Protestant view. Whereas theological virtue ethics is seen as completely at home in the Roman Catholic tradition, Protestant ethics is considered an ethics of divine law and human obligations and responsibilities, at most with the exception of Friedrich Schleiermacher and liberal theology in the nineteenth century.[17] Hauerwas, for instance, developed his initial research into an 'ethics of character' precisely as

---

11. G. Elizabeth M. Anscombe's essay "Modern Moral Philosophy," *Philosophy* 33 (1958), 1–16, reprinted in Roger Crisp and Michael Slote (eds.), *Virtue Ethics* (Oxford: Oxford University Press, 2001), 1–5, is generally considered to have initiated the revival of virtue ethics, whereas MacIntyre's *After Virtue* had much greater impact.

12. Stanley Hauerwas, *Character and the Christian Life: A Study in Theological Ethics* (San Antonio: Trinity University Press, 1975), a reworked publication of his doctoral dissertation *Moral Character as a Problem for Theological Ethics* (New Haven: Yale University Press, 1968)—notably several years before MacIntyre published *After Virtue*; Stanley Hauerwas, *A Community of Character: Toward a Constructive Christian Social Ethic* (Notre Dame: University of Notre Dame Press, 1981).

13. Richard J. Mouw, *The God Who Commands: A Study in Divine Command Ethics* (Notre Dame: University of Notre Dame Press, 1990).

14. Gilbert C. Meilaender, *The Theory and Practice of Virtue* (Notre Dame: University of Notre Dame Press, 1984).

15. Eilert Herms, "Virtue: A Neglected Concept in Protestant Ethics," in Eilert Herms, *Offenbarung und Glaube: Zur Bildung des christlichen Lebens* (Tübingen: Mohr, 1992), 124–37.

16. For example, Mouw, *The God Who Commands*, 2: "My main concern in this book is to set forth a case for divine command ethics in the comprehensive sense," that is, in which virtue ethics is incorporated; Meilaender, *Theory and Practice of Virtue*, makes a strong case for Luther's emphasis on grace which makes virtue always a secondary category; Herms, "Virtue: A Neglected Concept," 126: "In protestant orthodoxy the concept of virtue didn't play any prominent role."

17. For example, Jean Porter, "Virtue Ethics," in Robin Gill (ed.), *The Cambridge Companion to Christian Ethics* (Cambridge: Cambridge University Press, 2001), 104–5.

an alternative to a Protestant command ethics by returning to the classical virtue ethical representatives Aristotle and Aquinas. Although he also took the Protestant doctrine of sanctification of the believer in the theologies of John Calvin, John Wesley, and Jonathan Edwards as an adequate starting point, according to Hauerwas, these theologians lacked the instruments of classical virtue ethics to think through the actual meaning of sanctification in the life of the believer, in particular in terms of character formation and cultivation of the virtues.[18] More recently, Jennifer Herdt argued that early Protestantism developed a "hyper-Augustinian view" with an overemphasis on divine agency, which makes human agency into a stance of pure passivity. Martin Luther's insistence that prideful human agency is to be displaced by the indwelling Christ who is to renew the sinner from inside out is not understandable in terms of gradual human transformation and habituation of the virtues. Herdt concludes that in Protestantism the traditional Thomistic conception that grace can work through ordinary processes of habituation was lost.[19] In these views, if virtue ethics could be developed along Protestant theological lines, a profound revision of core concepts is needed. In itself the Protestant tradition does not seem to offer much to contribute to developing a virtue ethics.

Even more severe is the criticism that the Reformation has been a major factor in the final abandonment of virtue ethics, paving the way toward a modern deontological ethics and consequentialism as its counterpart. In this view, the characteristically Protestant account of the Ten Commandments, as the ordering of the moral life, furthered an emphasis on principles, rules, obligations, duties, and prescriptions. As a consequence, commands and obligations could become the sole and final measure for morality in which the cultivation of virtues gradually was neglected.[20] MacIntyre famously argued that the Reformation inaugurated a

---

18. Hauerwas, *Character and the Christian Life*, 193–4. In later work he has corrected this view: it would be a mistake to consider virtue ethics an alternative to a rule-based ethics, because this distinction has been the result of theories about the nature of ethics that should be left behind, namely those theories that see 'ethics' as an intelligible mode of investigation independent from the practices of communities in which thick notions of the good life are carried forward. See Stanley Hauerwas and Charles Pinches, *Christians Among the Virtues: Theological Conversations with Ancient and Modern Ethics* (Notre Dame: University of Notre Dame Press, [1997] 2009), ix. Yet, this study is mainly oriented to Aristotle and Aquinas, ignoring Protestant accounts of virtue ethics, for the 'Protestant tendency' is to deny both the content and form of virtue (27).

19. Jennifer A. Herdt, *Putting on Virtue: The Legacy of the Splendid Vices* (Chicago: The University of Chicago Press, 2008).

20. See, for example, Servais Pinckaers, *The Sources of Christian Ethics*, trans. Mary Thomas Noble (Edinburgh: T&T Clark, 1995), 284–85: Protestantism "discarded all the permanent faculties, particularly the virtues, from its broad general structure of moral teaching"; cf. Andreas Kinneging, *Geografie van goed en kwaad: Filosofische Essays* [Geography of good and evil: Philosophical essays] (Utrecht: Spectrum, 2005), Ch. 10.

process that led to what he calls "the breakdown of the teleological conception of life," a conception that formed the underlying framework of virtue ethics and its eudaimonistic conception of the good life in both Antiquity and Christianity.[21] The suggestion is that the Reformation paved the way toward a Kantian ethics of obligation, detached from a teleological conception of life in which ethical imperatives were derived from an understanding of the *telos* of human nature toward which untutored human nature had to develop. As MacIntyre argues, the Enlightenment project as the attempt to found morality without any notion of teleology was doomed to fail since such a rational justification of morality made moral precepts to be based on formal rationality, without any context of practical beliefs and supporting habits of thought, feeling, and action which makes such precepts intelligible. The attempt to ground morality in impersonal moral standards in fact resulted in rival and incompatible accounts of utilitarianism, Kantianism, and social contract theory. According to MacIntyre, the failure of this Enlightenment project becomes particularly clear from Søren Kierkegaard's *Either/Or*, in which morality no longer has any final rational foundation but in the end only depends on a "criterionless fundamental choice."[22] In line with MacIntyre, Brad Gregory more recently argued in his book *The Unintended Reformation* that the Reformation was the main cause of the shift from a teleological concept of morality to a formal morality of rights. Gregory in particular defends that "the religious disagreements and related sociopolitical disruptions of the Reformation era" are the fundamental historical realities that drove the central change from a substantive morality of the good to a formal ethics of rights, which finally resulted in late modern hyper-pluralism and the total subjectivization of morality.[23] According to these influential interpretations, the Reformation inaugurated a decline of virtue ethics ending up in the existence of unbridgeable rival conceptions of moral justification. In this narrative the Aristotelian-Thomistic teleological framework has dramatically broken down in the modern era, the Protestant Reformation being a major factor in this breakdown. It is clear that if this interpretation is correct, any Protestant account of virtue ethics would require a complete revision of the main tendency of its tradition.

Unfortunately, various Protestant theologians and philosophers consciously or unconsciously contributed to this narrative in their criticism of the concept of virtue. Neo-Calvinists and dialectical theologians, for instance, rejected the anthropological scope of nineteenth-century liberal theology, including the concept of 'Christian and societal virtues,'[24] and regarded the Reformation's

---

21. MacIntyre, *After Virtue*, 53–4.

22. Ibid., 49.

23. Brad Gregory, *The Unintended Reformation: How a Religious Revolution Secularized Society* (Cambridge and London: Belknap Press of Harvard University Press, 2012), Ch. 4, quote on 185.

24. Throughout the nineteenth-century 'Christian and societal virtues' (*christelijke en burgerlijke deugden*) belonged to the standard theological-ethical and moral-educational

doctrine of justification not just as prior but also as opposed to the concept of virtue. In particular the implied element of the selfishness of virtue as focused on human perfection and its capacity for meritorious action, as well as the anthropological presupposition of a relatively autonomous existence independent of God, were criticized. This criticism was intimately bound up with what was said to be the discovery of the Reformation: the doctrine of justification as being opposed to the concept of *gratia infusa* as effecting a habitual change in man. Virtue cannot render human beings good.[25] More recently, the Reformed philosopher Nicholas Wolterstorff argued that a biblical and Christian understanding of the call to do justice to the goods to which others have rights is opposed to any eudaimonistic view, that is, the view that the ultimate goal of life of each person is to live one's own life as well as possible, which is at the heart of all classical Greek and Roman ethical views, Aristotelian virtue ethics included. Wolterstorff argues that Augustine causes a break with eudaimonism, the Stoa in particular, in favor of an ethics of justice and rights, a line of thought followed by Protestants in later times.[26]

Deconstructive, Reconstructive, and Constructive Aims

In this book, I will challenge these and other virtue ethical evaluations of Protestantism as well as Protestant evaluations of virtue ethics by reinvestigating several important yet largely unnoticed voices from the Protestant tradition on virtue ethical core themes and by demonstrating how Protestant theology may contribute to the actual development of a contemporary virtue ethics. From this central aim follows a threefold task.

First of all, I will challenge dominant critical views about the relation between Protestantism and virtue ethics by *deconstructing* the underlying

---

vocabulary in Protestant circles, for instance in the Netherlands: Nelleke Bakker (ed.), *Tot burgerschap en deugd: Volksopvoeding in de negentiende eeuw* [For citizenship and virtue: People's education in the nineteenth century] (Hilversum: Verloren, 2006).

25. Herms, "Virtue," 124–37, summarizes this criticism in five points: (1) Virtue conceived of as a *habit* dissolves the unity of conscious intention and action. (2) The concept of virtue implies an element of *selfishness*, because the theory of virtue focuses on the perfection of the individual as a personal agent. (3) Perfection defined as *the capacity for meritorious action* ignores that salvation is granted to man by grace alone. (4) This misconception is supported by the anthropological presupposition about the human soul as *ens per se subsistens*, a kind of autonomy of existence which contradicts the Christian conviction that man as a creature is utterly dependent on God. (5) Where the New Testament speaks about *aretè* it speaks not of an attitude, but of an obedient response to the divine demand.

26. Nicholas Wolterstorff, *Justice: Rights and Wrongs* (Princeton and Oxford: Princeton University Press, 2008), Ch. 7 and 8.

narrative. If considered more closely, it appears that MacIntyre's and Gregory's narratives easily jump from the Reformation, its historical context and theology to modern philosophers, without clarifying how these modern ethicists precisely were influenced by the Reformation theology. Neither do they take into account the continuation of the traditional virtue ethical framework in Protestant theologies.[27] This makes the narrative quite general, lacking sufficient historical evidence about the development of modernity and its ethics from the Reformation onwards. Moreover, more material interpretations of Protestant theology and its ethics, such as Herdt's, are often restricted to the main figures, such as Luther and Calvin, following particular, sometimes contested lines of interpretation and neglecting the *post*-Reformation theology of, for example, Reformed scholasticism and its ethics. Part of the task is to deconstruct the dominant narrative of a general decline of virtue ethics caused by the Reformation by reinvestigating Reformation and post-Reformation theologies from the perspective of virtue ethics.

In doing so the deconstructive task is closely connected with a second concern, namely the *reconstruction* of Protestant theological ethics from the question in what respect virtue ethics is actually continued, criticized, and/or developed within this tradition. How do the Reformers and post-Reformation theologians understand virtue, the virtues, happiness, and human nature? Historically speaking, the virtues were not absent in Protestant theology and were even regarded by most of its representatives as a substantial part of the Christian life. Although Calvin chooses to outline the Christian moral life from the perspective of divine commandments, this choice is not by principle but practical. He explicitly states his full agreement with the old church fathers, who wrote so well and profoundly about the virtues, suggesting that he could also have taken the virtues as his starting point.[28] Furthermore, it is the almost completely unnoticed and neglected ethics of post-Reformation theology, Reformed orthodoxy, or scholasticism in particular, of the sixteenth, seventeenth, and eighteenth centuries which is even more relevant to the reconstructive task. To give but a few examples of great virtue ethical interest in the era of early Reformed scholasticism, a number of Reformed (and Lutheran) theologians, such as Peter Martyr Vermigli and Antonius Walaeus, published extensive commentaries on Aristotle's *Ethica Nicomachea*, others, such as Lambert Daneau and Bartholomaeus Keckermann, developed their philosophical ethics in terms of both (natural) law and virtue ethics, whereas others, such as Amandus Polanus, William Ames, and Peter van Mastricht, complemented their treatment of the Ten Commandments with an examination of the various virtues that correspond to these commandments or integrated these commandments in their

---

27. An exception is MacIntyre's *Whose Justice? Which Rationality?* (Notre Dame: University of Notre Dame Press, 1988), Ch. 12, on the Augustinian and Aristotelian background to the Scottish Enlightenment, but his overview is primarily based on secondary historical studies and his normative framework is strictly Aristotelian-Thomistic.

28. *Inst.* 3.6.1.

virtue ethical expositions of the Christian life. In seventeenth- and eighteenth-century Puritanism, John Owen made use of a metaphysics of goodness in which the human person becomes godlike, and Jonathan Edwards devoted a whole study, *The Nature of True Virtue*, to the virtues.

Although the field of Reformed scholasticism has been investigated extensively, studies have limited themselves to core systematic issues such as the doctrine of God, Christology or the doctrine of revelation and Scripture, leaving the field of ethics rather unexplored;[29] as Luca Baschera concludes in an overview of this field: "No modern scholar has yet attempted to give a comprehensive presentation of the history of Reformed ethics in the era of Orthodoxy."[30] Yet, things seem to be changing in a promising way. Recent studies on virtue and justification in Vermigli,[31] the virtue ethical content of Edwards's theology,[32] the influence of the Stoa in Protestant ethics,[33] virtue ethics from a Lutheran perspective,[34] and the continuation of natural law and Thomistic virtue ethics in Protestantism offer significant new insights.[35] Similarly, when it comes to the nineteenth and twentieth centuries, some recent interest in virtue ethical themes within Protestant theology can be observed, as for instance in Schleiermacher's philosophical and

---

29. For example, Richard A. Muller, *Post-Reformation Reformed Dogmatics*, 4 vols (Grand Rapids: Baker, 2003).

30. Luca Baschera, "Ethics in Reformed Orthodoxy," in Herman J. Selderhuis (ed.), *A Companion to Reformed Orthodoxy* (Leiden: Brill, 2013), 519–20. Exceptions are a few studies on single authors, Lambert Daneau and Bartholomaeus Keckermann in particular: Donald Sinnema, "The Discipline of Ethics in Early Reformed Orthodoxy," *Calvin Theological Journal* 28/1 (1993), 10–44; Christoph Strohm, *Ethik im frühen Calvinismus: Humanistische Einflüsse, philosophische, juridische und theologische Argumentationen sowie mentalitätsgeschichtlichen Aspekte am Beispiel des Calvin-Schülers Lambertus Danaeus* (Berlin: De Gruyter, 1996).

31. Luca Baschera, *Tugend und Rechtfertigung: Peter Martyr Vermiglis Kommentar zur Nikomachischen Ethik im Spannungsfeld von Philosophie und Theologie* (Zurich: Theologische Verlag, 2008).

32. Stephen A. Wilson, *Virtue Reformed: Rereading Jonathan Edwards's Ethics* (Leiden: Brill, 2005); Elizabeth Agnew Cochran, *Receptive Human Virtues: A New Reading of Jonathan Edwards's Ethics* (University Park: Pennsylvania State University Press, 2011).

33. Elizabeth Agnew Cochran, *Protestant Virtue and Stoic Ethics* (Enquiries in Theological Ethics) (London: Bloomsbury T&T Clark, 2018).

34. Joel D. Biermann, *A Case for Character: Towards a Lutheran Virtue Ethics* (Minneapolis: Fortress Press, 2014).

35. Stephen J. Grabill, *Rediscovering the Natural Law in Reformed Theological Ethics* (Grand Rapids: Eerdmans, 2006); David VanDrunen, *Natural Law and the Two Kingdoms: A Study in the Development of Reformed Social Thought* (Grand Rapids: Eerdmans, 2010); Manfred Svensson and David VanDrunen (eds.), *Aquinas among the Protestants* (Oxford: Wiley Blackwell, 2018).

Christian ethics.³⁶ This also applies to Kierkegaard's existential ethics³⁷ and even Karl Barth's ethics of divine commandments as showing interesting parallels and similarities to virtue ethics.³⁸ Building on these and other investigations, it is part of my reconstructive task to investigate how Protestant thinkers develop their understanding of virtue and the virtues. My aim is not to offer a comprehensive reconstruction of virtue ethics in the whole field of Protestant ethics. For the sake of limitation, I will focus on Calvin and (Neo-)Calvinism, Reformed scholasticism, and Kierkegaard as important representative instances that figure in or are relevant to MacIntyre's influential narrative about the breakdown of the teleological view of life.

Finally, this project is *constructive* in developing alternative accounts of virtue ethics as in line with Augustine and as taken up in distinctive ways by the Reformers, post-Reformation theologians, and later Protestant thinkers, including Kierkegaard. For this book is about 'virtue ethics after Protestantism,' not only in the sense of 'according to Protestantism' but also 'after taking into account Protestantism.' To put it somewhat differently, the aim is not only to consider Protestant theology and ethics through the lens of virtue ethics, but also to ask what specific contributions this theology and ethics can offer to contemporary virtue ethics. From this final perspective I try to offer constructive contributions to the actual development of virtue ethics. Again, the aim is not to be exhaustive. Many important aspects and voices will be left aside. I will particularly focus on four themes and aspects that are connected with the main shifts caused by Christianity and as rearticulated in Protestantism.

First of all, the emphasis on other-directed virtues and the *affirmation of ordinary life* has an impact on the perception of *moral exemplarity* as this functions in habituation and the cultivation of virtues. Similar to recent approaches in the social sciences³⁹ and in theology,⁴⁰ recent virtue ethical research shows a remarkable turn to the "moral phenomenology of ordinary life," as Chappell

---

36. Heleen Zorgdrager, "Mapping the Christian Character: Calvin and Schleiermacher on Virtue, Law and Sanctification," in Pieter Vos and Onno Zijlstra (eds.), *The Law of God: Exploring God and Civilization* (Leiden and Boston: Brill, 2014), 256–81.

37. John J. Davenport and Anthony Rudd (eds.), *Kierkegaard after MacIntyre: Essays on Freedom, Narrative, and Virtue* (Chicago and La Salle: Open Court, 2001).

38. William Werpehowski, *Karl Barth and Christian Ethics: Living in Truth* (Farnham: Ashgate, 2014); Kirk J. Nolan, *Reformed Virtue after Barth: Developing Moral Virtue Ethics within the Reformed Theological Tradition* (Louisville: Westminster John Knox Press, 2014).

39. Andrew Sayer, *Why Things Matter to People: Social Science, Values and Ethical Life* (Cambridge: Cambridge University Press, 2011), advocates a turn to everyday concerns in order to do justice to the 'things that really matter to people.'

40. Michael Banner, *The Ethics of Everyday Life: Moral Theology, Social Anthropology, and the Imagination of the Human* (Oxford: Oxford University Press, 2014), portrays the Christian life as both shaped by the imagination of concrete occasions in Christ's life and informed by the social sciences.

observes.[41] This turn to ordinary life is not fully understandable without the historical impetus of the Protestant affirmation of the ordinary that influenced modern understandings of the moral life. Furthermore, Protestant approaches offer alternative understandings of virtue ethical aspects that are not present in classical virtue ethics. I will demonstrate this in particular from the nature and the working of moral exemplars. A focus on ordinary life implies that moral exemplars are not only provided by exceptional characters and extraordinary stories of moral excellence, but also provided by those exemplars who represent the dilemmas, stories, and struggles of everyday life. Such exemplars may be more recognizable to those who try to cultivate the virtues as exemplified by these exemplars in their own lives than traditional exemplars, such as heroes, sages, and saints.

Secondly, and related to this, a perspective on the issue of *virtuous people showing moral flaws* will be offered from a Protestant view of sin, grace, and moral excellence. This also concerns the relationship between human and divine agency in acquiring the virtues. Both in Augustine's treatment of virtue and in Protestant interpretations the human being cannot realize the good life fully by his or her own powers alone but is in need of divine assistance. This has to do with the human will as a fundamentally divided human faculty. In the constructive part of this book these interpretations will be made fruitful in relation to actual virtue ethical concerns, in particular the issue of so-called situationism, that is, the empirical claim that the extent to which a person will act from virtue is highly dependent on situational factors. As a result, most people regularly have neither moral virtues nor moral vices but rather "mixed traits."[42] A Protestant account of virtue, in which human sinfulness is acknowledged and met with grace, will be related to the question whether exemplary virtues can exist alongside deep-seated vices. A Protestant contribution could consist in offering a different perspective on what counts as true human virtue, namely humility, as a paradoxical virtuous way to acknowledge that one never possesses the virtues in their fullness.

Thirdly, a Protestant *concept of the law* will be related to a Neo-Aristotelian *conception of 'practices'* as a fruitful attempt to understand the virtues as being part of complex social activities. In this approach, human beings are seen as socially embedded, functioning in practices and corresponding social roles. MacIntyre famously developed a concept of a practice as primarily determined by the good or *telos* internal to the social activity characteristic of a particular practice and virtues as the qualities that "enable us to achieve those goods which are internal to practices."[43] This concept will be taken up and be enriched by Calvinistic and

---

41. Chappell, "Virtue Ethics in the Twentieth Century," 168, who considers exploration of the place occupied by ideas of well-being and excellence in ordinary life one of the main tasks for future research in virtue ethics. See also Michael Austin and R. Douglas Geivett (eds.), *Being Good: Christian Virtues for Everyday Life* (Grand Rapids: Eerdmans, 2012).

42. Christian B. Miller, *The Character Gap: How Good Are We?* (New York: Oxford University Press, 2017).

43. MacIntyre, *After Virtue*, 191.

Neo-Calvinistic understandings of law and law spheres. A Calvinistic concept of law has the potential to add something that is less developed in MacIntyre's conceptualization: an external reference point for a critical assessment of existing practices. This may prevent practices from becoming conservative and self-referential.

Finally, the idea of the *transformation of the orders of life* will be made fruitful in relation to this potential weakness in virtue ethics, that is, its tendency to affirm what is given rather than to criticize what is unjust or wrong. A Protestant conception of virtue as characterized not just by formation but also by transformation, that is, by the need of continuous personal and communal reform, and as committed to social justice, may be a valuable and necessary additional contribution. The notion of transformation may open up a particular perspective on character formation from moral exemplars in terms of personal renewal and social reform that can prevent virtue ethics from deteriorating into conventionalism. Transformation is neither a matter of natural progress nor something that is achieved once and for all. It rather demands reform, that is, a continuous renewal. Transformation also designates a commitment to social justice, including a prophetic role full of commitment to challenge and influence current and future social arrangements. In this sense, the notion of reform may function as critical element of any virtue ethics.

Outline

The book is structured in the following way. The first two chapters form a preliminary investigation preceding the main body of this book. Various approaches of an ethics of the good life stemming from Antiquity and as rearticulated in contemporary thought are investigated, including Augustine's. This is necessary since the main body of this book explores the contours of a Protestant theological account of virtue ethics as significantly in line with Augustine and as related to present-day currents of thought. Chapters 3, 4, and 5 are in particular devoted to the deconstructive and reconstructive aims of this book by focusing on how Calvin(ism), Reformed scholasticism, and Kierkegaard think about the good life, virtue, and human nature. The final chapters of this book (Chapters 6 through 8) are mainly constructive, though reconstruction and deconstruction are still part of it, by focusing on the moral exemplarity of Christ in ordinary life, the frailty of human virtue, and the meaning of the transformation of life with regard to virtue, practice, and exemplarity.

Chapter 1 starts with an investigation of different 'sources of the good life' as represented by three currents of thought: the philosophy of the art of living, classical and Neo-Aristotelian virtue ethics, and a Christian account of virtue and the virtues in late Antiquity, Augustine's in particular. Although philosophy of the art of living relates itself to Aristotelian virtue ethics and its recent revival, late modern overtones predominate, in particular in its problematic emphasis on the manageability of life depending on the human will and individual choices, which distinguishes it importantly from classical virtue ethics and even more from the Christian virtue ethical tradition. This last tradition has something to offer that is lacking in the philosophy of the art of living: the idea of passivity or receptivity that is profound in both Augustine's and Aquinas' theologically based virtue ethics. Although the notion of passivity is present in Christian versions of the art of living, this idea is conceptually weakly developed, namely as a continuous dialectics of activity and passivity, love of the self and love of the other, without their internal relationship being adequately thought through.

However, the theological core notions explored in Chapter 1 not only include criticism of classical thought and late modern philosophy of the art of living, but also seem to have repercussions on virtue ethics and its teleology. According to Wolterstorff, Augustine, being one of the supreme theological representatives of the Christian view that entered Western thought, dismisses the eudaimonistic view of life in his criticism of the human aspirations inherent in all classical and Hellenistic philosophies. Therefore, the question is whether the good life can still be seen in terms of happiness and fulfillment through cultivation of the virtues and whether any form of teleology is maintained in an Augustinian view. *Chapter 2* first investigates how Aristotle's virtue ethics includes the necessity of external goods as constitutive of the good life and how his ethics of the good life is aimed at the goods of others. Next, contra Wolterstorff I argue that Augustine does adopt a eudaimonistic framework, in which he develops a non-competitive understanding of the common good.

In response to Alasdair MacIntyre's and Brad Gregory's claims that the Reformation's concept of morality in terms of obedience to divine commandments has been a major factor in a catastrophic breakdown in modernity of the teleological view of life and the virtues, *Chapter 3* aims to correct this criticism by a reconstruction of Calvin's understanding of virtue and law. Calvin's utterances about the nature of the law, virtue, the self before God, one's calling in the world, natural law, and reason appear to be much more in alliance with a teleological, virtue ethical view than MacIntyre suggests. This opens up the possibility of a fruitful interplay between a Reformed account of law and Christian virtue ethics. This will be illustrated by demonstrating how a Calvinistic concept of law may contribute to a Neo-Aristotelian understanding of 'practices.'

The reconstructive task is continued in *Chapter 4*, which is devoted to an investigation of the main characteristics of post-Reformation theological understandings of human nature and the human intelligibility of the good, teleology, and the virtues. I will show how in Reformed scholasticism both Aristotle's *Nicomachean Ethics* and medieval scholasticism function as important sources for a philosophical understanding of ethics and a theological account of the Christian life based on the biblical revelation, in which not only divine commandments but also virtue and the virtues are present as core concepts.

Since MacIntyre considers the Protestant theologian and philosopher Søren Kierkegaard's understanding of ethics as depending on a 'criterionless choice' as decisive turning point in the development toward emotivist ethics, *Chapter 5* focuses on Kierkegaard's ethics, in particular as represented in his upbuilding works. I will argue that the Danish philosopher and theologian represents a Christian conception of the moral life that is distinct from but—contrary to MacIntyre's claim—not completely opposed to Aristotelian-Thomistic virtue ethics. Although the realities of sin and salvation transcend a virtue ethics based purely on human nature, I will demonstrate that this does not prevent Kierkegaard from speaking constructively about human nature, its teleology, and the virtues, that is, showing the main elements of what I have called a 'grammar of virtue.' Yet, from a Christian 'upbuilding' perspective, general features of human nature must be transformed profoundly, which implies more than a harmonious perfection or completion of nature (Aquinas), but less than the complete replacement of nature by grace.

Although Chapters 3 through 5 already offer significant constructive contributions, the final three chapters are more directly devoted to developing constructive proposals. In *Chapter 6* I will take up Herdt's reading of Protestantism's 'hyper-Augustinian' inability to think through character formation and habituation of virtue as a challenge to develop a Protestant view of the imitation of Christ as part of 'participation in Christ' (based on Luther's understanding of 'union with Christ' and Calvin's *duplex gratia*). From this reconstruction, a constructive conception of the meaning of exemplarity in ordinary life is unfolded. Imitating Christ as moral exemplar does not mean copying him, as a human effort to emulate a high moral ideal, but loving the neighbor in the particularities of one's own life as Christ did in the particularities of his life. It is a striving rooted in Christ's lowliness, as Kierkegaard and Bonhoeffer show, which makes *imitatio Christi* an achievable though demanding ethical requirement for each individual.

The question to what extent moral growth in virtue is possible from a Protestant view is addressed in *Chapter 7* and is related to human frailty in acquiring the virtues. The potential weakness of the Protestant tradition, namely that the possibilities of human nature in acquiring virtue are seen as limited, may at the same time be its strength: by asserting that even 'the most holy' and morally exceptional person before God is still a sinner dependent on God's grace it is possible to do justice to human frailty and moral flaws. From an Augustinian interpretation of the unity of the virtues and a Protestant interpretation of moral growth in terms of the need of a continuous renewal I will argue that growth in moral excellence is possible in the acknowledgment that imperfection will still be part of one's character. This perspective will be made fruitful in relation to issues of situationism and observations about people showing mixed character traits and deep-seated vices alongside moral virtues.

In *Chapter 8*, the Protestant idea of the affirmation of ordinary life as well as the need to transform this life in all its social spheres will be taken up as a starting point to investigate the role of moral exemplarity in the cultivation of the virtues. Whereas the gap between classical exemplars like the sage, the hero, and the saint, on the one hand, and ordinary people, on the other, is difficult to bridge, the relocation of moral exemplarity in the sphere of ordinary life offers important possibilities to bridge this gap. From this perspective moral exemplarity can be understood as fully related to the complexities and ambiguities of ordinary life, which characterize not only our own lives but also the lives of exemplars. At the same time, exemplars may still be exceptional precisely with regard to the need to transform society. How this may be understood is pointed out by introducing the distinction between 'role exemplars' and 'existential exemplars' as different kinds of exemplarity that relate differently to our participation in social practices and to our existential concerns. In a final step I will relate this to the critical potential of the Protestant emphasis on transformation as designating a commitment to social justice and social reform, offering a constructive contribution to the shape of a contemporary virtue ethics.

Chapter 1

SOURCES OF THE GOOD LIFE

What does it mean to live well? This may count as the central question not only of classical virtue ethics but also of a philosophical current of thought that has emerged in the past decades, known as 'philosophy of the art of living,' which claims to retrieve a central concern of Antique philosophy. It is central to how the Christian faith was understood by Christian thinkers in late Antiquity as well and continues to be so in contemporary Christian ethics. These currents of thought provide contrasting as well as overlapping answers to the question. In this chapter, I will focus on these three different ways of understanding the good life: philosophy of the art of living, classical virtue ethics, and Christian thought in late Antiquity, by focusing on what each of them considers to be the sources of the good life.

Contemporary philosophy of the art of living can be traced back to Michel Foucault's work in the 1970s and 1980s, which discovered in the writings of Greek and Roman philosophers an argument in favor of a 'care of oneself' (*souci de soi*).[1] In an interview Foucault explains this interest: "What strikes me is the fact that in our society, art has become something which is related only to objects and not to individuals, or to life. . . . But couldn't everyone's life become a work of art?"[2] In a way close to Nietzsche's saying that one should create one's own life by styling it through long practice and daily work,[3] Foucault argues that "we have to create ourselves as a work of art."[4] Foucault refers to Pierre Hadot, who analyzed philosophy in Antiquity as a way of life rather than as a theory about life.[5] From

---

1. Michel Foucault, *The Care of the Self*, The History of Sexuality, Vol. 3 (London: Penguin Books, 1990), 37–68, originally: *Le souci du soi* (Paris: Gallimard, 1984).

2. Michel Foucault, "On the Genealogy of Ethics: An Overview of Work in Progress," in Paul Rabinow (ed.), *The Foucault Reader: An Introduction to Foucault's Thought* (London: Penguin Books, 1991), 350.

3. Friedrich Nietzsche, *Die fröhliche Wissenschaft*, in Friedrich Nietzsche, *Kritische Studienausgabe*, Bd. 3.2, ed. Giorgio Colli and Mazzino Montinari (München: De Gruyter, 1999), fragment no. 290.

4. Foucault, "On the Genealogy of Ethics," 351.

5. Pierre Hadot, *Philosophy as a Way of Life: Spiritual Exercises from Socrates to Foucault* (Oxford: Blackwell Publishers, 1995), originally: *Exercices spirituels et philosophie antique* (Paris: Études Augustiniennes, 1981).

these initial investigations of Greek and Roman philosophical schools, a popular philosophy of the art of living emerged, represented by, among others, the German philosopher Wilhelm Schmid, the Dutch humanistic philosopher Joep Dohmen, and the North American philosopher John Kekes.[6] In some respects, philosophy of the art of living is close to virtue ethics and its recent revival,[7] yet there are significant differences. In this chapter I will argue that the philosophy of the art of living resembles classical virtue ethics only in a limited sense.

Theologically, it is of interest that recently attempts have been made to develop a *Christian* art of living. In Germany, Peter Bubmann and Bernhard Sill presented a *Christliche Lebenskunst*,[8] and in the Netherlands, several proposals have been made to bring the philosophy of the art of living (*levenskunst*) in conversation with the Christian tradition.[9] These attempts are challenging, since in the philosophical presentations of the art of living Christianity—and any religiosity—is strikingly absent as a valuable source of wisdom for an art of living. Many of its features are even explicitly rejected. According to Foucault, in the Christian way of life as advocated after Hellenism, life was predominantly defined as the renunciation of all earthly ties, that is, of everything that includes love of

---

6. Wilhelm Schmid, *Philosophie der Lebenskunst* (Frankfurt: Suhrkamp, 1998); Joep Dohmen, *Tegen de onverschilligheid: Pleidooi voor een moderne levenskunst* [Against indifference: A plea for a modern art of living] (Amsterdam: Ambo, 2007), Ch. 7; Joep Dohmen, *Brief aan een middelmatige man: Pleidooi voor een nieuwe publieke moraal* [Letter to an ordinary man: A plea for a new public morality] (Amsterdam: Ambo, 2010); John Kekes, *The Art of Life* (Ithaca and London: Cornell University Press, 2002). For the sake of brevity, I limit myself to these three representatives. Other popular, more aesthetic versions of the philosophy of the art of living are provided by Richard Shusterman and Alexander Nehamas. Luc Ferry and Alain de Botton too may be regarded as philosophers of the art of living.

7. Joep Dohmen, "Philosophers on 'the Art-of-Living,'" *Journal of Happiness Studies* 4/4 (2003), 352. Kekes develops his philosophy of the art of living also in terms of virtue ethics, especially in his book *Moral Wisdom and Good Lives* (Ithaca and London: Cornell University Press, 1995). Cf. *The Art of Life*, 164–9 for a more critical approach.

8. Peter Bubmann and Bernhard Sill (eds.), *Christliche Lebenskunst* (Regensburg: Verlag Friedrich Pustet, 2008); Bernhard Sill and Peter Bubmann, *Schritte durch die Lebensmitte: Facetten christlicher Lebenskunst* (München: Gütersloher Verlagshaus, 2013).

9. Frits de Lange, "Schipperen met het eigen leven: Zelfsturing als normatief ideal [Giving and taking in one's own life: Self-direction as normative ideal]," in Theo Boer and Angela Roothaan (eds.), *Gegeven: Ethische essays over het leven als gave* (Zoetermeer: Boekencentrum, 2003), 59–77; Frits de Lange, "The Modern Life Course and the Ethics of the Art of Living," Guest Lecture University of Western Cape, South-Africa, July 27, 2004, retrieved from www.fritsdelange.nl on December 28, 2019. Together with Joep Dohmen he edited *Moderne levens lopen niet vanzelf* [Modern lives are not lived as a matter of course] (Amsterdam: SWP, 2006); Jochem Quartel and Jan Hoogland, *Levenskunst voor iedereen* [The art of living for everyone] (Utrecht: Kok, 2014).

oneself and relatedness to an earthly self.[10] In an interview he remarks: "From that moment on, the self was no longer something to be made but something to be renounced and deciphered."[11] Instead of care of the self and self-development, Christianity propagated self-renunciation and the denial of any self-interest for the sake of God and the other.[12] Dohmen follows this interpretation and adds that in the Christian understanding of life "the soul's purity, needed to be unified with God, has to be acquired by way of self-repentance, self-examination and confession, accompanied by an ascetic and repentant way of life attuned to this"[13]—features that entirely contradict ideals of autonomy and personal liberty in modern philosophy of the art of living. In a less historical exposition Dohmen states: "The Christian does not want to reach a state of autonomy at all, but aims to show that he dissociates himself from this world and from his own past."[14] Schmid, too, basically refers to Christianity in a negative way, for example, as responsible for the negation of the human being's bodily nature in a crusade against the lusts.[15] According to Kekes, the old "religious answer" did not tell the believer how life can be good in the present world, but it only told how to live here and now in order to enjoy the good life in the hereafter.[16]

In this chapter, based on an interpretation of some relevant aspects of the late Antique Christian thinker Augustine, I will argue not only that this criticism is largely unjustified, but also that the modern philosophy of the art of living itself contains problematic understandings of the good life as a manageable life project solely depending on my own human will and personal choices. The shortcomings that are contained in this conception can be corrected by taking into account core elements of the Christian tradition and its understanding of the good life and the virtues. Before exploring this, I will start with a short analysis of the philosophy of the art of living as basically modern in nature and as quite different from classical and Neo-Aristotelian virtue ethics. This is followed by an analysis of how contemporary theological accounts of the art of living address the challenges of the philosophy of the art of living. By bringing the premodern Christian tradition of Augustine into dialogue with two other currents of thought, we will gain an impression of the contours of a particular Christian virtue ethical framework

---

10. "L'étique du souci de soi comme pratique de liberté," in *Breekbare vrijheid: Teksten en interviews*, 192.

11. Foucault, "On the Genealogy of Ethics," 366.

12. Foucault, *Breekbare vrijheid*, 192.

13. Dohmen, *Tegen de onverschilligheid*, 101 (trans. mine).

14. Joep Dohmen, *Het leven als kunstwerk* [Life as a work of art] (Amsterdam: Ambo, 2011), 87.

15. Wilhelm Schmid, *Filosofie van de levenskunst: Inleiding in het mooie leven* [Philosophy of the art of living: Introduction to the beautiful life], trans. Carola Kloos (Amsterdam: Ambo, 2001), 40–1. Originally: *Schönes Leben* (Frankfurt: Suhrkamp, 2000).

16. Kekes, *The Art of Life*, 2.

that is continuated to a great extent in (post-)Reformation theology, as will be demonstrated in the course of this book.

Art of Living: A Modern Project

Wilhelm Schmid explains the popularity and relevance of the philosophy of the art of living from the current situation of late modernity: the end of the grand narratives and ideologies including their utopian dreams.[17] Late modern people no longer live in a world in which life is sustained by social ties and traditions or in which nature provides the human being with a *telos* according to which life is to be lived. Instead, they must take care of themselves as individuals, choosing how to live their life and according to which standards. Since traditional institutional and social structures are losing their normative regulating function, the human life course has increasingly become a matter of individual construction. Philosophy of the art of living starts from the late modern condition that life has become a void that must be filled, that it will have been in vain if we won't have shaped it ourselves. Art of living is an attempt to fill this void.[18]

According to philosophers of the art of living, modern people often do not have an adequate idea of what it means to live and how to find direction in their lives.[19] By returning to the classical ideas of practical wisdom and the good life, a philosophy of the art of living aims to offer what has been lost in modernity: care of the self, attention to the important existential questions, self-examination, self-improvement—in short, an art of living. It relates a modern conception of a self-regulating, autonomous self to the practical wisdom and 'care of the self' as central aims of classical philosophy. In Foucault's view, ἐπιμέλεια ἑαυτοῦ or *cura sui*, care of the self, was characterized by the fact that the art of existence—the τέχνη του βίου—was dominated by the principle that one must take care of oneself, which includes both care of the soul and care of the body as well as self-knowledge and self-examination in a series of clearly defined exercises, with the aim to 'convert' oneself to a state of self-mastery (ἐπιστροφή εἰς ἑαυτόν or *potestas sui*).[20]

Although philosophy of the art of living can be seen as a retrieval of classical philosophy, late modern conditions are in many respects decisive. These conditions imply that we can no longer accept the classical ideas of reality and human nature, which in the 'synoptic ethics' of the Greek and Roman philosophers determined how a human being should act. According to Dohmen, "Ideas about human

---

17. Schmid, *Filosofie van de levenskunst*, 7.

18. De Lange, "The Modern Life Course," 2.

19. For example, Schmid, *Filosofie van de levenskunst*, 20; Dohmen, *Brief aan een middelmatige man*, 15–16. In a somewhat different interpretation, Hadot argues that the ancient understanding of *philosophy* as a way of life has disappeared from our modern understanding of philosophy (*Philosophy as a Way of Life*, 107–8, 269–70).

20. Foucault, *The Care of the Self*, 43–67.

behavior cannot be derived from insights into nature or from human nature."[21] Hence, the philosophy of the art of living is basically organized around modern concepts like life project, self-direction, authenticity, autonomy, and personal will. Without pretending to give a fully fledged description of the whole branch of this philosophy, a short overview reveals that these modern conceptions are indeed predominant. Kekes, for instance, relates 'art of life' primarily to the notion of 'life project.' Each life involves numerous different activities, of which some are instrumental to the continuation of life, others are chosen because they reflect a person's interests, aspirations or values, and some of them endure and become a person's chief preoccupations throughout life. These last are a person's life projects.[22] Living a good life depends on engagement in personally satisfying and well-chosen life projects in a way that exemplifies one's ideal of personal excellence, according to one's will.

Characteristic of the philosophy of the art of living is the recognition of a fundamental plurality in people's personal life views. Life views have become a matter of individual choice and different people will make different decisions, "each of which may be reasonable, because their decisions must reflect the differences in the characters and circumstances of the deciders."[23] Although the decision for a life view does not imply a radical opposition to tradition, it emphatically depends on one's own choice and will: the conception of the good life should be one's own and not the result of influences over which one has no control.[24] And although living the good life requires a sense of one's limited ability to control reality and an understanding of one's vulnerability to contingency,[25] life basically appears to be a matter of self-mastery and self-management. Dohmen admits that many things befall us as fortune or misfortune, but what counts is "to determine *how much latitude one has within the concrete context of action*," and how to deal with both one's limitations and potential in a practical way.[26]

Life is seen as an art because it is a creative, imaginative, individual endeavor to make life into a good life, not as a life that is lived rightly in a moral sense, but as a life that is successful and looks beautiful. Although an ethical orientation is necessary to the good life, we no longer have an absolute standard: it "might be a

---

21. Dohmen, "Philosophers on the 'Art-of-Living,'" 356.
22. Kekes, *The Art of Life*, 4.
23. Ibid., 6.
24. Ibid., 14–15; Dohmen, *Tegen de onverschilligheid*, 160–82; Dohmen, *Brief aan een middelmatige man*, 113, 174; Schmid, *Filosofie van de levenskunst*, 25–6: "The art of living, independent of how its content will be developed, rests entirely on the choice that the subject of the art of living makes" (trans. mine).
25. For example, Dohmen, *Brief aan een middelmatige man*, 25; Dohmen, *Tegen de onverschilligheid*, 39, 151, 281; Schmid, *Filosofie van de levenskunst*, 47; Kekes, *The Art of Life*, 94.
26. Dohmen, "Philosophers on the 'Art-of-Living,'" 364. Cf. Schmid, *Filosofie van de levenskunst*, 22.

virtuous life or a duty-full life, a life of self-fulfillment, a beautiful life or a happy life, or something different."[27] Since there is no absolute standard for the good, we "have to discover ourselves, each in our own concrete situation, whether we really want to become beautiful or happy, virtuous or 'ourselves.'"[28] It is a matter of authenticity, a personal attitude, on the basis of which one can live the good life. What prevails is the aesthetic: the transformation of one's life into a work of art, albeit in accordance with a 'transcending' ideal of the good life, which however is reduced to a matter of personal preference rooted in one's subjective will. We can only ask from an authentic person that he is prepared to take responsibility for his choice and to legitimize his actions accordingly.

These central late modern characteristics of the philosophy of the art of living are at least partly in tension with the classical origins from which it is inspired. The aesthetic nature of the 'care of the self' is precisely one of the reasons why Hadot criticizes the way his work is adopted by Foucault and the philosophy of the art of living: "What I am afraid of is, that, by focusing his interpretation too exclusively on the culture of the self, the care of the self, and conversion toward the self—more generally, by defining his ethical model as an aesthetics of existence—M. Foucault is propounding a culture of self which is *too* aesthetic."[29] According to Hadot, Antique philosophy—at least Stoicism and Epicureanism—is wrongly interpreted as aiming for a cultivation of the self as an end in itself.

From his own Stoic point of view, Hadot points out the differences between the classical philosophers' and Foucault's 'care of the self.' First of all, Foucault's 'techniques of the self' are focused on the self, that is, as taking pleasure in oneself. For the Stoics, "happiness does not consist in pleasure, but in virtue itself, which is its own reward."[30] Second, the Stoic does not find his joy in his 'self,' but in "the best portion of the self," that is, in the "transcendent self." Differently from Foucault's account, the goal is to go beyond oneself. The awareness of "belonging to a whole" is essential in Stoicism.[31] Hadot criticizes the one-sidedness of "the movement of interiorization." From the perspective of Stoicism and its "universalist, cosmic dimension," he argues that a movement of exteriorization should be added: "This is a new way of being-in-the-world, which consists in becoming aware of oneself as a part of nature, and a portion of universal reason."[32] In sum, classical philosophy is not concerned with autonomy and personal choice but with self-transcendence

---

27. Dohmen, "Philosophers on the 'Art-of-Living,'" 367.
28. Ibid., 368.
29. Hadot, *Philosophy as a Way of Life*, 211.
30. Ibid., 207.
31. Ibid.
32. Ibid., 211. Responding to Hadot's criticism, Dohmen advocates autonomy in relation to a "horizontal transcendence": the self can learn in dialogue with others by which a person may transcend him or herself (*Tegen de onverschilligheid*, 157). However, this is more a reply to Hadot's personal conviction than to his interpretation of classical philosophy.

and conversion—not to a state of self-mastery but to a particular philosophical way of life.

Philosophy of the Art of Living and Virtue Ethics

The differences between classical philosophy and philosophy of the art of living become all the more apparent as soon as we compare the latter with Aristotelian virtue ethics, a current of thought not strongly represented in Hadot's account. These differences reveal several problematic features of the philosophy of the art of living originating from its modern presuppositions.

To distinguish virtue ethics from philosophy of the art of living is not to say that there are no commonalities between the two. It is precisely commonalities that make it interesting to engage both currents of thought in dialogue. First of all, this concerns the interest in the cultivation of personal character traits and the formation of a personal attitude from within.[33] Both in virtue ethics and in the philosophy of the art of living, the end of cultivating character is a kind of self-realization.[34] Furthermore, in both strains of thought the concept of *eudaimonia* is pivotal, designating 'a well-lived life' or 'the good life.' Finally, both in virtue ethics and in philosophy of the art of living much emphasis is put on the necessity of training good habits and personal qualities, including learning from exemplary exemplars.[35]

Yet, there are major differences. In the philosophy of the art of living the modern ideal of autonomous freedom of choice is predominant, as we have seen. The good life basically seems to be a matter of knowing what you want. Although in classical virtue ethics individual fulfillment and development are important too, the virtues are not just a matter of personal choice of a life project or a self-chosen lifestyle. In Aristotle's ethics, *eudaimonia* is conceived of in terms of a life that succeeds in being a good life in a general sense: it is directed toward a highest good.[36] This *telos* is bound up with the nature of the human being, which is rationality, and the virtues are the qualities that assist the achievement of the *telos* of living life in a rational way, both in wisdom (the intellectual virtues) and in emotion (the

---

33. Dohmen, for instance, values Aristotelian character formation through the development of virtues and the cultivation of good habits ("Aristoteles: De vader van de deugdethiek [Aristotle: The father of virtue ethics]," in Maarten van Buuren and Joep Dohmen, *Van oude en nieuwe deugden: Levenskunst van Aristoteles tot Nussbaum* (Amsterdam: Ambo, 2012), 71.

34. Cf. Paul van Tongeren, *Deugdelijk leven: Een inleiding in de deugdethiek* [Virtuous life: An introduction to virtue ethics] (Amsterdam: Sun, [2003] 2004), 43: "Virtue ethics is an ethics of self-realization" (trans. mine).

35. Dohmen, "Aristoteles: De vader van de deugdethiek," 71; in Kekes's book *The Art of Life*, examples of particular lives play an important role.

36. *EN* 1094a18–24 and 1097a28–31.

character virtues).³⁷ In Aristotle's eudaimonistic ethics it is presupposed that human beings share such a common essence, whereas in the philosophy of the art of living human beings choose their own *teloi*.³⁸

This is not to say that the 'metaphysical biology' on which Aristotle's account of human nature and the virtues rest is without problems from a late modern perspective. However, the alternative of transforming the *telos* into something that solely depends on the lifestyle, personal values, or life project one has chosen is more problematic, since it reduces morality either to a purely subjective preference for available alternatives or to transpersonal principles that have no intrinsic connection to the aesthetic 'care of the self.' Therefore, Alasdair MacIntyre proposed to counter Aristotelian metaphysical biology by understanding the human *telos* within the context of practices, narratives, and traditions in which we are located and which transcend the self.³⁹ It is not my intention to discuss these concepts here (I will take up them in Chapter 3), but at least these Neo-Aristotelian proposals face up to problematic aspects of premodern metaphysics, yet without abandoning any form of a given teleology as is the case in the philosophy of the art of living and its turn toward a self-determining and self-directing subject.

A second difference concerns the role of community and social relatedness. In Aristotle's view the realization of the best human opportunities in a certain form of life coincides with life as a citizen in the *polis*. The most important reason was that the good, as the *telos* of human life, was thought as a *common* good that could not be possessed by individuals but only jointly in community. Although tradition and social ties are not absent in the art of living, it is essentially an individual endeavor. Decisive is self-direction in order "to *control* the influences traditions have on the development of our individuality."⁴⁰ Schmid speaks of social and societal bonds, but interprets them immediately in terms of structures of power (Foucault!) that overrule the individual's freedom. Therefore, the philosophy of the art of living emphasizes that the individual has power too, so that he will not just become the slave of ruling powers.⁴¹ As a consequence, other people, communities, or traditions are neither really constitutive of the choices the individual makes, nor provide him or her with criteria or shared convictions for how to make these choices. Even when it is acknowledged that one's formation depends on others, in the end you

---

37. *EN* 1098a13–19.

38. Cf. Dohmen, "Aristoteles: De vader van de deugdethiek," 71–2, who affirms this major difference between his own philosophy and virtue ethics.

39. Definitions of these central concepts in MacIntyre, *After Virtue*, 187, 205, 222.

40. Kekes, *The Art of Life*, 26 (italics mine).

41. Schmid, *Filosofie van de levenskunst*, 25. In his book *Die Liebe neu erfinden: Von der Lebenskunst im Umgang mit Anderen* (Berlin: Suhrkamp, 2010), Schmid tries to think through relationality in the art of living, but again neither community nor tradition plays any meaningful role in his conceptualization.

yourself choose which 'significant others' are important and exemplary.[42] In this view, everything becomes a matter of choice, as the Dutch philosopher Paul van Tongeren comments, even the way one chooses and the criteria on the basis of which one chooses.[43]

Although virtue too is a personal quality of the individual, it is at the same time defined by a wider community which regards it as an excellence and embedded in a tradition and in particular social practices. And although the *polis* as a fixed community has disappeared, in Neo-Aristotelian virtue ethics it is still possible to locate the virtues in transcending social practices in which the virtues receive their shape from the internal goods that are aimed for in these practices.[44] These practices are by definition communal and socially determined, and are to be understood in relation to their respective traditions. From a virtue ethical point of view, without these 'transcending' entities the good life cannot be understood adequately.

Interestingly, Foucault admits that in taking up the Hellenistic notion of 'care of the self' as central to the art of living, this philosophy goes indeed beyond the communal in which classical virtue is embedded:

> I think that one of the main evolutions in ancient culture has been that this *technè tou biou* became more and more a *technè* of the self. A Greek citizen of the fifth or fourth century would have felt that his *technè* for life was to take care of the city, of his companions. But for Seneca, for instance, the problem is to take care of himself.[45]

Insofar as Foucault's philosophy of the art of living has its source in Antiquity, it resembles the Stoa, albeit in a very reduced sense as we have seen.

This brings us to a third difference: the philosophy of the art of living emphasizes self-mastery and the manipulability of the good life to a much greater extent than virtue ethics. Although Dohmen and Schmid acknowledge the vulnerability of life and admit that we are not able to manage everything in life, they still claim that it is possible to acquire self-direction, autonomy, and self-mastery by which you can arrange your life, if you really want it. The 'beautiful life' means that "you interfere in existence and consciously transform it into something meaningful."[46] Foucault refers to the new concept of virtue included in the Hellenistic concept of the 'care of the self' as consisting "essentially in perfectly governing oneself, that is,

---

42. Dohmen, *Brief aan een middelmatige man*, 62–3.
43. Van Tongeren, *Leven is een kunst*, 126.
44. Cf. MacIntyre, *After Virtue*, 187.
45. Foucault, "On the Genealogy of Ethics," 348.
46. Schmid, *Filosofie van de levenskunst*, 9. Epicurus, *Letter to Menoikos*, trans. Peter Saint-Andre (http://monadnock.net/epicurus/letter.html, 2011), 123, speaks of "the beautiful life (τοῦ καλῶς ζῆν)," but relates this life, among other things, immediately to belief in the transcendent god.

in exercising upon oneself as exact a mastery as that of a sovereign against whom there would no longer be revolts."[47] Whereas Aristotelian virtue ethics considers *eudaimonia* as something which cannot be fully realized in reality and depends upon external factors like lucky circumstances and conditions,[48] according to philosophers of the art of living, happiness seems to be in reach for everyone who wants it. In the end it depends on your own will.

In a sense the rise of 'art of living' may be seen as a reaction to modern ideologies of manipulability, but criticism is limited to specific appearances of manipulability, like the socialist salvation state or neoliberal free market. The idea of manipulability returns on the level of performing one's individual life. Dohmen speaks of "control based on good self-management,"[49] and Schmid argues for "the art of mastering life,"[50] which even seems to extend to suffering: "like lust pain must be incorporated into life and integrated in the coherence of the self."[51] Despite Hadot's Stoic criticism, in this respect the philosophy of the art of living is close to Stoicism, in which virtue was not only a necessary but also a sufficient condition for *eudaimonia* (thereby erasing the aspects of fortune that in Aristotelian ethics are seen as part of happiness—I will discuss this more extensively in Chapter 2). As van Tongeren demonstrates, in the philosophy of the art of the living the Stoic "true knowledge of the good" is replaced by "authentic knowledge and choice of the self," but the basic scheme is maintained: you are the one who is able to realize happiness, as long as you know yourself and act authentically according to your will. In virtue ethics, on the contrary, dependence on external factors is much more strongly emphasized.[52]

The irony is that this strong emphasis on self-mastery and manipulability of the good life increases the pressure upon the individual, since the extent to which your life is successful depends entirely upon the choices you yourself make and how you yourself direct your life. Givenness of life and the givenness of others as intrinsically part of your life are not determining factors. All that matters is how you choose to give them a meaningful place in your life or not. Relations are primarily a matter of personal choice based on indeterminate preference. Ironically, this endless requirement to choose may become an unbearable command to the autonomous self which makes life not so much a pretty convenient piece of art but rather a worrisome burden where one constantly asks: What do I want? Do I make the best choices?

---

47. Foucault, "On the Genealogy of Ethics," 363.
48. *EN* 1099a31–33.
49. Dohmen, *Tegen de onverschilligheid*, 39.
50. Schmid, *Filosofie van de levenskunst*, 22.
51. Ibid., 48.
52. Van Tongeren, *Leven is een kunst*, 125–33. In a response Joep Dohmen admits that his philosophy indeed tends to be too activistic ("De rol van deugden in een humanistische ethiek [The role of virtues in a humanistic ethics]," *Algemeen Nederlands Tijdschrift voor Wijsbegeerte* 106/2 (2014), 139–44.

Theology of the Art of Living

Until now we have discussed two sources of understanding the good life. It is time to add the third source, the Christian tradition, as a conversation partner to the art of living and virtue ethics. Let us start with recent theological accounts of the art of living, as brought forward in the introduction of this chapter, which correct some of the late modern presuppositions of the philosophy of the art of living. Departing from the Christian tradition in a broad sense, these accounts attempt to counter the criticism of Christian convictions about the self before God that according to secular philosophers of the art of living contradict the central aim of care of the self. Are these theological corrections and proposals convincing?

The theologians Bubmann and Sill are aware of the fact that art of living can easily be associated with the ideals of a luxurious life full of aesthetic high points or with the manipulability of life. In their view, in the philosophy of the art of living the subject as *Organisator der Lebenskunst* is indeed overestimated.[53] Similarly, Frits de Lange wants to keep away from the association with modern aesthetics and a seductive, 'beautiful' life. Art of living should not be reduced to providing one's life with "an attractive design."[54] Instead, Christian art of living articulates human freedom as based on God's acting. If freedom is founded in the Christian conception of redemption, nothing prevents us from developing a Christian art of living. Bubmann and Sill correct the aesthetic language of late modern art of living by adding theological notions of dependence on God, the gift-like character of human capabilities and human vulnerability: "Christian art of living has as its theme the finitude and vulnerability of human freedom and witnesses its indispensable conditions determined by God's acting."[55] According to de Lange, the art of living involves both mastering and letting go: "In the metaphor of the sailor—as old as classical philosophy itself—both come together: the activity, the mastering technique, the navigating, and the yielding to the uncontrollable and unpredictable wind and waves."[56]

In these theological contributions, the basic method is to correct particular aspects in secular philosophy of the art of living by adding Christian elements. Individual freedom, for instance, is not to be understood as absolute self-determination, but as given, communicative and cooperative freedom. This means that a 'successful' life is not completely manageable but is a matter of a "given ability" (*geschenktes Können*).[57] De Lange adds to the art of living in terms of self-direction "the art of surrender," as a proper attitude to the things over which we have little control. Instead of drawing on the Stoic virtue of equanimity, which

---

53. Bubmann and Sill, "Einleitung," 14–15.
54. De Lange, "Modern Life Course," 4. Cf. De Lange, "Schipperen met het eigen leven," 59–77.
55. Bubmann and Sill, "Einleitung," 14–15 (trans. mine).
56. De Lange, "Modern Life Course," 5.
57. Bubmann and Sill, "Einleitung," 14, 18.

requires a change of perspective of reality close to becoming indifferent to it, Christian faith speaks of acquiescence, of surrender, which implies a personal relationship with reality and in which struggle is not removed, although one's fate is put in the hands of God.[58] Furthermore, as de Lange argues, Christianity widens the classical notion of friendship as love of the other that broadens the circle of a potentially selfish 'care of the self': charity transforms friendship and robs it of its exclusivity and favoritism, widening the scope to every other, even one's enemy.[59]

In my view, these corrections are to be affirmed as important aspects that should be part of a critical and constructive theological discussion with the philosophy of the art of living. Christian art of living is not indeed directed toward strong, successful subjects, but rather to weak and vulnerable subjects. Instead of being interested in strong, self-conscious subjects, it takes the dignity attributed to each human being as its presupposition. Moreover, not the subject's own abilities and self-creation are the starting point, but God's acting as creator.[60] I think that these and other corrections are good starting points. However, the question is how these considerations are related to other goals of *Lebenskunst* that the theologians of the art of living articulate, like establishing one's own identity, forming a self-will, reflecting upon and strengthening one's own life, sharpening one's awareness of the realities, and possibilities of one's life, living a stylish life.[61] It is unclear whether and how these notions are related to the theologically motivated emphasis on vulnerability and receptivity.

In these approaches the Christian tradition basically *adds* something, whereas the radical *transformative* nature of Christian faith is undervalued. Hence, their theological accounts of the art of living are still deeply indebted to 'secular' articulations of the art of living by authors like Foucault, Schmid, Dohmen, Kekes, and others. Bubmann and Sill, for instance, explain their aim as that of discovering the beauty of one's own life and then giving it a form shaped by faith. They take it as a task of Christians to shape one's own life according to faith, provide it with beauty, and discover it as a God-given life that must be cultivated and developed.[62] In a Dutch popular work on the art of living, *Doornse levenskunst*, the argument is that art of living starts "with the invitation to me as a creature to help the creator in creating myself."[63] In both examples God is articulated as a necessary condition, but this theological presupposition doesn't substantially alter the view that one's

---

58. De Lange, "Modern Life Course," 9–10.

59. Ibid., 12.

60. Bubmann and Sill, "Einleitung," 15–16; Quartel and Hoogland, *Levenskunst voor iedereen*, 9, 36–7, 44.

61. Bubmann and Sill, "Einleitung," 10; Sill and Bubmann, *Schritte durch die Lebensmitte*, 117–22; Quartel and Hoogland, *Levenskunst voor iedereen*, 12.

62. Bubmann and Sill, "Einleitung," 9–10.

63. Aarnoud van der Deijl, Alida Groeneveld, and Stephan de Jong (eds.), *Doornse levenskunst: Mooi, goed en waarachtig leven* [Art of living from Doorn: Beautiful, good and truthful life] (Utrecht: Kok, 2014), 10 (trans. mine).

life is basically a self-created piece of art. Of course, God is our creator, but we cannot really depend on him since we have to help him. In the end it is not clear what we receive from God that we cannot realize ourselves.

Such theological accounts of the art of living vacillate uncertainly between views in which life is seen as a project that one can achieve by one's own efforts and views in which life rests in dependency and givenness. They are a hybrid mixture of modern ideals of self-realization, on the one hand, and Christian conceptions of life as a gift, on the other, without clarifying how these contrasting aspects are related. Mastery is aligned to vulnerability, ability to inability, succeeding in making life a successful project to acknowledging the profound human fallibility in performing life as an art. Bubmann and Sill reject perfectionism, but the aim is still to open up possibilities of a life that succeeds.[64] They consider Christian art of living to be a "stylish appropriation" of the reality of Christ and a way to follow him. Art of living in terms of *Nachfolge* means that Christ urges us to a new existence, to a life full of trust in God, of love for all life and of hope of shalom, but at the same time this life is defined in terms of shaping one's own life and giving direction to it.[65] In a similar way, de Lange interprets self-direction in terms of conversion, that is, the process of transformation in which a Christian is involved if he has *chosen* to devote his life to following Christ. Like philosophers of the art of living, he defines it in terms of choice: "Based on this existential choice for and commitment to an ideal, one organizes one's life and arranges and rearranges one's priorities in it."[66] The language of choice, lifestyle, and self-direction is mixed up with Christian concepts of following Christ, conversion, human vulnerability, and dependency on God, without their interconnection being theologically explained. My argument is not that it is unjustified to adopt such modern, secular concepts in theology, but at least it is a theological task to explain how such concepts can convincingly be understood as being part of the Christian grammar. This grammar is not just about God as a condition making life as an art possible, but also about transformative grace, language that is absent in these theological accounts of the art of living.

By aligning contrasting concepts quite uncritically, such theology of the art of living is still vulnerable to the problematic aspects of the philosophy of the art of living that I detected in the previous section, and that they try to counter, in particular the overemphasis on autonomous choice in a life project. Whether my

---

64. Bubmann and Sill, "Einleitung," 15: "Möglichkeitsräume gelingenden Lebens zu eröffnen." In the following chapters of their volume, in which all sorts of themes are addressed, the strategy is often to align two dialectically related terms, like being sick and being well, giving and taking, to foster a community and to go your own way, to approach the other and to distance oneself, remembering and dreaming, etc. Cf. Sill and Bubmann, *Schritte durch die Lebensmitte*, 181; Hoogland and Quartel, *Levenskunst voor iedereen*, 9 and 44.

65. Bubmann and Sill, "Einleitung," 17.

66. De Lange, "Modern Life Course," 12.

life will be successful is still a matter of my own choices and will. Though this 'will' may be seen as tuned in to God's will, it is taken as a quite unproblematic human agency. Therefore, instead of adding Christian notions to the modern framework of the philosophy of the art of living, a more profound reflection on the Christian understanding of life is needed in order to develop a convincing theological account of the good life. We are not the first to undertake this; it is already part of the Christian tradition. The way a Christian thinker like Augustine engaged in dialogue with ancient philosophers' conceptions of the good life, the virtues, and *eudaimonia* forms a more adequate and profound response to the problematic features of the philosophy of the art of living than is offered by the theological representatives of the art of living.

Will and Receptivity in Augustine's Thought

As we have seen, conceptions of the art of living connect modern elements with notions derived from classical philosophy. Strikingly absent in both philosophical and—to a great extent—theological accounts of the art of living is the period between Antiquity and modernity: the Christian thought of late Antiquity and the Middle Ages.[67] Not only is it impossible to understand modern concepts like will, choice, and self properly without taking into consideration how these and other concepts have emerged and developed within Christianity, but also valuable contributions are to be derived from Christian accounts of virtue ethics, especially in terms of those virtues that are not acquired by self-mastery but are received as gifts—the theological virtues of faith, hope, and love. I limit myself to Christian thought in late Antiquity, Augustine in particular. It is relevant how he discovers the central and problematic meaning of the human will, on the one hand, and the importance of receptivity and passivity, on the other, as indispensable to a truthful understanding of the good life. As we will see, this provides us with a profound framework for engaging with contemporary philosophy of the art of living.

These distinctive features presuppose both continuity and discontinuity between classical and Christian discourses on the good life and the virtues.[68] To start with the continuity, it is clear that several classical virtue ethical concepts were adopted in the Christian understanding of life. Importantly, Christian thinkers translated and interpreted classical virtues in Christian terms. For instance, in his reading of Cicero's *De officiis*, Ambrose understood the four cardinal virtues that Plato had

---

67. An exception is Hadot, who repeatedly demonstrates that an essential part of classical philosophy as a way of life as represented by the philosophical schools of Platonism, Aristotelianism, Epicureanism, and Stoicism, continued in Christianity. Christianity presented itself as *philosophia*, and as such "assimilated into itself the traditional practices of spiritual exercises" (*Philosophy as a Way of Life*, 107). Meanwhile, Hadot dissociates himself from the major transformations and corrections of classical thought in Christianity.

68. Cf. Van Tongeren, *Leven is een kunst*, 139–78.

distinguished and were incorporated in the Stoa—*prudentia* (φρόνησις), *fortitudo* (ἀνδρεία), *temperantia* (σωφροσύνη), and *iustitia* (δικαιοσύνη)—in a Christian sense: prudence concerns the love of God, courage is the virtue of the martyr, temperance is understood in terms of decency and purity, and justice is equated with love of one's neighbor.[69] Similarly, Augustine understands the cardinal virtues in Christian terms: *prudentia* serves to distinguish good from evil, *temperantia* to oppose earthly seductions, *fortitudo* to help the human being to endure adversity in life, and *iustitia* is the virtue that gives each one his or her due.[70] Note that it was not a 'pagan' thinker but the Christian theologian Ambrose who coined the term 'cardinal virtues'—these four virtues being the *cardo* or hinge on which all other virtues turn.[71] Furthermore, the Christian faith can be seen as a particular view of the good life, providing an alternative in the Antique world to other answers given to the shared question of what it means to live well. In the next chapter I will address the question whether and how Augustine continues the eudaimonistic framework.

The discontinuity consists in how Christian thinkers understand the sources of the good life and the virtues. This concerns, first of all, the understanding of the human will and the reality of evil, as becomes clear from Augustine's thought. In his view, the human will consists in the ability to want those things for which there are no good reasons and that do not have good effects on our well-being: evil.[72] Thus, the Christian doctrine of sin, in which the human will is pivotal, opens our eyes to an aspect of human acting that is not developed in classical virtue ethics and is remarkably absent in theological accounts of the art of living—that is, that the human will has the ability to oppose the good, and that evil can intermingle with the good we desire by nature. This can be explained from many instances in

---

69. Plato, *Republic, Vol. I: Books 1-5* (Loeb Classical Library 237), ed. and trans. Christopher Emlyn-Jones and William Preddy (Cambridge: Harvard University Press, 2013), 427a-e; Ambrose, *De excessu fratris Satyri* 1, PL 16, 1289-354; Ambrose, *De officiis* 1.27-50, PL 16, 60-102. As Jasmijn Bovendeert, *Kardinale deugden gekerstend: De vier kardinale deugden vanaf Ambrosius tot het jaar 1000* [Cardinal virtues Christianized: The four cardinal virtues from Ambrose to the year 1000] (Nijmegen: Radboud University, 2007), 33-40, 48-54, 68, demonstrates, Ambrose's use of the cardinal virtues is flexible; their content and meaning depend on the various contexts in which they are dealt with.

70. Bovendeert, *Kardinale deugden gekerstend*, 91, referring to *Sermo* 150 among other texts.

71. Ambrose, *Expositio evangelii secundum Lucam* 5.49, PL 15, 1649: "Hic enim quattuor velut virtutes amplexus est cardinales"; *De excessu fratris Satyri* 1.57, PL 16, 1309. Cf. Cicero, *De officiis* (Loeb Classical Library 30), ed. and trans. Walter Miller (Cambridge: Harvard University Press, [1913] 1968), 1.5.

72. CD 22.24. Quotes are from Dyson's translation: Augustine, *The City of God against the Pagans*, ed. and trans. R. W. Dyson (Cambridge and New York: Cambridge University Press, 1998); Bovendeert, *Kardinale deugden*, 103, 112.

Augustine's work. For the sake of brevity, I explain it here from his understanding of virtue and happiness in *De civitate Dei*.

In Augustine's view, virtue may be the best and most useful thing one can find on earth.[73] Nevertheless, virtue cannot achieve the highest good or perfection in temporal and finite human life. In book 19 of *De civitate Dei* the cardinal virtues are described as unsuccessful attempts to contribute to the *vita beata*, since, according to Augustine's famous dictum, virtue seems to have as its main task "to wage perpetual war against the vices (*perpetua bella cum vitiis*)."[74] This is due to the reality of evil affecting the human will, a thought that is alien to ancient philosophy. Although the Greeks have an understanding of the potentially tragic nature of human existence and though there are all kinds of circumstances that may prevent a person from realizing the good life, this is due to conditions outside the self. Insofar as the philosophy of the art of living acknowledges the notion of the tragic, the same is true. Christian faith, on the contrary, states that evil is not just a matter of bad luck or a lack of fortune, but of a wrong will that is in a battle with the good will.[75] Therefore, happiness is not within our reach, as Augustine states: "God forbid . . . that, for as long as we are engaged in this internal warfare, we should believe that we have already attained that happiness: that happiness which we seek to attain by our victory."[76] This statement seems to imply two things. First of all, the good life is something we long for, but it is not something we can achieve just by our own powers—it is a divine gift. Secondly, it seems that true happiness can only be fully realized in the eternal life. As a consequence, true virtues are eternal; we cannot reach the highest good on earth.

However, this last conclusion could be drawn too fast. Explaining Augustine's valuation of the virtues and the good life in terms of a *dichotomy* of the

---

73. In his works written in the first years after his conversion, Augustine conceives of the virtues in a Neo-Platonic outlook as the way to direct the soul to the highest, to God. Their task is to purify the soul, a concept that Augustine derived from Plotinus. In *De moribus ecclesiae catholicae et de moribus Manichearum* (1.15.25, PL 32, 1322) the cardinal virtues are described as four expressions of love. *Virtus* is perfect love of God, the sovereign good, and each of the cardinal virtues is a form of this love (Bovendeert, *Kardinale deugden gekerstend*, 91–6). Yet, as James Wetzel, *Augustine and the Limits of Virtue* (Cambridge: Cambridge University Press, 1992), 72, demonstrates, although love is thus related to a personal God, the actual description of virtuous love in *De moribus* is still intellectual, since this love results in illumination. The virtues serve the aim of freeing the soul from the body and reflect both Stoic and Neo-Platonic influences. This is corrected in his later work *De civitate Dei*.

74. CD 19.4.

75. Augustine, *Confessions*, trans. R. S. Pine-Coffin (London: Penguin Books, [1961] 1984), 8.22–27, where he speaks of a battle of myself against myself. Cf. Wetzel, *Limits*, 2: "Augustine removes good and evil from external space and places them in his newly discovered interior space, the realm of his will."

76. CD 19.4.

earthly and the heavenly is too limited. The question is what is really at stake in Augustine's treatment of the classical understanding. The standard view, as reflected in Foucault's, Dohmen's, and Schmidt's comments, is that Augustine opposes the philosophical attempts to found happiness on the achievements of virtue by depicting this life as an ineffectual struggle against temptation and vice.[77] Yet, this argument would not be very convincing to the philosophers of his time, with whom he is in a continuous conversation, since they would agree that virtue indeed has to cope with such external difficulties, either by Neo-Platonic intellectual contemplation or by a Stoic attitude of *apatheia*, which too can be regarded as forms of eternalization. The core of Augustine's argument is not to transport fulfillment toward an afterlife. Rather he has in mind a reformulation of virtue for life in this world, because he discovered that the ideal of *beatitudo* cannot be reached by virtue of one's own powers. James Wetzel illuminatingly points to two elements that persuaded Augustine to face this specific powerlessness: one is his analysis of inner conflict; another is given by his analysis of time.[78]

When it comes to *inner conflict*, Augustine emphasizes the vulnerability of human life to material loss and pain, in order to underscore the vulnerability of philosophical, intellectual *beatitudo* to the disorder of passion, since passion binds reason *involuntarily* to the perishable world. Ancient philosophy, especially Neo-Platonic and Stoic conceptions, can only answer passion's intrusion by having faith in reason's sovereignty over disordered affection. In this context, Augustine doubts whether virtue really has this power of sovereignty. It may be more vulnerable to the affections than is acknowledged. Augustine's dismissal of the philosophical conception of virtue in book 19 is based on his moral psychology as developed in books 9 and 14. Temperance, for instance, reveals virtue's continual struggle against vice, precisely because it desires to 'temper' a passionate desire. Reason cannot disown the 'irrational' desires, because such desires that motivate a vicious or disordered passion are our own.[79] Since passion embodies judgment, even reason is implicated in these very vices. This brings Augustine not to a radical otherworldliness, renunciation, and self-annihilation as much as to an acknowledgment of the ongoing struggle between vice and virtue in one's inner being.

Augustine's account of the 'powerlessness' of the virtues is also based on his analysis of human *temporality*. In our attempt to acquire the virtues we are still bound to our temporality, which includes our past of imperfect virtue and uncontrolled passion. The Stoic sage who tries to reach *apatheia*, on the contrary,

---

77. Similarly, Bovendeert, *Kardinale deugden gekerstend*, 96, sees an unbridgeable gap in book 19 between the cultivation of the virtues on earth, which is a laborious process, and the real perfection of the virtues in the one true *virtus* in heaven, the highest good, a gap which cannot be bridged on earth.
78. Wetzel, *Limits*, 107.
79. *CD* 19.4.

has to erase his own past of unmeasured passion and imperfect virtue. In this philosophy, reason receives extraordinary powers over passion because Stoic and Platonic philosophers fail to see how passion carries reason's past into its present. Reason is in conflict with itself in the field of memory and involuntary sin emerges from it. Because our lives extend over time, it is rather our willing that bears the impress of what we have been. Willing is an achievement of temporal synthesis but our will can fail in willing to integrate our desires. Interpreted in this fuller context of Augustine's moral psychology, Augustine's critique of classical virtue surprisingly has Stoic and other classical philosophy's *otherworldliness* as its target! For it is philosophers like the Stoics who try to project virtue and beatitude from temporal dissolution by situating subjects of virtue and beatitude outside of time's influence. Augustine's alternative is to redirect attention to the intricacies of *time-bound willing*.[80]

This implies a break with classical conceptualizations of the good life and virtue, but at the same time Augustine offers an alternative conception.[81] Augustine's 'negative' evaluation of the classical understanding of the good life and the virtues from his theological doctrine of sin and grace is philosophically relevant. By relating the good life and virtue to God, he pretends that classical philosophy and virtue ethics should be transformed radically, that is, from its *radix*. The theological word for this transformation is redemption. Augustine doesn't deny that virtue expresses the ideal form of our self-defining activity in the world, but he does deny that virtue reflects resources of power that *we ourselves* generate to maintain our virtuous integrity in the world around us, where time and change promise us only entropy and dissolution.[82] For "that which makes the life of man blessed is not something derived from him, but something above him. And this is true not only of man but of every heavenly power and virtue whatsoever."[83] Through the grace of Christ, "who is God with the Father, and human with us . . . we are reconciled with God in the spirit of love . . . Divinely endowed, then, with these virtues, *we can lead a good life now*."[84] Augustine's invocation of grace proposes a solution beyond the self-

---

80. Wetzel, *Limits*, 109–10.

81. Ibid., 113, 116.

82. Ibid., 124–5. So, unlike Paul Ramsey, *Basic Christian Ethics* (Louisville: John Knox Press, [1950] 1993), 212–13, who states that Augustine's criticism of classical virtues is not based on 'metaphysics' but on the ethical ground that it is concern for the neighbor that makes Christian virtue true virtue, I think that this ethical concern is intrinsically related to Augustine's theological conception of human will and divine grace, which in turn is deeply related to what we may call his moral psychology.

83. *CD* 19.25.

84. *Ep.* 155.16 (italics mine), transl. Augustine, *Political Writings*, ed. and trans. E. M. Atkins and Robert J. Dodaro (New York: Cambridge University Press, 2001).

contradictory human will throughout time: to define ourselves without having to appeal to self-generated sources of power.[85]

In short, Augustine's emphasis on the laborious or even failing achievements of the cardinal virtues in *De civitate Dei* 19.4 demonstrates virtue's vulnerability to time and to our limited or self-contradictory will. As a consequence, his emphasis on grace is not to be seen as obscuring the good life and the virtues making this life possible, as well as complicating the way the virtues can be achieved and the good life can be lived: we are in need of a source beyond our own capabilities. The divided will and God's healing grace intervene between the ideal of the full union of beatitude and virtue, on the one hand, and the optimistic, illusory attempt to realize this by one's own power, on the other. This illusion is depicted as 'pride.'[86] Thus, the overstressed ideal to realize the good life in a successful life project and by one's own power, which readily leads to either oppression of the passions and of radical temporality or complete defeatism through lack of success or bad luck, is abandoned.[87] Augustine's eschatological approach leads to a more realistic account of the good life which can do justice to human temporality and inner conflict without giving up hope of human flourishing and fulfillment.

That the good life is rooted in receptivity to what God gives is expressed in the particular nature of the theological virtues as the broader horizon of the cardinal virtues. Limiting myself again to Augustine's understanding, it is the virtues of faith, hope, and love that put the cardinal virtues in the right perspective. They provide the eschatological horizon from which the good life is to be lived: human life "is happy in the hope of the world to come, and in the hope of salvation." Again, this is hope for *this* life, for "it is in hope that we *have been* made happy (*beati facti sumus*)." Moreover, in faith or "true piety" we acquire the true virtues of prudence, patience, temperance, and justice.[88] Though the supreme good is eternal and perfect peace, "if any man uses this life in such a way that he directs it toward that end which he so ardently loves and for which he so faithfully hopes, he may without absurdity be called happy *even now (dici nunc beatus potest)*."[89] The cardinal virtues receive their meaning from the right end, which is *amor Dei*. From this true love the good life can develop and the virtuous character can be cultivated, since it is "good and bad loves that make good and bad characters,"

---

85. Wetzel, *Limits*, 126.

86. For although virtues which have reference only to themselves, and are desired only on their own account, are true and genuine virtue, they are nevertheless "puffed up and proud, and so are to be adjudged vices rather than virtues" (*CD* 19.25). These virtues are still caught up in the spectacle of a self *incurvatus in se*.

87. Wetzel, *Limits*, 55. Hence Wetzel speaks of "limits of virtue," which refers "negatively to Augustine's dissatisfaction with classical virtue and its blindness to the psychology of inner conflict, and positively to his theistic reformulation of virtue as the motivational integrity of graced willing" (16).

88. *CD* 19.4.

89. *CD* 19.20 (emphasis mine).

as Augustine writes in one of his Letters.⁹⁰ Real development is possible precisely because God is the source and because the final fulfillment is eschatological: "If you recognize the source of the virtues you have been given . . . all your virtues will be real ones. They will develop and be perfected in this way through the assistance of God, whose generous gift they are."⁹¹

These key Christian concepts may contribute to a profound conception of the good life and the virtues distinguished from the other two conceptions. First of all, it becomes clear that the modern emphasis on the human will cannot be understood unless the history of Christian thought is taken into account. When the philosophy of the art of living relates modern conceptions of autonomy to classical philosophy, this cannot be achieved without consciously or unconsciously presupposing Christianity as a link between the two. While philosophers of the art of living criticize the 'will-less Christian' because of his or her adherence to God and consider Augustine a preeminent example of self-renunciation instead of self-development, Augustine is in fact the first to establish the will as an independent human faculty. The modern emphasis on the human will in the philosophy of the art of living is indebted to the Christian tradition, but this heritage is perverted, since the ambiguous nature of the human will is not taken into account. As van Tongeren remarks: "The one who thinks that the good life is just a matter of knowing what you want, perhaps does not know what 'the will' actually means."⁹² Whereas the modern philosophy (and theology) of the art of living is quite naïve about the human will as the unproblematic, univocal source of a good and beautiful life, Augustine demonstrates how divided the human will is and that it therefore does not suffice as the ultimate source for realizing the good life. Taking seriously the Augustinian understanding of the will, including human fallibility, implies a critique of the manageability of the self and the good life in the philosophy of the art of living.

Secondly, the theological virtues make us aware of the fact that in the end the good life is something which is given to us. As van Tongeren puts it, referring to Augustine and Aquinas in particular:

> The theological virtues warn . . . against an overstressed moral activism and remind us of the importance of a certain passivity. If life is an art, then this art consists not only of doing what we can to become 'good,' but also of the cultivation of the ability to become receptive to what is given to us, or to carry what is withheld to us.⁹³

---

90. *Ep.* 155.13. Slightly changed quotation from Atkins' and Dodaro's translation.
91. *Ep.* 155.12.
92. Van Tongeren, *Leven is een kunst*, 163 (trans. mine).
93. Ibid., 174. Van Tongeren also points to an obverse side: the theological virtues could be *dangerous* as well, insofar as they may deteriorate not only into too great a passivity ending up in quietism, but also into fanaticism due to the lacking delimitation of what these virtues may reasonably ask from me. In van Tongeren's view, the theological virtues

The Dutch theologian Erik Borgman states more boldly "that, thus, art of living in a religious sense is in particular the shaping of the ability to receive, to be open to what befalls us and to devote oneself to it."[94]

Conclusion

In the philosophy of the art of living, the individual deploys his or her own life, is not embedded in tradition and community unless these are self-chosen, and strives for a life that can be managed in a self-chosen direction; it is basically a matter of 'knowing what you want.' This philosophy differs from (Aristotelian) virtue ethics, which includes a teleological view of life, a communal understanding of the good, and an awareness of the dependency on the non-manageable nature of human happiness. It differs even more from a Christian understanding of the good life and the virtues, as explained from Augustine, who acknowledges the problematic nature of the human will, human dependency upon God and the gift-like character of the theological virtues.

At first sight, this Augustinian approach seems to imply a transportation of the good life to eternal life. As a consequence, Augustine's continuous insistence in his late works that the ultimate good is to be found in the heavenly kingdom seems to confirm Foucault's, Dohmen's, Schmid's, Kekes's, and others' impression that a Christian account of the good life consists in a permanent renunciation of earthly ties. However, this eschatological view can only be rightly understood if it is seen as related to the present life. Augustine not only criticizes classical thought and its virtue ethics from a theological perspective, but also contributes profoundly to developing a viable conception of the good life, a conception that acknowledges the human condition as marked by temporality, deficiency, passion, and internal division. An Augustinian theological account of the human will, of sin, and grace appears to be relevant to re-envisioning a philosophy of the good life and the virtues. The good life is something we long for, not because it is only available in an afterlife, albeit that its final fulfillment is in the *beatitudo* of the eternal life, but because our actual life is marked by temporality and deficiencies. Therefore, we receptively depend upon God as the ultimate source of the good life. Augustine's Christian criticism of Stoic self-sufficiency is relevant not only to classical thought, but also to contemporary philosophies of the art of living. The good life is not something we can realize solely by our own activities. Augustine helps to understand that any account of the good life in which all emphasis is put on autonomous activity will fail. It will fail because the human capacity to manage

---

are only prevented from such a deterioration into fanaticism or even "holy madness" if they are connected to the classical virtues (174).

94. Erik Borgman, "Leven is een kunst [Life is an art]," in Hans Weigand (ed.), *Het volle leven: Levenskunst en levensloop in de moderne samenleving* (Zoetermeer: Boekencentrum, 2005), 14.

one's own life is overstressed. It is an unrealistic, 'otherworldly' view, because it violates radical human temporality and vulnerability.

However, the theological core notions explored in this chapter not only include criticism of classical thought and late modern philosophy of the art of living, but also seem to have repercussions for classical virtue ethics and its teleology. Augustine seems to dismiss the eudaimonistic view of life in his criticism of the human aspirations inherent in all classical and Hellenistic philosophies. Therefore, the question to which we turn in the next chapter is whether in his view the good life can still be seen in eudaimonistic terms. This will deepen our understanding of Augustine's Christian thought and the way it is adopted and interpreted in Protestantism.

Chapter 2

CHALLENGING EUDAIMONISM

Why should we care for the good of the other? To what extent does an ethics of the good life motivate us to strive for the good in the lives of others? Isn't ethics in need of a radically different perspective—that of general justice and universal human rights—altogether different from an ethics of the good life?

Such critical questions are raised in Nicholas Wolterstorff's book *Justice: Rights and Wrongs*. In this seminal work the Reformed philosopher offers an account of justice as grounded in inherent rights, a conception that originates not just from modernity with early roots in fourteenth-century nominalism but also from the Hebrew and Christian Scriptures. In this view, it is because the other has rights to goods that I have the duty to take care of these goods and the other's well-being. According to Wolterstorff, such a biblical conception of justice is opposed to classical Greek and Roman eudaimonism that I presupposed as common ground in the previous chapter. According to Wolterstorff, the eudaimonistic view, shared by all thinkers of Antiquity, albeit developed in a variety of ways, presupposes that the ultimate goal of each person is to live one's life as well as possible; the εὐδαίμων life is the well-lived life. Εὐδαιμονία—usually translated as 'happiness'—is understood as activity: happiness "does not consist in what happens to one but is what one makes of what happens to one. Living well consists of acting well."[1] As a consequence, in the eudaimonistic view it is important to choose good actions, actions that will either be chosen as goods in themselves or as a means to those actions that I choose as ends in themselves. The aim for each of us is to perform those activities that will make one's own life a well-lived life. Hence, according to Wolterstorff, eudaimonism offers an agent-oriented account of the good life. Although it is not incompatible with altruism, it nevertheless describes actions in terms of the way they contribute to the agent's living well. Rights, on the contrary, de-center the agent: "Instead of the agent's happiness determining his action, the worth of the recipient and of those others who will be affected by the action is to determine what the agent does."[2] According to Wolterstorff, it is Augustine who causes a break with the eudaimonistic view by radically addressing the needs of the neighbor to whom we must do justice.

---

1. Wolterstorff, *Justice*, 152.
2. Ibid., 178.

In this chapter I will take up Wolterstorff's criticism of eudaimonism as a starting point for deepening our understanding of how a Christian account of the good is related to classical philosophy and its ethics of virtue and *eudaimonia*. Does Augustine's critique of Greek and Roman ethics imply a break with an ethics of the good life? The discussion with Wolterstorff is relevant to my project because as an influential Neo-Calvinist philosopher he defends an ethical view of rights and justice as radically opposed to the eudaimonistic framework underlying classical and contemporary versions of virtue ethics. In doing so, he offers a critique of virtue ethics that is regularly voiced, namely that it is in fact self-centered, focused on the agent's own happiness and aimed at optimal self-realization. Moreover, in relating a modern discourse to the Christian tradition, Augustine in particular, he is doing something similar to what I am trying to do with regard to Protestantism and virtue ethics, but with a different outcome, since my project presupposes not just discontinuity of the Christian tradition with ancient thought but also continuity with its eudaimonistic and virtue ethical framework. Therefore, core issues are whether a theological account of virtue ethics necessarily presupposes a eudaimonistic framework and how this relates to a biblical understanding of the moral life in terms of justice.

Since Wolterstorff's criticism applies to eudaimonistic philosophy in general, it includes Aristotle as well, who is generally regarded as the main source of virtue ethics, Neo-Aristotelian virtue ethics in particular, which is this book's main conversation partner. Hence, in this chapter I will first discuss Wolterstorff's criticism of eudaimonism from a reading of Aristotle's ethics. This concerns in particular the questions how Aristotle values external goods as conditional for *eudaimonia* and whether his eudaimonistic ethics allows the good of the other to be pursued as an aim in itself, rather than as something that contributes to one's own *eudaimonia*. These investigations will lead us to a more nuanced view of eudaimonism. Next, we turn again to Augustine's criticism of classical conceptions of the good life. For, according to Wolterstorff, it is Augustine who breaks decisively with classical eudaimonism and replaces it by a biblical account of justice. I will argue that rather than causing a break with eudaimonism, Augustine transforms it and offers a non-competitive view that enables us to broaden our conception of the good life and the virtues as fully encompassing the good of the other. Finally, some implications for an ethics of the good life and virtue ethics will be outlined in terms of sharing in a common good and acquiring the virtue of justice, an interpretation which differs significantly from Wolterstorff's.

Aristotle: Virtuous Activity and External Goods

Wolterstorff's main problem with eudaimonism is that this view cannot account for all the goods to which we have rights, since it restricts happiness to activities (of a virtuous kind). The eudaimonist holds that the ultimate goal of each of us is that we live our lives as well as possible. "The good life is constituted of activities;

and what characterizes those activities is that together they make one's life a well-lived life."³

In opposition to eudaimonism, Wolterstorff argues that there are goods to which I have rights, for example, being treated fairly, and these goods do not consist of activities but are 'passivities.' Because such goods are not part of my own activity, they are not constitutive of my happiness, of how my life is lived. "So it is in general. Rights against others are rights to the good of being treated by them in certain ways. None of those goods is constitutive of one's happiness, for none of them is an activity on one's part."⁴

It is true that rights and the universality of human worth change the ethical perspective importantly. Nevertheless, the question is whether Wolterstorff doesn't present eudaimonism too narrowly. In the previous chapter we have seen that an Aristotelian conception of the relationship between virtue and *eudaimonia* differs from a Stoic conception precisely insofar as it does not identify happiness and virtue. Although nowadays most virtue ethicists follow Aristotle's rather than the Stoic conception of virtue and happiness, Wolterstorff pays much more attention to the latter—for this is the version Augustine struggled with—than to Aristotle. Therefore, the Stoic conception of eudaimonism appears to be predominant in his construction and, as a consequence, of his evaluation—of the eudaimonistic view in general.

Nonetheless, Wolterstorff is of course aware of the fundamental debate in Antiquity between the Peripatetics (Aristotelians) and the Stoics on this point. The Peripatetics held that the well-lived life and virtue depend on fortune, since *achieving* the aim of one's virtuous actions is a constituent part of *eudaimonia* and this achievement depends partly on good luck. For the Stoics, on the contrary, happiness and virtue are achieved simply by *aiming* at the right goals: what counts is protecting one's tranquility from emotional disturbance. Thus, the two strains of thought differ in how they value the dependency on 'external goods.' According to the Peripatetics, whether or not one succeeds in living one's life well depends not just on inward intentions, as with the Stoics, but also on external goods: "for it is impossible, or at least not easy, to play a noble part unless furnished with the necessary equipment."⁵ According to Aristotle, living in straitened circumstances necessarily impairs virtuous activity. Although a person living in such circumstances can act virtuously, nonetheless his virtuous activity is necessarily of a deficient sort. The Stoics held that circumstances could not prevent the virtuous person from acting virtuously. Hence, the Stoics affirmed that virtue was sufficient for happiness, whereas the Peripatetics denied it.⁶

Although Wolterstorff acknowledges the importance of the difference between these two versions of eudaimonism, in his view this does not affect the agent centeredness of both Stoic *and* Aristotelian eudaimonism: "All agreed that

---

3. Ibid., 151.
4. Ibid., 176; cf. 207.
5. *EN* 1099a31.
6. Wolterstorff, *Justice*, 169–71.

virtuous activity is necessary and sufficient for the well-lived life, the happy life; they disagreed over whether *virtue (being virtuous)* is necessary and sufficient."[7] Moreover, in eudaimonism "none of those goods of being treated a certain way to which one has a right against others are *constitutive* of one's living well; and only some are *conditions* of one's living well."[8]

In my view, these conclusions are questionable. For the dependency of *eudaimonia* on external goods and outward circumstances obviously implies that not only the virtuous habitus but also virtuous activity is, though necessary, *not* sufficient for the good life, since these external goods and outward circumstances cannot be achieved by one's own activity. In Wolterstorff's argument, the presupposed definition of eudaimonism as exclusively consisting of virtuous *activity* seems decisive in his evaluation rather than that it is informed and corrected by Aristotle's non-identification of virtuous activity and *eudaimonia*. Therefore, it is worthwhile to reconsider Aristotle's conception of happiness. I will demonstrate that in his understanding (1) *eudaimonia* is at least partly dependent on external goods, (2) these goods are constitutive of the good life, (3) *eudaimonia* is dependent on the activity of others, and (4) in the end it has at least partly the character of a gift.

First of all, as Martha Nussbaum analyzes in a profound argument, Aristotle's view of *eudaimonia* is something that "also requires external goods in addition."[9] Aristotle develops his position in relation to two 'extreme' positions that are commonly held. On the one hand, some people believe that living well is just a matter of having good fortune. In that case good living is a gift of the gods that has no connection with human effort or the goodness of a stable character.[10] *Eudaimonia* would just mean 'having a good *daimoon*.' On the other hand, other people hold that good luck has no power at all to influence the goodness of a human life. The factors relevant to living one's life well are all within the agent's grasp. This position includes two variants: the first route, associated with Platonism, is to narrow down the good life by acknowledging as intrinsically valuable only activities that are maximally stable and invulnerable to change; the second route is to deny that activity is any part of living well and to consider a virtuous condition or state to be sufficient for *eudaimonia*. Nussbaum argues that Aristotle's strategy is to take both extremes seriously, as motivated by something that appears in reality and therefore "neither class is likely to be altogether mistaken,"[11] without identifying himself completely with either. This helps him to arrive at a position that does justice to the motivating concerns in each of the extreme positions, while avoiding their excesses.[12]

---

7. Ibid., 171.

8. Ibid., 177.

9. *EN* 1099a31-33. Martha Nussbaum, *The Fragility of Goodness: Luck and Ethics in Greek Tragedy and Philosophy* (Cambridge: Cambridge University Press, 1986), 318-42.

10. *EN* 1099b7-11.

11. *EN* 1098b28-29.

12. Nussbaum, *Fragility*, 319-20.

In dealing with the first view Aristotle argues "that the greatest and noblest of all things should be left to fortune would be too contrary to the fitness of things."[13] This argument is not based on an empirical survey but on a deliberation in which what we believe about what makes our life worthwhile is important—namely, that human life is worth living only if a good life can be secured by some effort that lies within our capabilities. Though this effort is the most important element, it will not be sufficient for *eudaimonia*, as Aristotle demonstrates in dealing with the opposite view: the view that the good life is completely invulnerable to *tuchè*, since *eudaimonia* consists simply in having a good ethical condition or state. Although Aristotle sympathizes with this view, purchasing complete invulnerability is at too high a price. Good states are not by themselves sufficient for the good life. *Eudaimonia* requires actual activity and not just good *hexis*, condition or state,[14] for "living well and acting well are the same as *eudaimonia*."[15] Good character finds its natural fulfillment and flourishing in activity.[16]

So far the argument does not bring us really beyond how Wolterstorff portrayed Aristotle and the Peripatetics, since activity indeed seems to be central in this view. However, Nussbaum adds that in Aristotle's view the good life is vulnerable—the 'fragility of goodness' in the title of her book: making the good life dependent on acting or doing well, also makes this life vulnerable to impediment, while "only the lying-in-wait that is *hexis* can escape disturbance."[17] Moreover, in Aristotle's view the good life depends on external goods:

> No activity (*energeia*) is complete if it is impeded; but *eudaimonia* is something complete. So the *eudaimoon* person needs the goods of the body and external goods and goods of luck, in addition, so that his activities should not be impeded. Those who claim that the person who is being tortured on the wheel, or the person who has encountered great reversals of fortune, is *eudaimoon*, so long as he is good, are not saying anything—whether that is their intention or not.[18]

In this fragment it becomes clear that not only doing or acting is necessary for *eudaimonia* but also external goods, goods of the body, of social context, and of resources. In short, *eudaimonia* "requires external goods in addition (ἐκτὸς ἀγαθῶν προσδεομένη)."[19]

---

13. *EN* 1099b24–25.
14. *EN* 1176a33–35.
15. *EN* 1095a19–20, trans. Nussbaum, *Fragility*, 323.
16. Nussbaum, *Fragility*, 320–4.
17. Ibid., 326.
18. *EN* 1153b16–21, trans. Nussbaum, *Fragility*, 325.
19. *EN* 1099a29–31; Nussbaum, *Fragility*, 330. Cf. Roger Crisp, "Rights, Happiness and God: A Response to *Justice: Rights and Wrongs*," *Studies in Christian Ethics* 23/2 (2010), 156–62, who acknowledges "that there may be room even within Aristotelian eudaimonism for non-activity-based goods."

So far so good, but with Wolterstorff we can still ask what the nature of the 'additional need' of external goods is: Are they just conditional or are they constitutive of *eudaimonia*? At first sight, these goods are not actual constituents of good living, for it is activities according to excellence that are in charge of *eudaimonia*.[20] However, Aristotle continues by asking in what ways this stable good life is vulnerable. His answer is that great misfortunes will "crush and mar our bliss both by the pain they cause and by the hindrance they offer to many activities."[21] Nussbaum rightly argues that "this seems to be about *eudaimonia* itself and *its constituents*, not some supervenient good."[22] This becomes clear from a fragment in the *Ethica Eudemia* where it is argued that "practical wisdom is not the only thing that makes acting well according to excellence (εὐπραγίαν καὶ ἀρετή, [the definiens of *eudaimonia*]), but we say that the fortunate, too, do well (εὖ πράττειν), implying that good fortune (εὐτυχία) is a cause of good activity just as knowledge is."[23]

In concluding this second element of Aristotle's view of *eudaimonia*, we can say that in his view external goods are indeed constitutive of the good life. Although great disruptions of the good life will be rare since human excellence, once developed, is stable, external goods are not just (and partly) conditional, as Wolterstorff holds in his interpretation of eudaimonism, but constitutive of the good life. Because this 'passivity' is part of *eudaimonia* it is more proper to maintain the traditional description of Aristotelian ethics as an ethics of the 'good life' which includes what is 'given' as good as constitutive, rather than of the 'well-lived life,' as Wolterstorff does, in which all emphasis is on the activity of the agent as the only constituent.

Thirdly, in Aristotle's view the good life is related to the activity of others and not exclusively actor centered. This becomes manifest in his treatment of *philia*—which includes many relationships that we would not classify as friendship and therefore is hard to translate. *Philia* is "the greatest of external goods,"[24] as Aristotle insists:

> Nobody would choose to have all possible good things on the condition that he must enjoy them alone; for man is a social being (πολιτικὸν γὰρ ὁ ἄνθρωπος), and designed by nature to live with others (συζῆν); accordingly the happy man must have society... Therefore the happy man requires friends.[25]

---

20. *EN* 1100b8–10.

21. *EN* 1100b23–30.

22. Nussbaum, *Fragility*, 332 (italics mine).

23. Aristotle, *Eudemian Ethics* (Loeb Classical Library 285), trans. H. Rackham (Cambridge: Harvard University Press, [1935] 1982), 1246b37–1247a2 (here trans. Nussbaum). The same nuanced view is repeated at the end of book X of *Ethica Nicomachea* on the 'contemplative life' (*EN* 1178b33–1179a7).

24. *EN* 1169b10.

25. *EN* 1169b17–22.

The underlying argument is that the good life fundamentally is a *common* good life, as Aristotle states in his *Politica*, *where* he uses different phrases to refer to the good of the *polis*, including "common good (κοινὸν ἀγαθόν)"[26] and "common advantage (κοινῇ συμφέρον)."[27] The *polis* is a "partnership of similar people (κοινωνία τῶν ὁμοίων), and its object is the best life that is possible," that is, *eudaimonia* as "the greatest good."[28]

From this understanding of the good life as living with others and the common good follows that *philia* is not merely necessary to one's own good, but rather intrinsically good. Aristotle presupposes that we do in fact love others for their own sake and not just for the sake of some other benefit.[29] For those who love because the other is useful or gives them pleasure "do not love by reference to the way the person loved *is*, but to his being useful or pleasant."[30] According to Aristotle, there is a kind of human love that really cares for the good of another and this kind of love links activity with passivity, one's own aspiration with receptivity to the actions of the other. In conclusion, *philoi* and *philia* are constitutive parts of human *eudaimonia* and not just instrumental to a self-sufficient well-lived life.[31]

Finally, one other element of Aristotle's account of *eudaimonia* should be highlighted as relevant to the debate on the nature of *eudaimonism*, which is the gift character of *eudaimonia*. In their account of Aristotle's ethics, Stanley Hauerwas and Charles Pinches point out that "those who are happy cannot think of happiness as only their own achievement. They must always acknowledge that they might not have been so fortunate as they have been."[32] The same holds for virtue, since virtue isn't something one earns as one earns wages for one's work. *Eudaimonia* is not something we accomplish *by* being virtuous, but appears more like a gift, even "a gift of the gods," or "divinely given," as Aristotle suggests without elaborating: "Still, even if happiness is not sent us from heaven, but is won by virtue and by some kind of study or practice, it seems to be one of the most divine things that exist. For the prize and end of goodness must clearly be supremely good—it must be something divine and blissful."[33]

From this perspective, Hauerwas and Pinches understand Aristotle's claim that *eudaimonia* "requires both complete goodness and a complete lifetime."[34] *Eudaimonia* seems to involve the whole duration of one's life, since life can go awry even if steered by the stability of virtue. This does not imply that happiness

---

26. Aristotle, *Politica* 1268b31, 1279b. Trans. *Politics* (Loeb Classical Library 264), trans. H. Rackham (Cambridge: Harvard University Press, [1932] 1989).
27. Aristotle, *Politica* 1279a17.
28. Aristotle, *Politica* 1328a36.
29. *EN* 1155a 4 and 29–31.
30. *EN* 1156a14–17, translation slightly changed.
31. Nussbaum, *Fragility*, 356–66.
32. Hauerwas and Pinches, *Christians among the Virtues*, 12.
33. *EN* 1099b10–17.
34. *EN* 1100a3–5.

is just some ideal in the future, for "happiness is not so much the end, but the way."[35] According to Hauerwas and Pinches, Aristotle helps to understand that *eudaimonia* "comes as we acquire and live the virtues necessary to transverse the dangers and opportunities of our existence—dangers and opportunities that are intrinsic to our being essentially timeful."[36]

Aristotle helps to understand that, theologically speaking, it makes sense to desire *eudaimonia*, but not without distinction. From a Christian perspective our presumptions about happiness are profoundly challenged. However, the difference between Aristotle and Christianity does not consist in the emphasis on happiness, but in different accounts of *the kind of person* we must be if we are to become happy, and therefore in their respective *material* conceptions of happiness.[37] *Eudaimonia* is something we grow into, it is like a gift infused into our lives of which we become only aware in those occasional moments when we notice how small the efforts of our life are to its goodness. It is clear, however, that in this approach eudaimonism itself is not canceled out—it is fundamentally *transformed*.

Doing Justice for the Sake of the Other

The argument so far nuances the actor centeredness of Aristotelian eudaimonism, but does not suffice to counter Wolterstorff's criticism entirely. For he identifies another important 'structural' problem with eudaimonism: the subordination of the other's well-being to the good of my own well-lived life. My living my life well may require that I seek to promote the happiness of the other as an aim in itself, but the question I must ask is: "What contribution will this make to my own life being well lived?"[38] Wolterstorff argues: "I take it to be of the essence of eudaimonism to claim that my recognition that your being healthy would be a natural good in your life is not sufficient reason for me to seek ... *to bring about the natural good of health in your life*."[39] Although in eudaimonism the other's *health* does not have to form part of my good for me to perform it, but my *pursuing* the other's health does. "The condition on my performing any action as an end-in-itself is that I judge that it will enhance *my* eudaimonia."[40] Rights, on the contrary, de-center the agent: I am to do what you have a right to my doing. Instead of the agent's happiness determining his action, the worth of the recipient and of those others who will be affected by the action is to determine what the agent does.

---

35. Hauerwas and Pinches, *Christians among the Virtues*, 13.
36. Ibid.
37. Ibid., 14–16.
38. Wolterstorff, *Justice*, 177.
39. Ibid., 154.
40. Ibid., 211. Cf. Nicholas Wolterstorff, *Justice in Love* (Grand Rapids/Cambridge: Eerdmans, 2011), 12.

Again, the question is whether Wolterstorff's portrayal of the self-centeredness in pursuing the good of the other is correct with regard to Aristotle. As we have seen, *philia* is directed toward the good of the other. In her careful analysis Jennifer Whiting argues that "we need not read the 'eudaimonist axiom' as requiring that all actions be performed ultimately for the sake of the agent's *own eudaimonia*: for Aristotle's account of *philia* shows how, given human nature, it is *possible* to act directly for the sake of *another's eudaimonia*."[41] Julia Annas too argues that the fact that I aim at my own final end makes this ethics formally agent centered or self-centered, but does not make it self-centered in content, for "the good of others ought to matter to me *because* it is the good of others, not because it is part of my own good."[42] This can only be understood from a community-defined conception of the good. Wolterstorff's evaluation of eudaimonism underestimates the meaning of the community centeredness of the good life in Aristotle, as we have seen. Yet, full participation in a well-functioning *polis* is not only a necessary condition for the development of the individual's excellences, but also an intrinsic good or end without which a human life is incomplete.[43] We only acquire a full understanding of the good of *eudaimonia* if it is also understood in terms of a *common* good. The good life of a single person and the quality of the common life persons share are closely linked:

> For even though it be the case that the Good is the same for the individual and for the *polis*, nevertheless, the good of the *polis* is manifestly a greater and more perfect good, both to attain and to preserve. To secure the good of one person only is better than nothing; but to secure the good of a nation or a *polis* is a nobler and more divine achievement.[44]

Aristotle clearly considers the good realized in social relationships to be superior to the good achieved in the life of an individual apart from the larger community.[45]

Interestingly, Wolterstorff himself deals with a relevant potential objection to his argument against eudaimonism by referring to the virtue of justice: one could say that since acting in accord with virtue is constitutive of the good life, eudaimonism requires treating you justly, that is, as you have a right to my treating

---

41. Jennifer Whiting, "The Nicomachean Account of *Philia*," in Richard Kraut (ed.), *The Blackwell Guide to Aristotle's Nicomachean Ethics* (Malden and Oxford: Blackwell, 2006), 302.

42. Julia Annas, *The Morality of Happiness* (Oxford: Oxford University Press, 1993), 224. Woltertorff considers this argument at odds with the whole structure of eudaimonism as outlined by Annas herself. However, in this explanation Wolterstorff neglects the fundamental concern for the other included in *philia* and justice.

43. Nussbaum, *Fragility*, 348–9.

44. *EN* 1094b8–12.

45. Cf. David Hollenbach, *The Common Good and Christian Ethics* (Cambridge: Cambridge University Press, 2002), 3–4.

you. Therefore, treating you unjustly cannot be a way of living my life well. I think that this argument makes sense, as we will see, but according to Wolterstorff it has limited impact since the eudaimonist has no good reason for holding that justice always has to take precedence over other virtues like magnanimity. In my view, this conclusion is unjustified. For why does Aristotle devote a whole chapter to the virtue of justice, whereas he deals with all the other virtues of character, like magnanimity, in one single chapter? This is because justice is not a virtue like the other virtues, but the "chief of the virtues, and more sublime 'or than the evening or the morning star.'"[46] This is so precisely because persons can exercise it in "their relations with another (πρὸς ἕτερον δύναται)."[47] Aristotle explicitly speaks of "the good of others." Since justice relates to "someone else," justice alone of the excellences is thought to be directed to "the good of others (ἀλλότριον ἀγαθὸν)," because the just person does what is "for the advantage of another (πρὸς ἕτερον), either a ruler or an associate."[48] A just action in the general sense is an acting owed to all concerned and with respect for the law. General or universal justice—of which we are speaking here, as distinguished from specific or particular justice— may be regarded as a 'meta-virtue' that not just subsumes the other virtues, but is "virtue as a whole."[49] According to Nussbaum, Aristotle here claims that "with only solitary concerns, without the excellence that consists in having an appropriate regard for the good of others, a human being will lack not just one important human end, he will lack all of the excellences."[50] For the best person is not he who exercises his virtue "in relation to himself (πρὸς αὑτὸν)" but the one who exercises it "in relation to the other (πρὸς ἕτερον)."[51]

Aristotle does not elaborate on general justice, but rather focuses on specific justice (distributive and corrective justice). Nevertheless, it is clear that he not only acknowledges the external normativity on which justice rests (laws),[52] but also regards the good of the other—and not just the good of one's own life—as the

---

46. *EN* 1129b27–29.
47. *EN* 1129b34.
48. *EN* 1130a3–7.
49. *EN* 1130a10.
50. Nussbaum, *Fragility*, 351.
51. *EN* 1130a7–8. This is not to say that self-sufficiency is completely absent in Aristotle's account of virtue and the virtues. The virtue of magnanimity indeed has essentially to do with valuing one's own worth: the magnanimous person is worth great goods, honor in particular (*EN* 1123b3–30). This view threatens to undermine Aristotle's communal understanding, for instance of how virtue is passed on in formational practices, as Herdt, *Putting on Virtue*, 38–43, argues. However, this element can be corrected within a virtue ethical framework.
52. I leave out of consideration the potentially problematic nature of Aristotle's equation of justice with lawfulness. See Charles M. Young, "Aristotle's Justice," in Richard Kraut (ed.), *Blackwell Guide to Nicomachean Ethics*, 182. What interests me here is the broadening of justice as universal beyond being just a particular excellence of character among others.

aim of the virtue of justice. Furthermore, a widening of the concept of *eudaimonia* toward the community as a whole is inherent in justice: according to Aristotle, we call anything just that produces or preserves *eudaimonia* and its constituents "for the political community (τῇ πολιτικῇ κοινωνίᾳ)."[53]

Here is not the place to deal in full detail with Aristotle's complex treatment of justice, but at least it is clear that in his conception justice is directed to the good of the other to which I have to do justice, that is, precisely to what Wolterstorff considers lacking in any account of eudaimonism.[54] This may be true in some variants of eudaimonism, but in Aristotle's account other related concerns are constitutive of both virtue and *eudaimonia*. As Nussbaum puts it: "Without making political and other-related concerns ends in themselves, one will lack not only justice but also true courage, true moderation, true generosity, greatness of soul, conviviality, and so forth."[55] One cannot choose these excellences as ends in themselves without choosing the good of others as an end. Without this end we lack not just a part of the good, but the good as a whole.

Meanwhile, Wolterstorff's own account of justice in terms of 'rights' is not without problems. Since my concern is the defensibility of eudaimonism, I will not deal in detail with his argument, but limit myself to two aspects. First, as Bernd Wannenwetsch has asked,[56] by thinking through justice in terms of rights, is it really possible to counter the dominant use of rights as strongly associated with what we may call 'possessive individualism'? Although Wolterstorff defends an earlier, 'better' understanding of rights, it is still the question how this language relates to today's rights language. Secondly, can Wolterstorff distinguish his focus on 'primary justice,' that is, distributive or communicative justice instead of rectifying or corrective justice, sufficiently from the privileging of 'procedural justice' with its prime interest in just states of affairs (to prevail) rather than just works (to happen) as predominant in today's rights language? As Wannenwetsch puts it: "You can do wrong, and you can do justice, but you cannot 'do rights': to do 'right'—in the singular—*is* to do justice. Hence to understand justice in terms of rights—in the plural—appears to have an inherent tendency of promoting the

---

53. *EN* 1129b18–19.

54. Wolterstorff, *Justice*, 135–6, too admits that in Aristotle's concept of distributive justice a person's worth is presupposed, but in his general evaluation of eudaimonism this is undervalued.

55. Nussbaum, *Fragility*, 352. That justice is not just one of the virtues next to others is generally acknowledged. For example, André Comte-Sponville, *A Short Treatise on the Great Virtues*, trans. Catherine Temerson (London: Vintage, [1996] 2001), 61: "Of the four cardinal virtues, justice is probably the only one that is an absolute good in itself." It is not a virtue like the others, but rather the boundary that defines them or the principle that allows them to exist: "It cannot replace happiness (how could it?) but there can be no happiness without it" (62).

56. Bernd Wannenwetsch, "But to *Do* Right . . . Why the Language of 'Rights' Does Not Do Justice to Justice," *Studies in Christian Ethics* 23/2 (2010), 138–46.

idea of *producing* justice rather than of *doing* it."⁵⁷ To phrase it in my own words, it is the Aristotelian distinction between activity as *poièsis* (production) and as *praxis* (doing) that draws our attention to the credits of a eudaimonistic account of justice over against a view of justice based on individual rights.

Nevertheless, Aristotelian eudaimonism too shows considerable deficiencies, since this ethical program is restricted to free, male citizens in the specific paternalistic sociopolitical context of the Greek *polis*, without paying any attention to the domain of ethics that pertains to the care for the other, to the role of women, and to the care of the elderly, the sick, and the distressed.⁵⁸ Whereas these people still live within the *polis* though without being really part of it, all people living outside the *polis* can only be considered barbarians. Justice seems not to be directed to the goods of these 'barbarians.' Moreover, it seems that Aristotle's philosophy doesn't offer any good possibilities and reasons to transcend given social structures. Here, Wolterstorff's point makes sense: the universality of the worth and dignity of each human being, as rooted in the biblical message and ethos. The Christian *caritas* tradition maintains from the outset the fundamental equality of *all* people, irrespective of their social position, and establishes a universal account of justice and care for the good of the other (that is to say, this view is in principle present in the Christian tradition, in practice it has often been violated). Therefore, again the question is whether the introduction of the language of love of God (*amor Dei*) and the neighbor and the whole Christian paradigm is to be regarded as a break with eudaimonism or rather as a transformation. Since Augustine is generally considered to be the most important Christian thinker of the first centuries on these matters and since Wolterstorff too makes a strong case for him, we will turn to some important aspects of his thought.

Augustine: Love's Concern for the Good of the Other

Wolterstorff claims that Augustine's philosophical affirmation of the emotion of compassion in his later works marks a fundamental departure from the agent orientation of eudaimonism.⁵⁹ In this interpretation, Augustine's turn toward a deep concern for the material good of the other caused a break with eudaimonism in general and Stoic eudaimonism in particular. Wolterstorff starts his argument from Augustine's account of love, on which his anthropology rests: to be human is to love. Whereas the Stoics put all emphasis on the intellectual side of the self, Augustine emphasizes the affective side. Hence the fundamental human ailment is

---

57. Ibid., 143.

58. Cf. Victor van den Bersselaar, *Bestaansethiek: Normatieve professionalisering en de ethiek van identiteits-, levens- en zingevingsvragen* [Existential ethics: Normative professionalization and the ethics of questions of identity, life and meaning] (Amsterdam: SWP, 2009), 89–90, 96, 402.

59. Wolterstorff, *Justice*, 207.

not false judgments of worth, but misplaced loves—our loves must be reoriented.[60] This love includes love of our fellow human beings. A crux in Wolterstorff's interpretation is that Augustine gradually emphasizes compassion for the other's material well-being, especially in his *Confessiones* and in *De civitate Dei*. In *Confessiones* 3.2 Augustine urges compassionate joy over the moral and religious excellence of our fellow human beings and compassionate grief over their turpitude. As he puts it from the perspective of the subject who receives compassion: "True brothers are those who rejoice for me in their hearts when they find good in me and grieve for me when they find sin. They are my true brothers because whether they see good in me or evil, they love me still."[61] Christ's command to love not only God but also one's neighbor as oneself taught Augustine to enhance the well-being of another on the same level as one's own. According to Wolterstorff, Augustine continues this line of thought and deepens it in *De civitate Dei*:

> It is not only for their own sakes that the citizens of the City of God are moved by these feelings [of pain, desire, and joy]. They also feel them on behalf of those whom they desire to see redeemed and fear to see perish. They behold Paul "rejoicing with those who rejoice and weeping with those who weep."[62]

From these and other instances Wolterstorff concludes that Augustine breaks entirely with Stoicism, especially on the level of the emotions. In this interpretation, Augustine's view changed from an initial emphasis on love of the other as confined to desire for the moral and religious flourishing of his or her *soul*, to a love for the other as related to both mental *and physical* well-being. Whereas in his early work *De vera religione* Augustine argues that we should love the *souls* of the neighbors because their souls are what is eternal in them,[63] this has completely changed in *De civitate Dei*. Now we read that "we do not so much ask whether (*utrum*) a pious soul is angry, as why (*quare*) he is angry; not whether he is sad, but whence comes his sadness; not whether he is afraid, but what he fears."[64] Augustine now speaks of our worry over others lacking 'external goods' such as "famine, war, pestilence, or captivity, fearing that in slavery they may suffer evils beyond what we can conceive."[65] Wolterstorff concludes: "There has been a sea-change in his thinking. The break with Platonism and Stoicism is now complete: virtue is not sufficient for happiness."[66] We are no longer enjoined to love our neighbor for her soul alone, but the other's material well-being is worthy of disturbance as well: "If

---

60. Ibid., 191.
61. Augustine, *Confessiones* 10.4. Quotations are from Augustine, *Confessions*, trans. R. S. Pine-Coffin (London: Penguin Books, [1961] 1984).
62. CD 14.9.
63. Augustine, *De vera religione* 46.86–47.90, PL 34, 160-3.
64. CD 9.5.
65. CD 19.8.
66. Wolterstorff, *Justice*, 198.

we felt no such emotions at all while subject to the infirmity of this life, we should then certainly not be living righteously."[67]

Although I think that Wolterstorff is right in emphasizing Augustine's concern for the material well-being of others based on his Christian understanding of love rooted in divine love, his overall interpretation is contestable. I leave behind the question whether there is so much difference between the early and the late Augustine when it comes to concern for the material well-being of others as Wolterstorff assumes. The core issue is whether Augustine's turn to a concern for the goods of one's fellow human beings implies an entire break with eudaimonism. I will defend that it is rather an alternative form of eudaimonism.[68]

First of all, it is noteworthy that Wolterstorff's own valuations of *eudaimonia* and eudaimonism in Augustine are in fact more ambivalent than his conclusion suggests. He acknowledges that Augustine "never gave up his conviction that tranquility is a condition of happiness, *nor his conviction that we all yearn for happiness.*"[69] Moreover, Wolterstorff states that the late Augustine understands well-being in terms of the life that goes well: "The conception of the good life implicit in Augustine's late thought was that of the good life that goes well—what I shall call the flourishing life."[70] I would say that "yearning for happiness" and "the flourishing life" are fitting descriptions of eudaimonism!

Furthermore, the presence of the eudaimonistic paradigm in Augustine's late work can easily be demonstrated from many instances. In book 13 of *De Trinitate*, for instance, happiness is regarded as the universal aim of humans:

> If he [the poet Ennius] had said 'you all want to be happy; you do not want to be unhappy (*omnes beati esse vultis; miseri esse non vultis*)' he would have said something that no one at all could fail to recognize in his own will. Whatever else anyone may wish for secretly, he never forgoes this wish which is well known to all and in all (*quae omnibus et in omnibus satis nota est*).[71]

In his argument, Augustine presupposes that happiness is what all people want. In doing so, he clearly adopts the eudaimonistic point of view as shared by all

---

67. *CD* 14.9; cf. 19.8.

68. As also is argued by, for example, John Burnaby, *Amor Dei: A Study of the Religion of St. Augustine. The Hulsean Lectures for 1938* (London: Hodder and Stoughton, 1938); Oliver O'Donovan, *The Problem of Self-Love in St. Augustine* (New Haven: Yale University Press, 1980), 137–59; Eric Gregory, *Politics and the Order of Love: An Augustinian Ethic of Democratic Citizenship* (Chicago: University of Chicago Press, 2008), 319–62; Herdt, *Putting on Virtue*, 50–6.

69. Wolterstorff, *Justice*, 200 (emphasis mine).

70. Ibid., 222.

71. Augustine, *De Trinitate* 13.6. Quotations from Augustine, *The Trinity* (The Works of Saint Augustine: A New Translation for the 21st Century I.5), trans. Edmund Hill (Brooklyn: New City Press, 1991).

philosophers of Antiquity. Departing from this common ground he tries to bring his readers to an awareness that the good life is related to goodness and to its source, the highest good, God.

He starts from the observation that "all who are happy have what they want," although, as he adds, "not all who have what they want are for that reason happy,"[72] for we can lack what we want or we can have what we ought not to have wanted. Thus, Augustine offers two conditions for happiness: that we have what we want and that we want nothing inappropriate or evil. Yet, it is still an open question in what happiness, positively speaking, consists. Although all people want to be happy, there is an enormous variety of opinions about *where* happiness is to be found: does it consist in conscious virtue, in bodily pleasure, in both, or in other things? The core question, then, is what *true* happiness is.

As Maarten Wisse explains, Augustine's argument in *De Trinitate*, book 13 is twofold.[73] First, the fact that happiness is found in strikingly different things suggests that not all people know where to find happiness, nor in what it consists. Yet, since all people want to be happy, considering happiness the only thing they love, and since one cannot love something one does not know, it follows that all know what the happy life is. The diversity is not a matter of knowledge but of will. For it is clear that true happiness consists of the virtuous life, a life devoted to goodness. Here Augustine establishes the connection between happiness and goodness, simply following a central presupposition of classical philosophy. True happiness consists not only in having what one wants, but also in willing *good* things rather than bad things. As a consequence, if someone wants what he wrongly desires, he is even further away from the happy life than someone who does not get what he rightly desires. Therefore, it is pivotal to have a good will: one needs to choose the good over attaining short-term happiness like pleasure. True pleasure consists in true happiness and true happiness is defined by justice.[74]

Secondly, Augustine demonstrates that true happiness can only be found in perfect justice and everlasting life, that is, in God. True happiness can only be reached in eternal life; it requires immortality because our present life is marked by sin, loss, and suffering. "Now who is there who would not want any kind of life that he enjoyed and thus called happy to be so in his own power that he could have it last forever? And yet who is there in such a position?"[75] Since no one can establish such an enduring happy life, all who pursue true happiness are in need of eternal life, which can only be found in the Christian faith.[76] Nonetheless, *eudaimonia* is maintained as the end and Augustine develops his apologetical argument within

---

72. Augustine, *De Trinitate* 13.8.

73. Maarten Wisse, *Trinitarian Theology Beyond Participation: Augustine's* De Trinitate *and Contemporary Theology* (T&T Clark Studies in Systematic Theology 11) (London: Bloomsbury, 2011), 262–7.

74. Augustine, *De Trinitate* 13.7 and 13.10.

75. Augustine, *De Trinitate* 13.10; Wisse, *Trinitarian Theology*, 266.

76. Augustine, *De Trinitate* 13.12; Wisse, *Trinitarian Theology*, 263 and 266.

a eudaimonistic framework. As he states in one of his late sermons, "Christians are at one with the philosophers" who "in their studies, their questionings, their arguments, their lives, have sought to apprehend the happy life."[77] The ways part not in the search for the good life as a happy life but in the answers to the question where this happy life is to be found.[78]

Therefore, although Wolterstorff may be right that Augustine breaks with *Stoic* eudaimonism, its *apatheia* ideal, and verdict on negative emotions, this does not imply a break with eudaimonism as such. As Wolterstorff himself acknowledges, the Stoics differed from the Peripatetics, who held that negative emotions must *be kept in check* rather than *eliminated*.[79] Whereas Augustine only encountered Aristotelianism as mediated by the Peripatetics represented by Varro, he is directly influenced by (Neo-)Platonists and kept faithful to aspects of Neo-Platonism, especially the notion of a highest good. In the end, Wolterstorff's argument for speaking of Augustine causing a "break with eudaimonism" rests on his presupposed overall definition of eudaimonism as holding an instrumental view of external goods and as being actor centered, that is, that love of the other is allowed in one's life, "but only if that love passes the test of contributing to one's own life being well-lived."[80] As we have seen, it is not justified to attribute these characteristics to eudaimonism as a whole.

Common Good as Non-competitive Eudaimonia

It is especially the eudaimonistic conception of a *common good* that illuminates the relation between the well-being of the self and that of the other. That the good is regarded as a common good indicates that a non-competitive view of the promotion of another's well-being as constitutive of one's own is possible. As Joseph Clair argues, Wolterstorff's opposition to the agent orientation of eudaimonism presupposes a competitive view in which "the self and the other compete in a zero-sum game over limited and indivisible goods."[81] A non-competitive view, on the contrary, takes the good as something held in common by the self and the other and appeals to their mutual relation to it. Wolterstorff doesn't refer to any conception of the common good and hence his account of the "well-lived life" and his argument against eudaimonism vacillates uncertainly between non-competitive and competitive views.

Pivotal to Augustine's Christian view is to think of the self and of the other as standing in a fundamental relation to God as the highest good. From this point of

---

77. Augustine, *Sermones* 150.4, quoted from Burnaby, *Amor Dei*, 46.
78. Cf. Herdt, *Putting on Virtue*, 51.
79. Wolterstorff, *Justice*, 156.
80. Ibid., 210.
81. Joseph Clair, "Wolterstorff on Love and Justice: An Augustinian Response," *Journal of Religious Ethics* 41/1 (2013), 158.

view, Augustine does not break with eudaimonism, but criticizes and transforms it from within. Not the goods to which the other has rights is the starting point, but God as the highest good to which both the self and the other relate. In Letter 155, for instance, Augustine argues in a non-competitive way about virtue in relation to God:

> What should we choose to love particularly, if not the one thing we can find that is unsurpassed? This is God; and if in loving anything else we make it preferable or equal to him, we have forgotten how to love ourselves. The nearer we approach him, the better it is for us; for nothing is better than him. We approach him, however, not by moving, but by loving.[82]

This fragment affirms Augustine's understanding of love as the only 'virtuous activity' to approach the ultimate object of one's desire, God. At the same time, he identifies such love as 'proper self-love.' However, this love is not directed to a *bonum private*, but it is a good that can be possessed only by being shared.[83] Or to put it differently, self-love precisely consists in loving the other as oneself, as the way one's self is ordered under God. In *De civitate Dei* 19.14 Augustine not only emphasizes the command to "harm no one" and to "do good to all," as Wolterstorff rightly emphasizes, but also explains that the two love commandments include three things to love: God, oneself, and one's neighbor.[84] The proper interrelationship between these three loves is a common theme in Augustine's entire work. In Letter 155 he explains that

> the love with which someone loves himself is exactly the same love as that with which he loves God. If he loves himself in any other way, we ought rather to say that he hates himself: for whenever someone, by turning away from a greater and more excellent good and turning towards himself, turns towards what is inferior and in need, he is deprived of the light of justice and becomes unjust. Then the very true words of Scripture become true of him: *Whoever loves injustice, hates his own soul.* (Ps. 11:5)[85]

This passage can be regarded as a paradigmatic instance of Augustine's eudaimonistic interpretation of the love commandment. God is identified as the highest good and communication with God is conceived of as the end of human flourishing. At the same time, one can alienate oneself from this end by acting unjustly toward the other and acting unjustly is precisely also a way of not loving oneself.[86]

---

82. *Ep.* 155.13. I refer to the translation by Atkins and Dodaro in: Augustine, *Political Writings*.
83. Burnaby, *Amor Dei*, 127.
84. *CD* 19.14.
85. *Ep.* 155.15.
86. Clair, "Wolterstorff on Love and Justice," 159–61.

Augustine's conception of the highest good is Neo-Platonic, but his reflections on love and grace are not just addenda to Platonism, but radical reformulations of our relationship with the good.[87] In books 8 to 10 of *De civitate Dei* he treats both Plato and Neo-Platonists like Plotinus, Porphyry, and Iamblichus approvingly: "Plato says that the true and highest good (*verum ac summum bonum*) is God, and he therefore wishes the philosopher to be a lover of God; for philosophy aims at the happy life, and he who loves God is happy in the enjoyment of God (*fruens Deo sit beatus qui Deum amaverit*)."[88] The vision of the highest good found in the Platonists is in agreement with Christianity and therefore "we place these above all others, and confess that they approach closest to us."[89] Augustine clearly acknowledges that their view is eudaimonistic: "The Platonists . . . assert that that which all men desire—that is, a happy life—cannot be achieved by anyone who does not cling with the purity of a chaste love to that one Supreme Good which is the immutable God."[90] In phrasing it this way, Augustine approves the Platonic understanding of the highest good as the end of the good life and transforms it from his Christian view. This approval is part of his rhetorical strategy in which he leads the reader to the Christian faith. For what the Platonists lack is proper worship of God, who is the source of true happiness. In making this theological point Augustine maintains the underlying Platonic eudaimonistic framework in one and the same argument: "In order that a man may know what it is to love himself (*se diligere*), an end (*finis*) has been appointed for him to which he is to refer all that he does, so that he may be happy; for he who loves himself desires nothing else than to be happy. And this end is attained by drawing near to God."[91] This means that to love the neighbor and to treat him justly is both to act for the good of the neighbor and to pursue one's own well-being. For to act unjustly toward the neighbor is both to wrong the neighbor and oneself, since by acting in this way one turns away from the highest good. Therefore, compassion is not a matter of self-renunciation or self-alienation, but of obedience to the double love commandment. Self-love and neighborly love are harmonized in the pursuit of the good itself, which is God. As Clair concludes, this passage "makes clear that, for Augustine, there is no difference between the agent-orientation of eudaimonism and the self-love presupposed in the double commandment of love."[92] Therefore, Wolterstorff's statement that all 'eschatological' forms of eudaimonism are implausible and even offensive because neighborly love would be a means to eternal reward[93] is wrong because it presupposes a competitive view.[94]

87. Cf. Wetzel, *Limits*, 10 and 13.
88. *CD* 8.8; cf. 8.12.
89. *CD* 8.9.
90. *CD* 10.1.
91. *CD* 10.3, Dyson's translation slightly changed.
92. Clair, "Wolterstorff on Love and Justice," 162.
93. Wolterstorff, *Justice*, 212.
94. This does not exclude all possible conflicts between the promotion of one's own well-being and the neighbor's in *acting*. From an Augustinian perspective, discerning the

Another aspect of Augustine's account of the common good as related to God as the highest good is that it enables him to develop a theologically informed view as an alternative to classical thought, that the good of the *polis* or *civitas* is the highest good. Augustine develops his thought in particular in relation to Cicero's conception, but the same may hold with respect to Aristotle. In Cicero's view, a republic is founded on agreement among people about right and just, about the required virtues and values, and about the good shared in common.[95] In *De civitate Dei* 2.21, Augustine refers to this definition when he develops his alternative view. In his view, a true commonwealth is a community of people united in worship of the only true God, which gets its moral expression in true love of the neighbor, as we have seen. Therefore, the only republic that fully embodies Cicero's definition is the city of God. However, this makes Augustine neither a theocrat nor a religious separatist. On the contrary, Augustine's theological conviction that human fulfillment can only be attained in the eschatological reality of the community of saints rather desacralizes politics. Precisely because of the transcendence of the city of God and its ultimate realization, every social good achievable in history is a limited good. The perfect good and fullness of love will ultimately be realized in the heavenly kingdom, but earthly societies can be more or less approximations of the heavenly city, depending on how they reflect the love of that city.[96]

Note that, contrary to Wolterstorff, Augustine does not take a conception of 'individual rights' as his starting point for thinking about justice, but still adopts the framework of the cardinal virtues, as we have seen in Chapter 1, the virtue of justice in particular. Three aspects are important in how he deals with the virtue of justice, which reveals a profound change of the classical concept without it being abandoned. First, he treats justice explicitly as the most important of the cardinal virtues, because it provides harmony or order both by establishing it among the other three cardinal virtues and by giving each one its due.[97] Secondly, *iustitia* is the virtue he most often redefines in a Christian way, by relating it closely to *caritas*, which is interpreted not only as charity (for instance, justice means using "our wealth to assist the needy"[98]), but also as having a universal scope. It is from the perspective of love, both of God and the neighbor, understood in terms of a common good, that doing justice reaches toward the *entire* world, and not just one's relatives or one's own social or political community. It is by virtue of loving God and the neighbor that one learns to see *all* human beings as "fellows . . . by reason of nature—by the law, that is, of our shared birth, not our shared business" and that one becomes oneself "the neighbor of every other human being."[99] Here

---

best course of action in love requires that one views each case of conflict within a broad theological framework that includes healthy self-love as rooted in creation, an awareness of the sinful human condition, and the hope of eternal happiness.

95. Cicero, *De re publica* 1.25.39.
96. Hollenbach, *Common Good*, 120–8.
97. Bovendeert, *Kardinale deugden gekerstend*, 108–9.
98. *Ep.* 155.12.
99. *Ep.* 155.14.

Augustine articulates the universal humaneness included in the Christian life view which goes really beyond the classical understanding of justice, as present in Aristotle and others. Thirdly, the virtue of justice decisively depends on God's justice, for he is the highest justice. Therefore, if we do justice we in fact participate in God and in doing so the true end of the human life will find its fulfillment.

All this does not mean that outside the Christian faith there is no understanding of justice. On the contrary, doing justice is the end of human life and all human beings have an innate capacity for knowing this. A sensitivity to the good is built into human nature and is not destroyed by sin although this sensitivity may be damaged. At the same time, knowing the good does not mean that we actually *do* the good, at least not to a sufficient degree. Here the specifically Christian understanding comes to the fore: faith in Christ includes a moral restoration of human beings, so that we are restored according to the image of God, a transformation that also restores our relationships with other human beings and the world. Augustine's soteriology is related toward becoming just and doing justice, yet avoiding the anthropological optimism of human perfectibility we find in classical thought, including Aristotelian virtue ethics.[100] The core of his soteriology is the restoration of *iustitia* through God's grace in Christ.

The connection between salvation and justice as well as its relation to nature can be explained as follows. As Wisse demonstrates in his reading of *De Trinitate*, justice is an absolute requirement for the vision of God and seeing God consists precisely in doing justice: "Blessed are the pure of heart, for they will see God" (Mt. 5:8).[101] On the one hand, justice is required in order to be able to see God. On the other hand, we need God to become pure of heart: since God is the only one who is really good and just, purity of heart, that is, becoming just, depends on God's goodness. This paradox can only be solved from Christ who restores our purity of heart. Yet, this is not something entirely new, as if grace creates a completely new human being that was not there before. Rather, it links up with our natural access to God that has been curbed ever since the Fall. Grace is not needed because there is no natural access to God but because our natural abilities malfunction and need to be repaired.[102] In this sense, Augustine is a virtue ethicist in the core of his soteriology: the happy life is the good life and what we need is to become good and just, but this is not within our reach. Since we cannot establish the good and just life by ourselves, grace is needed. This prevents virtue ethics from deteriorating into a plain optimism about our capacity to realize the good life by our own efforts.

In sum, Augustine's acknowledgment of the good includes at the same time an acknowledgment of the highest good, which is God. In this ontology there is no competition between love of the self, love of the other, and love of God. Interpreted according to this 'rule of love,' Augustine's account of eudaimonism is

---

100. Wisse, *Trinitarian Theology*, 13–14.
101. Ibid., 123, 174; *De Trinitate* 8.6.
102. *De Trinitate* 8.13; Wisse, *Trinitarian Theology*, 181, 269–70.

an innovative one and not a rejection of its framework.[103] The way he develops his thought of the good life and the virtues as dependent on God is a radical Christian reformulation of Antique thought, yet in such a way that he continuously appeals to our natural inclinations and to those outside Christianity who share a concern for the common good.[104]

Conclusion

My analysis of Aristotle and Augustine demonstrates that there is no need to abandon eudaimonism because of its agent centeredness, as Wolterstorff argues. Though Aristotle's virtue ethics suffers from several deficiencies and needs to be corrected and transformed, in his conception *eudaimonia* is dependent on external goods, basically directed to a common good and the good for others is an end in itself. In addition, I have argued that Augustine did not cause a break with the eudaimonistic framework. What he offers is a transformation of the meaning of happiness and the good life: the good life is a common good life from which no one is excluded. Justice is at the heart of it and therefore the most important virtue of the four cardinal virtues. The just and good life that we long for depends on God, who is himself the ultimate good. As Wolterstorff rightly argues, Augustine's acknowledgment of the biblical love commandment implies a break with the ideal of Stoic *apatheia*, but this does not imply a break with the ideal of the good life as such. Wolterstorff's criticism appears to be informed by a competitive view of the good, which is reflected in his account of rights that is vulnerable to possessive individualism, whereas Augustine basically adopts a non-competitive view of the common good, based in the biblical conception of love. Finally, Augustine acknowledges both our natural inclination toward the good and the need for grace since we cannot establish the good and just life by ourselves. We are longing for the good life; its fulfillment depends on God.

Augustine's view is to a great extent represented in Protestantism, for instance in Calvin's work. It is his view to which we turn in the next chapter. Does Calvin adopt an Augustinian eudaimonistic teleology? How does he deal with virtue and the virtues? What may his approach contribute to a viable virtue ethics?

---

103. Clair, "Wolterstorff on Love and Justice," 163. Clair also demonstrates that Wolterstorff's presentation of the incompatibility of the command to love the neighbor as oneself and the agent orientation of eudaimonism in *Justice* is in tension with his argument for the legitimacy of self-love presupposed in his careagapism in his book *Justice in Love*. Clair advocates an Augustinian account of human worth and dignity as grounded in ontological participation in the good, which in his view is superior to Worterstorff's conception of justice as natural inherent human rights contingent on the freedom of divine desire (Wolterstorff, *Justice*, 26–33). Cf. O'Donovan, *Problem of Self-Love*, 157.

104. Wisse, *Trinitarian Theology*, 269.

Chapter 3

CALVINISM AND THE BREAKDOWN OF TELEOLOGY

In this chapter I begin to counter Alasdair MacIntyre's and Brad Gregory's claim that the Reformation has been a major factor in a catastrophic breakdown in modernity of the teleological view of life, which resulted in the abandonment of the eudaimonistic conception of the good life and the virtues making this life possible.[1] According to MacIntyre, the teleological conception consisted of a threefold scheme in which (1) untutored human nature needs to be transformed (2) by practical reason (rational precepts, virtues) (3) into human-nature-as-it-could-be-if-it-realized-its-*telos*. When this Greek scheme was placed within the Christian theistic framework, the precepts of ethics were understood not only as teleological, but also as God's commands directing human beings toward their *telos*. Yet the threefold scheme was kept intact. In the Christian view throughout the Middle Ages, no gap existed between what is commanded in the divine law and what human beings would decide to do on the basis of rational reflection.[2]

MacIntyre—a similar line of thought can be traced in Gregory's work—argues that in modern ethics, from David Hume to Immanuel Kant and from Adam Smith to Søren Kierkegaard, only two elements of the traditional scheme remained: a conception of untutored human nature, on the one hand, and a set of moral precepts, on the other, which, however, human nature is no longer inclined to obey.[3] As the concept of *telos* was lost, the only element upon which moral principles might be grounded was *un*tutored human nature, that is, the autonomous individual. As a result, rational justification of moral principles became problematic: moral value judgments lost their factual character and terms like 'good' and 'justice' became meaningless because they were no longer rooted in a shared tradition and narrative.[4] This development finally wound up in the now

---

1. Alasdair MacIntyre, *A Short History of Ethics: A History of Moral Philosophy from the Homeric Age to the Twentieth Century* (London: Routledge, 1974), 121–7. In *After Virtue*, 53–4, MacIntyre offers a compacted version of the lengthier treatment in *A Short History*; Gregory, *The Unintended Reformation*, Ch. 4.
2. MacIntyre, *After Virtue*, 53.
3. Ibid., 55.
4. MacIntyre, *After Virtue*, 110–11.

common conviction that all value judgments are non-rational, and that the moral agent is sovereign in his choices ('emotivism' or 'expressivism').[5]

MacIntyre argues that three problematic modern concepts in particular stem from the Reformation period.[6] First, the late modern idea of moral rules being unconditional in their demands but lacking rational justification echoes the Reformers' insistence on God's sovereignty making his commands arbitrary. In Luther's ethics, "The only true moral rules are the divine commandments; and divine commandments are understood in an Occamist perspective—that is to say, they have no further rationale or justification than that they are the injunctions of God."[7] And Calvin does not interpret God's commandments as designed to bringing us to the *telos* to which our own desires point. Since human reason and will are enslaved by sin, only God and his commandments provide us with the true end of moral life, asking only for human obedience. Gregory differs from MacIntyre insofar he admits that the Reformers still held a teleological conception of the good, but they diverged greatly on how the ultimate end of life was related to what God said elsewhere in the Bible.[8]

Secondly, the moral agent as being sovereign in his choices stems from the Reformation concept of the un-roled self, standing naked before God. The moral agent stands alone, stripped of all social characteristics. According to MacIntyre, this idea paved the way toward the modern concept of the dislocated self, "totally detached from all social particularity."[9] The autonomous self has no given continuities and is set over against the social world.

Thirdly, the autonomy of the secular realm developed from the Reformers' attempt to free the political and economic spheres from ecclesiastical control. Luther handed over the secular world to its own devices, and "although Calvin's theocracy makes clergy sovereign over princes, it sanctions the autonomy of secular activity at every level where morals and religious practice do not directly conflict with such activity."[10] The history of Calvinism is the history of the progressive realization of the autonomy of the economic. The same holds for the state, to which the individual is no longer related via a web of social bindings in a set of linked associations in which everyone has his own status, but only as a self-determining subject.

---

5. Ibid., 6–35; Gregory, *Reformation*, 180–9. In his recent *Ethics in Conflicts of Modernity: An Essay on Desire, Practical Reason, and Narrative* (Cambridge: Cambridge University Press, 2016), MacIntyre repackages his former critique of emotivism (C. L. Stevenson and F. P. Ramsey) as a critique of expressivism (Simon Blackburn and Allan Gibbard).

6. MacIntyre, *Short History*, 126–7.

7. Ibid., 121. Cf. Gregory, *Reformation*, 201–5, who, more than MacIntyre, emphasizes the social divergence and dramatic disagreement in Christianity resulting from the doctrinal controversies of the Reformation.

8. Gregory, *Reformation*, 203.

9. MacIntyre, *After Virtue*, 32.

10. MacIntyre, *Short History*, 123.

MacIntyre's 'solution' to modern disengagement and 'criterionless' emotivism and expressionism resulting—at least partly—from the Reformation is to return to the Aristotelian and Thomistic teleological conception of life and to redefine this conception under present conditions. In virtue ethics human beings are seen as socially embedded, functioning in practices and corresponding social roles. What may count as a practice is primarily determined by the good or *telos* internal to the social activity characteristic of this practice and virtues are the qualities that "enable us to achieve those goods which are internal to practices."[11] Furthermore, it is necessary to envision life as a narrative unity in which various (conflicting) practices can be integrated in relation to the *telos* of human life as a whole. Finally, the human being, as a story telling animal searching for the good for his life, asks at the same time: What is the good for the human being as such? The good of one's life is related to and defined by a concept of the good for the human being in general as this is articulated in traditions. One realizes that one is, in being what one is, part of a living tradition and a community in which this tradition is embodied. All these basic concepts are teleologically structured.[12]

Important questions can be raised against the backdrop of MacIntyre's argument. His thesis about the general decline and breakdown of teleology in modern *philosophical* thought has already been nuanced.[13] Less attention has been paid to the question whether the Reformation indeed caused a breakdown of the teleological view of life.[14] How do *Protestant theological* conceptions of law and divine commands relate to the teleological conception of life and to classical and Christian virtue ethics? Furthermore, if teleological and virtue ethical concepts are still intact in the theology of the Reformation, what may this theology positively contribute to a viable virtue ethics or what may it correct in such an ethics?

In this chapter I focus on some aspects of Calvin's theology and Calvinism, as representing at least one important stream of Protestantism, in dealing with these

---

11. MacIntyre, *After Virtue*, 191.

12. Ibid., 181–225. See for a broad overview of how these core concepts have been taken up in theology: Nancy Murphy, Brad J. Kallenberg, and Mark Thiessen Nation (eds.), *Virtues and Practices in the Christian Tradition: Christian Ethics after MacIntyre* (Notre Dame: University of Notre Dame Press, 1997).

13. Cf. the summary of the outcome of this debate at this moment by Chappell, "Virtue Ethics in the Twentieth Century," 149–71: "MacIntyre seems wrong to claim that 'the key Enlightenment thinkers' abandoned teleology as a basis for ethics. If anyone deserves to be called 'key Enlightenment thinkers' Rousseau and Locke do—both of whom present political theories based wholly on the notion of the natural. Curiously, MacIntyre mentions neither Rousseau nor Locke at this point in his argument. But even the thinkers he does mention here—Pascal, Kant, Hume, Diderot, Adam Smith, Kierkegaard—are not uncontroversially nonteleological ethicists" (163). In Chapter 5, I will make a case for Kierkegaard.

14. An exception is Mouw, *The God Who Commands* and more recently Marco Hofheinz, *Ethik - reformiert! Studien zur reformierten Reformation und ihrer Rezeption im 20. Jahrhundert* (Göttingen: Vandenhoeck & Ruprecht, 2017), 64–113.

questions. My aim is first of all to counter MacIntyre's and Gregory's criticisms by correcting the most important arguments in their representation, based on a different reading of Calvin. This may be seen as a contribution to the reconstructive and deconstructive aims of this book. Secondly, a constructive contribution is based on a rereading of Calvin from the perspective of virtue ethics and its teleology. Calvin's utterances about virtue, the self before God, one's calling in the world, natural law, and reason will appear to be much more in alliance with a teleological, virtue ethical view than MacIntyre, Gregory, and others suggest, albeit not without distinction. This will open up the possibility of a fruitful interplay between a Protestant account of law or command ethics and virtue ethics.

Divine Command and Human Flourishing

When it comes to MacIntyre's first criticism—the arbitrariness of God's commands lacking any rational justification in the Reformed concept of law—this reading appears to be at least one-sided. The way reason and nature figure in the Reformation's concept of law and moral life is much more complicated than MacIntyre suggests.

First, it may be correct that Calvin justifies obedience to God's commandments as a matter of pleasing the divine lawgiver, but we should understand it as the response of the human subject to what God has already done and to whom he is. It matters what the divine lawgiver's attributes are. We obey God's legislative demands because we learned to know God as just, as the good creator who wants us to flourish.[15] Obedience is embedded in a narrative context, in the covenantal and relational story of God with his people, as is indicated, for example, by the prologue of the Decalogue. Covenant is the factor that holds the Calvinistic voluntarist impulse in check, as Richard Mouw puts it. The covenant theme accomplishes "to surround God's sovereign will with a divine character in which fidelity is a prominent feature."[16] In short, Calvin's theocentric bias is not in contradiction with what counts as 'good' in the good life. He does not fall into the trap of the Euthyphro-dilemma (does God command things because they are good, or is what God commands good because God commands it?). God rather commands what is necessary for human flourishing, which is in conformity with his own righteous and holy character.[17]

---

15. Mouw, *The God Who Commands*, 28–9.
16. Ibid., 100.
17. In *Inst.* 3.23.2, for example, Calvin states on the one hand: "God's will is so much the highest rule of righteousness that whatever he wills, by the very fact that he wills it, must be considered righteous." On the other hand, he says: "We fancy no lawless god who is a law unto himself . . . but the will of God is not only free of all fault but is the highest rule of perfection, and even the law of all laws." Cf. Guenther H. Haas, "Calvin's Ethics," in Donald K. McKim (ed.), *The Cambridge Companion to John Calvin* (Cambridge: Cambridge

Furthermore, for Calvin reason and human will are still active in the way human beings respond to God. The Christian life is not a matter of responding mindlessly to what MacIntyre typifies as "the arbitrary fiats of a cosmic despot."[18] And the law is not something outside of the believer and foreign to his will. In sanctified life, the law has become an internal enterprise, for the will has assimilated the law to itself.[19] Therefore, when Calvin deals with the *usus tertius legis* (the law as rule for the right life of the believer) he emphasizes the believer's increasing understanding of the *purpose and unity* of God's commandments—his mind being illuminated by the Holy Spirit. To understand the full meaning of the commandments, Calvin proposes that attention be directed to the reason and purpose of each commandment.[20] In Latin he uses the words *ratio* and *finis*, the latter being the translation of *telos*. This means that in each commandment we should ponder *why* it was given to us. Calvin recognizes the literary device of *synecdoche*, where the part is used to signify the whole: while the commandments prescribe or forbid particular acts, there are broader implications for their practice. One must go beyond the exact words in order to understand God's will and intention revealed in them. Karl Barth's interpretation of the law in terms of 'direction' (*Weisung*) points to a similar feature. God's commandments do not dictate exactly how to act, but provide general directions and imply human freedom and reasonability in personal response to God's command and the very situation in which one has responsibility.[21]

In short, the fullness of the divine will cannot be discovered without using our reason in interpreting God's revealed commandments. At the same time, reason is not autonomous but has become part of "the renewal of our mind" as Paul puts it in Rom. 12:2.[22] Reason is not replaced but submitted to the Holy Spirit, so that one oneself may no longer live but Christ within one (Gal. 2:20). When one is thus transformed, one's reason is transformed as well, but it is still *reason*. The work of the Spirit is not merely to regenerate people's hearts, but also to illuminate their minds so that they *understand* what is revealed as God's will in Scripture.

The meaning of 'divine command' can be demonstrated from a different angle as well. Advocates of the so-called divine command ethics, which can be considered as a renewal of the Reformation's claim that true morality is conceivable only as response to God's initiative, defend that morality is rooted in obedience. As Oliver O'Donovan comments, this does not necessarily mean that morality is *definitionally* equivalent to God's command, "but that since among things we rightly judge to be

---

University Press, 2004), 97, explaining Calvin's view: "The law is the authority because God wills it to be so, but he wills it to be so because it expresses his righteousness and holy character. The law is as firm and constant as God's own character."

18. MacIntyre, *Short History*, 123.
19. John Hesselink, *Calvin's Concept of the Law* (Allison Park: Pickwick, 1992), 256.
20. *Inst.* 2.8.8.
21. Cf. Werpehowski, *Karl Barth and Christian Ethics*, 23–32.
22. *Inst.* 3.7.1. Cf. Hauerwas, *Character and the Christian Life*, 209.

good some goodness lays claim on our action in a way that not all goodness does, God's command accounts for this morally transcendent claim."[23] The meaning of 'divine command' is neither that it founds what is good, nor that it explains why anything is good, but simply that it explains why this or that good *rests upon me as an obligation*.[24] The concept of divine command accounts for a sense of responsibility, the demand of unconditional and overriding responsibility itself, prior to any content. Although a reference to God is not inescapable—God enters moral reasoning by inductive inference—responsibility points to a 'reality' that holds me answerable. Being responsible presupposes openness to a demand I have not laid on myself.[25] This may be a relevant account of unconditional responsibility included in a Calvinistic concept of divine command.

Natural Law and Triplex Usus Legis

The relative importance of reason is also apparent in Calvin's concept of natural law. Calvin believed that God had displayed his moral will in the *lex naturalis* (natural law) or in the *lex interior* (internal law) as it is engraved upon the hearts of *all* people, as a part of human consciousness (Rom. 1:19 and 2:14): "There is nothing more common than for a man to be sufficiently instructed in a right standard of conduct by natural law."[26] God has displayed his moral will apart from his written law in natural law, though the latter is far more obscure in comparison with the first.[27]

The interpretation of Calvin's appeals to natural law has long divided scholars. August Lang, Karl Barth, Michael Walzer, Jochem Douma, James Torrance, Paul Lehmann, John Hesselink, and others, all emphasize the discontinuity of the Reformed view with natural law thought throughout the Middle Ages. According to these authors, natural law is in fact peripheral in Calvin's thought. Emil Brunner, John T. McNeill, Richard A. Muller, Gerard Th. Rothuizen, Paul Helm, Stephen J. Grabill, and David VanDrunen emphasize the continuity of Calvin's thought on natural law with the tradition, as well as its distinctiveness.[28] I follow the latter line, for natural law appears not to be peripheral but essential to Calvin's

---

23. Oliver O'Donovan, *Finding and Seeking: Ethics as Theology*, Vol. 2 (Grand Rapids/Cambridge: Eerdmans, 2014), 28.

24. Robert M. Adams, *Finite and Infinite Goods* (Oxford: Oxford University Press, 1999), 249–52.

25. O'Donovan, *Finding and Seeking*, 31.

26. *Inst.* 2.2.22. Cf. 2.2.17: it can still be seen "among all mankind that reason is proper to our nature; it distinguishes us from brute beasts."

27. *Inst.* 2.8.1: "inward law . . . as written, even engraved, upon the hearts of all, in a sense asserts the very same things that are to be learned from the Two Tables."

28. See VanDrunen, *Natural Law and the Two Kingdoms*, 93–5, for this overview.

legal and political views.[29] In my view, the place and meaning of natural law in Calvin's theology can be understood in light of his concept of the *triplex usus legis* (threefold use of the law). In the three uses of the law, the law functions in various ways, but is still one law revealed by God. This makes it possible for Calvin, and other Reformers, to recognize in the Decalogue a proclamation of natural law while not separating this notion from the theological meaning of the *usus elenchticus*: "The purpose of natural law . . . is to render man inexcusable."[30] At the same time, Calvin positively expresses the *primus usus* (in the *Institutes* labeled as *secundus*) in terms of natural law. His different evaluations of the use of natural law as both positive in various cultural achievements and as negative in leaving people inexcusable in their sin also has to be understood from the perspective of the doctrine of the two kingdoms: through natural law even pagans form good laws and produce other social goods in the civil kingdom, but are completely incapable of producing true spiritual good in the realm of the spiritual kingdom.[31]

Rothuizen has argued that the first use of the law is relatively independent (the qualification 'Christian' is not necessary; the notion 'society' is not absorbed in 'Christianity'), but not isolated from the other uses of the law (it is connected with God as the one lawgiver).[32] Therefore, the recognition of nature has different implications in the *primus usus legis* and the other *usus*. What is 'virtue' in the first case is 'need' in the second use of the law. In Rothuizen's formulation, the *usus elenchticus* convinces the human being of sin (in his being human, the human being is *peccator*), the *usus didacticus* imposes the requirement of holiness (in being *peccator* the human being must be holy), the *usus politicus* confronts sinner and human being (in being *peccator* the human being remains a human being).[33] The *usus elenchticus* and the *usus didacticus* guard against isolation of an exclusively natural conception of the *primus usus*. At the same time, this does not imply an exclusively Christian conception of the *usus politicus*, which would also be one-sided. In short, natural law is part of human consciousness in general, but does not exist at the expense of its vertical relation to God but by the grace

---

29. Cf. J. Todd Billings, *Calvin, Participation, and the Gift: The Activity of Believers in Union with Christ* (Oxford: Oxford University Press, 2007), 145: "It is simply not the case that Calvin represents a break with the 'whole tradition' of natural law" (contra Paul Lehmann).

30. *Inst.* 2.2.22.

31. VanDrunen, *Natural Law*, 110–14.

32. Gerard Th. Rothuizen, *Primus usus legis: Studie over het burgerlijk gebruik van de wet* [Primus usus legis: Study of the civil use of the law] (Kampen: Kok, 1962), 24–9, 58–9; relatively (*quodammodo*) independent, for the *lex naturalis* will sooner or later knock against the *lex Christi*.

33. Rothuizen, *Primus usus*, 23. Cf. *Inst.* 2.16.3: "However much we may be sinners by our own fault, we nevertheless remain his creatures."

of this connection, as fruit of 'common grace.'[34] In Calvin's view, nothing exists independent of God, whether one acknowledges it or not.

Natural Law and Grace

Against the backdrop of MacIntyre's criticism, it is important to notice that Calvin's view of the written divine commandments as expressing and clarifying natural law is basically in harmony with the traditional conception, though not without distinctiveness. David VanDrunen has demonstrated the incorrectness of the popular view, going back to Troeltsch and advocated by many scholars including MacIntyre and Gregory, that Aquinas as a realist was the great defender of natural law, Scotus weakened it and Ockham as representing nominalism and voluntarism, finally destroyed the theological foundations of natural law and thereby ushered modernity—incited by the Reformation—and its moral relativism.[35] In different ways, natural law served both for Aquinas, Scotus, and Ockham, as well as for the Reformers, as foundation for ethics and civic law. Whereas Aquinas rooted natural law in divine reason, Scotus located natural law in the divine will, but not in such a way that God's freedom is limitless; in Scotus's view, natural law is immutable and not arbitrary at all.[36] The same holds for Ockham. Natural law was affirmed and utilized in both Thomistic and nominalist circles. It was part of a common, Catholic inheritance.

This common conception is reflected in Calvin's use of the concepts "moral law (*lex moralis*)," "divine law (*lex Dei*)," "natural law (*lex naturalis*)," and "nations making laws" (which points at the Thomistic concept of *lex humana*, the human law), for example, when he deals with civil government using the concept of equity (*aequitas*): "the law of God which we call the moral law is nothing else than a testimony of natural law and of that conscience which God has engraved upon the minds of men. Consequently, the entire scheme of ... equity ... has been prescribed in it."[37] Equity is the basis on which every nation is free to make laws, that is, in conformity with the perpetual rule of love, the moral law, "the true and eternal rule of righteousness, prescribed for men of all nations and times." This rule is not different from God's will, which is also identified as the double commandment of love for God and the neighbor.[38] More precisely, Calvin understands love of the

---

34. Rothuizen, *Primus usus*, 30–2. Cf. *Inst.* 2.2.10-17.

35. VanDrunen, *Natural Law*, 42–55.

36. Scotus distinguishes God's ordained power from his absolute power. God cannot act against those general laws, which order things rightly and are established beforehand by divine will and intellect, as something antecedent to any act of divine will (ordained power). However, according to his absolute power God actually can act beyond these pre-established laws (VanDrunen, *Natural Law*, 50).

37. *Inst.* 4.20.16.

38. *Inst.* 4.20.15.

neighbor in terms of the concept of equity. In his view, the best summary of the moral law or the second table of the Decalogue is found in Mt. 7:12, where Christ teaches the love of the neighbor in terms of what is commonly designated the Golden Rule: "In everything, do to others what you would have them to do to you, for this sums up the Law and the Prophets."[39]

Furthermore, there is no fundamental contradiction between a Calvinistic theology of grace (common and special) and a so-called Thomistic theology of nature and grace or a teleological conception of life in general. Although Thomas distinguishes the cardinal virtues acquired by a human being from the theological virtues infused by divine grace, he acknowledges that even the virtuous capacity in human nature is a gift from God. The concept of nature is not naturalistic, autonomous, or rationalistic; human nature and the human capabilities are also the work of God the creator.[40] Moreover, it is only on the strength of the supernaturally infused virtues that the naturally acquired virtues direct human action to man's eternal destiny.[41] Finally, both with Thomas and with Calvin it is only because, prior to special revelation, we do have a conception of the good, that we can be held accountable by God.

The difference between Rome and the Reformation does not lie in the use of the nature-grace scheme—Calvin, for instance, reuses the scheme and transforms it in terms of common and special grace—but in the *harmonization* of common and special grace. Reformation and Rome have a common trust in the human capabilities as good gifts from the creator, but different from medieval scholastic theology the Reformers more boldly emphasize that human reason and human capabilities are useless when it comes to justification and, as a consequence, sanctification of life. Whereas in Roman Catholic theology a more gradual development is possible, the Reformation emphasizes the break between what the human being can endeavor thanks to God's common grace, on the one hand, and his total corruption and need for salvation and renewal, on the other. Calvin can subscribe to both a relatively positive conception of natural human capacities and man's total corruption by using the traditional Augustinian distinction between the natural (*ratio*, which enables the human being to distinguish between good and evil, to understand and to judge, as well as *voluntas*) and the supernatural gifts of the soul (faith, love of God, neighborly love, striving for sanctity and justice). Due to the Fall the human being *lost* the supernatural gifts completely, whereas the natural gifts of reason and will are still present, though *corrupted* by sin in their

---

39. *Inst.* 2.8.50 and 53; Haas, "Calvin's Ethics," 102–3. See also Paul Helm, "Nature and Grace," in Manfred Svensson and David VanDrunen (eds.), *Aquinas among the Protestants* (Oxford: Wiley Blackwell, 2018), 233.

40. Cf. *ST* II-I 55, 4 ad 6: "As to those things which are done by us, God causes them in us, yet not without action on our part, for He works in every will and in every nature."

41. *ST* II-I 65 ad 2.

actual use.⁴² According to Aquinas, however, the reason why grace is needed in addition to nature is not corruption due to the fall into sin, but the inherent limits of nature itself. According to Calvin, sin is not a matter of natural limitations, but an interruption that corrupts (not destroys) natural goodness and our moral understanding. Hence, it is human sin rather than the limits of human nature that requires supernatural revelation.⁴³ Reason in the end only functions effectively in a proper relationship with God; in this sense it is in need of redemption. To Calvin it is crystal clear that man "hardly begins to grasp through this natural law what worship is acceptable to God."⁴⁴ In full accord with Augustine, Calvin insists that the renewal of the human will is needed, which requires divine intervention.

Does all of this imply that Calvin actually holds a teleological conception of life? My answer would be in the affirmative, though not without distinctiveness, since he doesn't adopt an Aristotelian naturalistic scheme. Thanks to God's presence in the world all human beings can have a general idea about the human *telos*, the good, and the good life, but it is only in relation to God and in dependence on his special grace and revelation that we discover this *telos* properly. In Calvin's view, the *true* end is evangelical perfection (*evangelica perfectio*), which we find in God and consists in a life that is lived to God's glory (*gloria Dei*).⁴⁵ Differently from the Aristotelian framework and in accord with Augustine, this end is located outside the human being, making the glorification of God the proper end of human life (*Gloria Dei summus finis est*).⁴⁶ The glorification of God is the human being's *summum bonum*. It is through mediation of the coming life (*meditatio futurae vitae*) that we become directed to this *summum bonum*, which will be completed in the eternal life.⁴⁷

Given this framework, MacIntyre is wrong in his claim that according to the Reformers we can have no comprehension of man's end and that reason's power to discern that *telos* was destroyed by the Fall, but he is right insofar as, according to Calvin, we can have no comprehension of man's *true* end without revelation.⁴⁸ However, it seems that the same holds for Aquinas and the entire teleological conception of life throughout the Middle Ages! The difference is relative. In comparison with Aquinas, the Reformers tempered the trust in the human capabilities and what human beings would decide to do on the basis of rational reflection. The Reformers saw the dangers of optimism about the capabilities of human reason, as they sensed it coming up in the modern age. Hence, Calvin's evaluation of reason is more ambivalent than Aquinas'. From this perspective it

---

42. *Inst.* 2.2.12. Cf. Augustine, *De natura et gratia* 3.3; 19.21; 20.22, *PL* 44, 249 and 256-7. Cf. *Inst.* 2.2.25.
43. VanDrunen, *Natural Law*, 107; Helm, "Nature and Grace," 234.
44. *Inst.* 2.8.1. Cf. 1.6.1-4.
45. *Inst.* 3.6.5.
46. *CO* 51, 147 (commentary Eph. 1,4).
47. See for this explanation of Calvin's teleology: Hofheinz, *Ethik - reformiert!*, 92-6.
48. MacIntyre, *After Virtue*, 53.

could even be said that it is not Calvin but Aquinas who paved the way toward the autonomy of reason in modernity: Kant is Aquinas-without-God. Of course, this would be much too rash, but it illustrates that an alternative narrative, different from MacIntyre's, can plausibly be told.[49]

Calvin and the Virtues

My next consideration is about the status of virtue and the virtues in Calvin's theology. His treatment of virtue appears to follow Augustine's double evaluation of virtue as the most perfect and useful we can find on earth on the one hand, and as in need of redemption on the other, since no one can realize the good life on his or her own powers.

In line with his concept of natural law and the relatively independent status of the *primus usus legis* is Calvin's acknowledgment of "persons, who, guided by nature, have striven toward virtue throughout life" and of people who "not only excelled in remarkable deeds, but conducted themselves most honorably throughout life."[50] Calvin fully values these features, but they do not contradict the *corruptio totalis* of human nature (which does not mean that the human being is totally bad, but that every part of the total person is affected by sin). For it is only God's grace that restrains human corruption and by his providence God bridles perversity of nature (note that 'bridle' is the word Calvin also uses to describe the nature of the *primus usus legis*). Again, nature is not seen as independent of God's (common) grace: "these are not common gifts of nature (*communes naturae dotes*), but special graces of God (*speciales Dei gratiae*), which he bestows variously and in certain measure upon men otherwise wicked" (in this case 'special graces' does not mean 'special grace' but something like 'special gifts').[51] All these 'natural' virtues are gifts of God that extend to 'non-believers' as well. There is really a difference between the justice (*iustitia*), moderation (*moderatio*), and equity (*aequitas*) of Titus and Trajan, and the madness (*rabies*), intemperance (*intemperies*), and savagery (*saevitia*) of Caligula, Nero and Domitian. In a similar way to Augustine, Calvin praises the qualities of heroes of the Roman republic like Fabricius, Scipio, and Cato, albeit that these qualities are limited because they are not directed to God who gives them.[52]

Furthermore, in Calvin's view virtue is not contradictory to law, but has similar meanings as the law in its *triplex usus*. On the one hand, virtue is given by the Lord

---

49. Mouw, *The God Who Commands*, 67–70.
50. *Inst.* 2.3.3.
51. *Inst.* 2.3.4. In this section Calvin speaks of the personal virtues of people like Camillus (446–365 BC, celebrated by Horace, Vergil, and Juvenal) in which nature is "carefully cultivated" as "gifts of God," though their nature is still corrupted. Thus, instead of 'special grace' these "gifts" or "graces" are rather a matter of 'common grace'.
52. *Inst.* 3.14.2 and 3; *CO* 50, 255 (commentary Gal. 5:22).

to restrain all human beings from following their lust, to bridle perversity. On the other, the excellence and virtuousness of natural man makes him not righteous before God, for in these virtues is "no zeal to glorify God" and "the chief part of uprightness is absent."[53] Therefore, as in Augustine's view, a complete renewal of the human will is needed—otherwise the virtues will deceive us with their vanity. As Berkouwer has pointed out, Calvin does not aim at a quantitative reduction of what the human being may endeavor due to God's grace.[54] His evaluation is qualitative: from the perspective of justification, the virtues are worthless if they are not related to the right end. The core question is how the good gifts of the virtues are being used: are the virtues and virtuous deeds applied to the end of true righteousness or not, because what ought to be done is "weighed not by deeds but by ends."[55] The 'pagan' virtues are good in themselves, but become wrong by how they are used (*per accidens, per modum operationis*); they are no sins in themselves (*peccata in se*).[56]

Here, we discover again a teleological way of thinking. In line with Augustine's distinction between the two cities, Calvin emphasizes the importance of the entire direction of one's life before God (*coram Deo*). Decisive is the God relationship, which opens up any anthropocentricity to a theocentric orientation. We cannot understand the human being and his or her virtuous qualities apart from God's acting. Calvin agrees with Augustine that from the human part obedience to God (in the sense of *responding* to God) is what counts, as this is "the mother and guardian of all virtues" and "their source."[57]

The parallelism between Calvin's explanation of virtue and his third use of the law becomes clear when he sets out the features of Christian moral life. Here, we find a surprisingly positive account of virtue and the virtues. Unlike what is often assumed and as we find it in MacIntyre's descriptions of Reformation ethics, Calvin's choice to outline Christian moral life from the perspective of *law* is not based on principle but on practical reasons. In *Institutes* 3.6., he starts his treatment of the Christian life by suggesting that he could also have taken the virtues as his starting point. He explicitly refers in full agreement to the old church fathers, who wrote so well and profoundly about the virtues in their homilies. Calvin himself decides not to deal with the virtues in detail, because his intention "is not to extend it so far as to treat of each virtue specially, and expatiate in exhortation."[58] He limits himself to showing "the godly man how he may be directed to a rightly ordered

---

53. *Inst.* 2.3.4.

54. Gerrit C. Berkouwer, *De mens het beeld Gods* [The human being as image of God] (Kampen: Kok, 1957), 161.

55. *Inst.* 3.14.3.

56. Herman Bavinck, *Gereformeerde ethiek* [Reformed ethics] (Utrecht: Kok Boekencentrum, 2019), 125–6.

57. *Inst.* 2.8.5; *CD* 14.12. Cf. Hofheinz, *Ethik - reformiert!*, 98.

58. *Inst.* 3.6.1. Cf. Jochem Douma, *Grondslagen* [Foundations], Christelijke ethiek, Vol. 1 (Kok: Kampen, 1999), 227.

life," and briefly to setting down "some universal rule with which to determine his duties."[59] Note that Calvin speaks not only in terms of rules and duties but also in more teleological terms of "man directed to a rightly ordered life." The division followed by Calvin is that, on the one hand, "the love of righteousness, to which we are by no means naturally inclined, may be instilled and implanted into our minds,"[60] and, on the other hand, we are prescribed a rule which does not make us err: to obey God and his commandments.[61] One might say that virtue ethics (to cultivate love for righteousness) goes hand in hand with a command ethics (to follow God's commandments).

Although Calvin cannot be regarded as an Aristotelian or a Thomist, in his view it is not the law of God as such that is the core of the Christian life, but the *personal* dedication of our lives to God, "in order that we may thereafter think, speak, mediate, and do nothing except to his glory."[62] From this starting point it is possible to describe Christian life in terms of the cultivation of virtues.[63] Moreover, Calvin positively clarifies how his view on the virtues differs from philosophical accounts of the virtues. To give but one example, whereas philosophers like Cicero and Seneca announce merely that we should live in accordance with nature, Scripture draws its exhortation to be virtuous from the "true fountain: Christ who has been set before us as an example."[64] The notion of determining the right state of character, which we call virtue, by imitating a prime example, is in line with the tradition of classical virtue ethics and the Christian transformation of this tradition (Christ as "the true fountain").

From this particular Christian perspective, Calvin mentions a number of virtues, often in contrast with vices, to outline what Christian life looks like. Marco Hofheinz lists eight virtues that Calvin most frequently names in his eclectic and non-systematic treatments.[65] The first one is love (*caritas*), which Calvin, following Augustine, understands as the "choir in which all virtues consonance."[66] Humility

---

59. *Inst.* 3.6.1.
60. *Inst.* 3.6.2.
61. *Inst.* 3.7.2.
62. *Inst.* 3.7.1.
63. In the 1970s, Raymond K. Anderson already wrote a dissertation on order, grace, and virtue in Calvin: *Love and Order: The Life-Structuring Dynamics of Grace and Virtue in Calvin's Ethical Thought* (Chambersburg: Wilson College, 1973). One of his observations is: "Calvin always values the virtues he sees." Yet, he concludes that the virtues belong to the periphery of Calvin's thought. "They appear . . . as natural corollaries of the three theological virtues 'moderated' with them by orientational reflection on the several aspects of one's situation in life with God" (397). They function in a flexible way in his Scriptural understanding of human excellence, that is, "as a function of God's virtue—as God's own goodness, power and majesty communicated somehow by his Spirit" (315).
64. *Inst.* 3.6.3. I will elaborate on this in Chapter 6.
65. Hofheinz, *Ethik – reformiert!*, 76–80, which I follow here.
66. *CO* 52, 123 (commentary Col. 3,14).

(*humilitas*) is the virtue that directs our attention completely to God as the sole source of our justification and justice.[67] Together with modesty (*modestas*) it is the salt that makes the other virtues tasteful.[68] Similarly, other virtues can be counted as equally important: self-renunciation (*sui abnegatio*) as the virtue that redirects our attention from ourselves to God in order to do the good not for our own sake,[69] temperance (*temperantia*) as the decisive virtue of the believer, obedience (*obedientia*) as "the mother and guardian of all virtues,"[70] and patience (*patientia*), which we learn from sufferings and at the same time enables us to endure these sufferings.[71] Finally, godliness or fear of God (*timor Dei*) is the virtue that brings us to confession of our sins in order to rely on God's grace.[72] Other virtues could be listed,[73] but more important is that Calvin does not elaborate systematically on all these virtues. For what matters is just to persevere in the path of Christian simplicity. Therefore, Calvin cannot be called a virtue ethicist in the narrow sense of the word. Rather we should say that there are clearly virtue ethical traces in his work, retaining "a vestige of sympathy with the Stoic virtues."[74] These virtues have their proper place in the locus of sanctification. In Chapter 6, I will show that this includes human activity and habituation. At the very least, all this indicates that virtue and the virtues are in principle at home in Calvinistic ethics.

More challenging than the question whether theology in the wake of the Reformation 'allows' for virtue and virtue ethics is the question what Protestant theology may contribute positively to a viable virtue ethics. One of these contributions may be Calvin's significant use of a new term which adds something to the virtue ethical tradition and may function as a bridge to modernity. This concerns the term *moderatio*, which appears everywhere in his writings and is often misunderstood as 'moderateness' or 'mediocrity', as Anderson demonstrates. Rather, the word describes something which is preserved in the modern use of the English word 'moderator', that is, someone who guides and orders procedures, taking care that they are appropriate and efficient with regard to the purpose at hand. For Calvin, 'moderation'—other related terms he uses are 'integrity' and 'honnêteté'—describes a kind of guidance, an ordering process through which our actions are relevant and efficient in terms of their purpose. It describes a responsive process by which one draws one's life to its calling to exist in Christ. Rather than thinking in terms of abstract and fixed rules that need to be applied in moral issues, Calvin seems to be thinking of the living orientation and order the

---

67. *Inst.* 2.2.11.
68. *CO* 30, 541 (sermon 1 Sam. 25:14–28).
69. *Inst.* 3.7.2.
70. *Inst.* 2.8.5.
71. *Inst.* 3.8.4.
72. *Inst.* 3.3.7.
73. See for a more extensive overview: Anderson, *Love and Order*, 336–67.
74. Anderson, *Love and Order*, 315. Elizabeth Cochran, *Protestant Virtue and Stoic Ethics*, makes a strong case for Stoic influences on Calvin's thought on virtue and the virtues.

human being receives in relationship with God, which enables one to find one's way in the specific context one is involved in.[75] In this interpretation, moderation or integrity is a kind of virtue which is close to prudence, with the difference that moderation is not defined from the exemplar of the 'prudent man,' as in Aristotle, but seems to be more creative, dynamic, flexible, and open to what is uniquely given in one's situation and possibilities. This makes this virtue more appropriate in modern life, which is less defined from pre-given social orders from which one may derive what is prudent and what is not.

Another relevant contribution may be that law, *telos*, and virtue can be conceived of as connected in a particular way. Although Calvin develops his ethics basically in terms of law and commandments, the material content of what may count as the good life cannot be envisioned without any account of the virtues, as we have seen. This interconnectedness of virtue and law has advantages over against an exclusively virtue ethical approach, as sometimes advocated in contemporary virtue ethics. Calvin's tempered evaluation of human reason, his doctrine of sin, and his emphasis on moral precepts as divine commands are relevant as a necessary counterpart of a viable virtue ethics. In line with the medieval tradition, MacIntyre too acknowledges the need for precepts and law in ethics, but he does not so much take into account that human nature needs to be *restrained* by external norms, as seen in Calvin's approach.[76]

This is a promising element in regard of the question how a viable ethics of the good life and the virtues can be developed under late modern conditions. More than MacIntyre's harmonious three-partite naturalistic scheme, Calvin's approach is sized to the post-Nietzschean acknowledgment that nature, including human nature, is not *in se* well-ordered, but also dangerous and threatening and therefore in need of control. In a Calvinistic ethics, it is acknowledged that human nature is not inclined to a flourishing life, that is, to the love of righteousness as its true *telos*, and therefore needs to be not only transformed radically but also restrained by norms and laws. A Calvinistic perspective offers the possibility to envision virtue ethics as not being contrary to an ethics of divine commands or obligations. Commandments are the necessary, complementary external precepts in relation to virtues as dispositional traits of character.

A third contribution concerns the relevance of a Calvinistic or Neo-Calvinistic account of law in relation to MacIntyre's concept of 'practices.' Before I elaborate on this, I briefly turn to the other two claims in his criticism of Protestantism.

Selfhood, Roles, and God's Calling

MacIntyre's second claim concerns what he considers the Protestant idea of a pre-rational self, standing naked before God, stripped of all social roles.

---

75. Anderson, *Love and Order*, 320–2.
76. MacIntyre, *After Virtue*, 150, 200.

Protestantism's celebration of the individual's direct relationship to God indeed seems to be parallel with the modern portrayal of the emotivist self, whose naked will makes criterionless choices. According to MacIntyre, in the transition *from* the premodern concept of the self in its full roled-ness *to* the modern concept of identity as de-roled, Calvin would have to be placed on the side of modernity.

However, an alternative narrative can also be told on this point. First, the roled-ness of the self in premodern times is not as strong as it seems. As Peter Berger has argued, the understanding that there is a humanity behind the roles is not a modern idea. We find it also in the Bible and in ancient tragedies.[77]

Secondly, and more importantly, we should not limit the interpretation of the Calvinistic conception of the self to the aspect of being the naked self before God. To obtain a true picture of the social-ethical implications of Calvin's concept of selfhood, it is illuminating to look at his elaboration of the notion of vocation. In his *Institutes* 3.10.6, Calvin sees each particular way of life as a calling of God. God's calling is not opposed to nor completely identified with our social role in our profession. Calvin was aware of the societal changes in an increasingly mobile society which for many caused doubts about their social and occupational roles. On the one hand, he pleads for openness and freedom in interpersonal relationships, criticizing the hypocritical discrepancy between what one is inwardly, and what one appears to be outwardly because of one's role. On the other hand, he assures that we must not choose our own roles to play; God calls us, so to say, to enact them.[78] The starting point is that our calling is first of all to be citizens of this kingdom. Each individual has his calling "as a sentry post" in the kingdom of God. At the same time, our various callings in life commit us to duties fitted to our situation and possibilities assigned to us by God. We should not transgress our limits.

Important concepts here are order and harmony, even "harmony among the several parts of . . . life," which sounds familiar to a MacIntyrian conception of the unity of life as the way one has to order one's participation in the various practices and its virtues in which a person may be involved. One's life will best be ordered when it is directed to the goal, that is, God's calling to serve his kingdom. This teleological idea gives scope to one's life and, even more, it is an acknowledgment of each person's social role. Furthermore, in Calvin's theology we find a strong sense for the given order in society and in human practices as ordered by laws and principles as these are rooted in creation: "There exist in all men's minds universal impressions of a certain civic fair dealing and order. Hence no man is to be found

---

77. Peter Berger, "On the Obsolescence of the Concept of Honor," in Stanley Hauerwas and Alasdair MacIntyre (eds.), *Revisions: Changing Perspectives in Moral Philosophy* (Notre Dame: University of Notre Dame Press, 1983), 172–81, cited by Mouw, *The God Who Commands*, 71.

78. Mouw, *The God Who Commands*, 72. Cf. André Biéler, *Calvin's Economic and Social Thought*, trans. James Greig (Geneva: World Council of Churches, [1961] 2005), 356–9.

who does not understand that every sort of human organization must be regulated by laws, and who does not comprehend the principles of those laws."[79]

In conclusion, the naked self, standing before God is not identical with an un-roled self. In a Calvinistic view, we all have our specific roles in the creational order. Nevertheless, one's social role is not absolute, but linked to God's calling of the believer to be a pilgrim on the way toward the heavenly kingdom. As such, the God relationship transcends or relativizes all given social roles. In his roles and life choices, the self is first of all responsible to God—a responsibility to make responsible decisions in light of God's revealed will.

Life Spheres and Societal Responsibility coram Deo

In response to MacIntyre's evaluation of the third feature that he attributes to the Reformation—the secularization of various domains of social life—we can argue that Calvin's separation between ecclesiastical and civil authority did not imply the removal of civil society from under the rule of God. Rather, both preacher and prince stand in direct responsibility *coram Deo*. Civil rulers, freed from ecclesiastical authority, still need to do the will of God.[80]

Although, contra MacIntyre, Calvin and other Reformers did not espouse secular autonomy, it may be argued that they made it at least *easier* for other thinkers simply to absolve civil rulers and economic agents from a sense of responsibility to anyone but themselves.[81] In response to this, it is illuminating to take notice again of the nature of Calvin's moderate voluntarism as interconnected with the notions of justice and covenant. First of all, Calvin's insistence on the need for human beings to surrender to the will of God does not imply uncritical surrender to human rulers, for rulers are themselves human beings who must surrender to God's Word. Since we can observe that human rulers commit serious offenses against divine will, civilians must face the possibility that resistance is sometimes needed.[82] The theocentric approach shapes various responsibilities in the political domain.

Furthermore, the covenant theme is important here. Covenant does not only accomplish to surround God's will with a divine character in which fidelity is prominent, as we have seen, but is also applied to the social and political domains.[83] In this case covenant has the meaning of the agreement of an association, or its leaders, to conduct the life of the association in accordance with the primordial

---

79. *Inst.* 2.2.13.
80. Mouw, *The God Who Commands*, 65–6.
81. Ibid., 66.
82. *Inst.* 4.20.32.
83. Mouw, *The God Who Commands*, 100.

essence of group life (Johannes Althusius).⁸⁴ It commits a group of associates to abide by laws that facilitate the realization of prevenient social designs. God's commands are viewed as directing people toward a lawful conformity to creational purposes.⁸⁵ Several Calvinists developed the idea of 'creation ordinances,' thereby depicting God's relationship to creation as a legislative one, in a universe that is as law-filled as Thomas's is.

Finally, in early and later Calvinism we find an insistence on the richness of associational life in a plurality of forms, like family, guild, university, and so on, which exist by virtue of God's created designs. In Reformed thought, not only the polity of ecclesial community is related in many ways to the larger society, God also calls us to *integrate* the roles associated with the variety of these communal contexts. Against the danger of complete segmentation of social roles, Calvinists tried to reintegrate the individual into the double order of the religious and the political, bound together in a corporate community, which was neither purely religious nor purely secular, but a compound of the two.⁸⁶

Social Practices and Law Spheres

From these perspectives it can be clarified how a Calvinistic concept of law has the potential to add something that lacks in MacIntyre's Neo-Aristotelian account of virtues in terms of practices and the narrative unity of life. To explain this, we must recall that from Calvin's view explored so far, it follows that 'law' appears on two distinct levels. First, as 'natural law' it designates an "order of nature" by which creatures, both non-living and living, non-human and human, in all their diversity obey God. For in the act of creation God brings into existence not only all creatures, but also "the very order of things" directing them. In his explanation of Rom. 2:14-15, Calvin explains that all creatures are subject to the divinely established order of nature as the moral law for human life.⁸⁷ Secondly, since creation is subject to the Fall and in need of renewal, we are in need of true knowledge of God's will, which is provided in the law as revealed in Scripture as "one everlasting and unchangeable rule to live by" and "a perfect pattern of righteousness."⁸⁸ I will briefly explain how these two theological notions of law may enrich a MacIntyrian concept of practices in a philosophical sense, namely, by adding some Neo-Calvinistic notions as can be derived from Herman Dooyeweerd's transcendental analysis in terms of the

---

84. Cf. John Witte, *The Reformation of Rights: Law, Religion, and Human Rights in Early Modern Calvinism* (Cambridge: Cambridge University Press, 2007), 181–96.

85. Mouw, *The God Who Commands*, 102.

86. Ibid., 111–13.

87. *CO* 49, 37–8 (*Comm. Rom.* 2, 14-15); cf. *Inst.* 1.14.2, 1.14.20, and 2.2.12. See Haas, "Calvin's Ethics," 93.

88. *Inst.* 1.6.1-4 and 2.8.5; cf. Haas, "Calvin's Ethics," 93.

'Cosmonomic Idea' and 'modal law-spheres,' which he in turn developed from Abraham Kuyper's notion of sphere sovereignty.[89]

MacIntyre defines practices (sports, arts, sciences, games, and political and productive activities) first of all as socially established cooperative human activities, which have developed during a historical process and thus exist before an individual practitioner is initiated into one of these practices. The structural element of an established cooperative activity we call a practice is part of the very nature of this practice itself. Secondly, through a set of activities that may count as a practice, goods internal to that form of activity are realized—that is, a practice has a certain finality, a *telos*. The end of the activities is to be found *in* these activities (*internal* good). The *telos* of a practice is not an *external* end to which these activities are just means. The *telos* of the practice of medicine, for instance, is not to make money but the care and cure of patients. Thirdly, the human activities that constitute a practice can be seen as a rule-guided behavior in which the rules are understood as "standards of excellence" for that practice. Practitioners of a practice have a way of doing things, which can be interpreted as following a set of standards or rules. Finally, virtues are the qualities that enable us to achieve those goods which are internal to practices, and these qualities are extended by participating in these practices.[90]

What a Calvinistic concept of creational ordinances or law spheres may add to MacIntyre's definition is, in the first place, an ordering of different types of principles and rules, in order to specify the nature of the standards of excellence in practices. Dutch Calvinistic philosophers Jan Hoogland, Gerrit Glas, and Henk Jochemsen developed the so-called normative practice model, in which MacIntyre's concept of practice is enriched with a Dooyeweerdian concept of modal aspects representing irreducible ways of being, including social structures.[91] In this view, all practices function in all modal aspects, but the modal aspects do not function in the same way in all practices: one of these aspects functions as the qualifying principle of a certain kind of a practice. This *qualifying* principle can be identified with the *telos* of that practice. For example, the economic principle

---

89. Herman Dooyeweerd, *A New Critique of Theoretical Thought*, 4 vols., trans. D. H. Freeman and W. S. Young (Amsterdam and Philadelphia: Paris/The Presbyterian and Reformed Publishing Company, 1953–1958).

90. This is a brief explanation of MacIntyre's famous definition in *After Virtue*, 187: "By a 'practice' I am going to mean any coherent and complex form of socially established cooperative human activity through which goods internal to that form of activity are realized in the course of trying to achieve those standards of excellence which are appropriate to, and partially definitive of, that form of activity, with the result that human powers to achieve excellence, and human conceptions of the ends and goods involved, are systematically extended."

91. Henk Jochemsen and Gerrit Glas, *Verantwoord medisch handelen: Proeve van een christelijke medische ethiek* [Accountable Medical Practice: An Account of Christian Medical Ethics] (Amsterdam: Buijten & Schipperheijn, 1997), 64–99.

functions as the normative principle in the practice of an entrepreneur, whereas other principles such as the technical, the social, the juridical, the ethical, and so on, are all important *conditional* aspects that are necessary to perform the practice of the entrepreneur. A practice requires the simultaneous realization of all the structural rules as part of an integral normativity of that practice. These rules can be followed even without a conscious decision of the practitioner. The rules have a tacit, implicit character and are part of the normative attitudes, that is, the virtues, of the practitioner. Virtues are the embodiments of normative principles in stable attitudes of the practitioner of a practice.[92]

Up to this point Neo-Calvinistic thought is in line with MacIntyre's Neo-Aristotelian understanding, but from Dooyeweerd's philosophy a second, more important, aspect is to be added: the directional or regulative side of 'the order of things.' This may again be explained from the concept of practice. Any performance of a practice involves a specific interpretation of the rules, which takes place from a broader interpretative framework on the meaning of the practice for human life and for society, that is, worldview beliefs and religious beliefs. In MacIntyre's terms, it depends on a wider view on the *telos* of human life. The specific contribution of the regulative aspect, however, is to be found in its *critical function*. The beliefs pertaining to the regulative side of practices form the reference points for a critical assessment of existing practices. This critical function of the regulative side as an integral part of the concept of a normative practice prevents a practice from becoming conservative and self-referential.[93]

Here we discover the credits of a (Neo-)Calvinistic account of *external* normativity over against MacIntyre's concept of normativity that is in principle *internal* to practices. To put it in the words of Jochemsen and Hegeman: "The fact that a certain community of practitioners accepts certain standards of excellence does not mean that those standards are the best possible. In the light of other regulative ideas, they may need revision."[94] Although MacIntyre acknowledges that the relation between (conflicting) practices should be valued from the perspective of the unity and good of one's life as a whole and in relation to a concept of the good for man in general as articulated in traditions, his starting point is the individual's question of how to relate properly to various potentially conflicting practices. It is not clear how, in MacIntyre's view, these concepts may critically influence the *internal* normative rules of a practice. On this point, the Neo-Calvinistic approach has more to offer than the Neo-Aristotelian—namely, the possibility of *criticizing* social practices from a transcendent point of view. Interpreted in this way, the law of God functions as a transcendent point of view from which we can undertake such criticism.

---

92. Henk Jochemsen and Johan Hegeman, "Connecting Christian Faith and Professional Practice in a Pluralistic Society," in Bram de Muynck, Johan Hegeman and Pieter Vos, *Bridging the Gap: Connecting Christian Faith and Professional Practice in a Pluralistic Society* (Sioux Center: Dordt College Press, 2011), 76–80.

93. Ibid., 81–2.

94. Ibid., 82.

Conclusion

In response to Alasdair MacIntyre's and Brad Gregory's claim that the Reformation's concept of morality in terms of obedience to divine commandments has been a major factor in a catastrophic breakdown in modernity of the teleological view of life and the virtues, this chapter has offered an alternative interpretation from a reading of Calvin. This criticism is to be corrected from a covenantal (narrative framework), reasonable (the interpretative role of the actor and the meaning of natural law), and teleological (divine commands as aimed at human flourishing) interpretation of the nature of divine law. Calvin's utterances about the nature of the law, virtue, the self before God, one's calling in the world, natural law, and reason appear to be much more in alliance with a teleological, virtue ethical view than MacIntyre suggests.

This opens up the possibility of a fruitful interplay between a Reformed account of law and virtue ethics. On the one hand, the concept of creational order and law spheres accords with a conception of goodness that is rooted in a coherent and ordered reality as this is presupposed both in theories of natural law and in a MacIntyrian conception of internal goods as constitutive of social practices. On the other hand, in addition the distinctive notion of divine law opens up the possibility of criticizing particular practices from a transcendent point of view. Furthermore, it explains why a particular good rests upon us as an obligation, as a demand that I have not laid on myself, but that nevertheless accounts for an unconditional responsibility beyond established social practices or what counts as virtuous in these practices. Finally, Calvin's characteristic use of the virtue of 'moderation' or 'integrity' as a redefinition of prudence is particularly appropriate in modern life, because it is not defined from pre-given social orders from which one may derive what is prudent, but rather enables to find one's way to the *telos* in the specific context one is involved in.

At the same time, a Calvinistic approach shows potential weaknesses. Calvin does not elaborate on the virtues and does not well explain how in the Christian life of sanctification habituation may take place. His choice of the law as the dominant framework for his explanation of the Christian moral life could easily lead to a neglect of virtue and the virtues. Hence, throughout the ages Protestant ethics at times has shown an ambivalent and limited adaptation of the Christian virtue ethical tradition, resulting sometimes in an overemphasis on duty and moral obligation outweighing the notion of virtue. That this is not a necessary outcome and that natural law, virtue, and the virtues are an integral part of mainstream Protestant ethics throughout the sixteenth and seventeenth centuries will be shown in the next chapter, which is devoted to an account of a highly neglected tradition: Reformed 'Aristotelianism' and virtue ethics as found in the ethics of a great number of Reformed scholastic theologians. An understanding of this tradition even more undermines the dominant narrative of the dramatic decline of virtue ethics since the Reformation.

Chapter 4

RETRIEVING REFORMED SCHOLASTIC VIRTUE ETHICS

In his book *The Unintended Reformation* Brad Gregory argues that the Protestant rejection of the authority of the Roman Church and the turn to Scripture as the only source created an open-ended range of rival truth claims about the biblical message, ending up in "bitter disagreements among early modern Christians about the objective morality of the good."[1] Gregory does not specify very precisely who were involved in these bitter disagreements about the morality of the good. In fact, his argument is based on two general theses. The first is that *doctrinal controversies* and religious wars of the Reformation era *in general* created a social reality that undermined the shared conception of the common good. For instance, "because their standoff on the Lord's Supper divided Lutheran from Reformed Protestantism in social terms, it also divided them as moral communities."[2] Gregory's second line of argument is that Protestants explicitly rejected core concepts of the traditional Christian anthropological and soteriological view. Although they still held eternal life as the ultimate end, they differed from this tradition on other essential points: "In sixteenth century Lutheran and Reformed Protestant theology, salvation had nothing to do with the virtues because it had nothing to do with human freedom or the human will."[3] According to Gregory, Protestant theologians rejected the Roman Church's view of human nature, the value of pagan ancient virtue ethics and the existence of any remnant of the image of God (*imago Dei*) in the human will. There was no longer any sense of a gradual habituation and rational disciplining of the passions, and the ordering of the virtues from *caritas* was replaced by faith as the cornerstone of the Christian life.

As we have already seen in Calvin, most of these claims can be countered as overstated and unjustified as soon as we take a closer look at early modern Protestant theology. In fact, there was much more continuity of the Christian medieval teleologically structured view of life, natural law, virtues, and the good in Protestant views. New historical-theological research demonstrates not only that Aquinas played a significant role in Protestant theology,[4] but also that the

---

1. Gregory, *The Unintended Reformation*, 188.
2. Ibid., 205.
3. Ibid., 206.
4. Svensson and VanDrunen (eds.), *Aquinas among the Protestants*.

Nicomachean Ethics still offered a crucial ethical framework in post-Reformation Reformed orthodoxy.[5] Gregory largely ignores this whole tradition of what we may call 'Reformed scholastic virtue ethics' in his broad narrative of the decline of virtue ethics. Although he points to Melanchthon, who reintroduced Aristotle's *Ethics* into the university curriculum of Wittenberg, Gregory states that this was only possible because of a radical distinction between law and gospel, on the basis of which morality could be separated from theology.[6] Although there is much to be said for Gregory's claims about the social impact of the religious controversies after the Reformation, resulting in the pluralization of communities, it is highly contestable that this development is intimately bound up with an alleged rejection of large parts of the teleological and virtue ethical framework in the Reformation. Of course, this does not mean that no changes took place in the understanding of the good and the virtues. Therefore, the question is to what extent the framework is continued and in what respects there is discontinuity.

Importantly, already *before* the Reformation, significant differences occur about how to understand natural law, the relation between reason and will and virtue and grace. Since the twelfth century, important controversies had existed in how the virtues are to be understood from a theological perspective. Peter Lombard identified virtue with grace in a particular interpretation of Augustine, an interpretation that was very influential, for instance his famous definition of Augustine's understanding of virtue as "a good quality of the mind, by which we live rightly, of which no one can make bad use, which God alone works in us (*quam Deus solus in homine operantur*)."[7] Very differently, Peter Abelard took up the Aristotelian concept of virtue as the core of his approach to virtue ethics. In his philosophically oriented account, virtue is a habit through which one is able to act morally right and to merit supreme beatitude.[8] Although Thomas Aquinas succeeded in connecting both approaches in an all-encompassing system, there existed significant controversies that qualify the view of there being just one undivided virtue ethical tradition. After Aquinas, scholastic analysis of the virtues was still dominated by controversies over free will and the relationships between will, intellect, and the passions. In these controversies, some took rational judgment as determining the choice of the will, others defended versions of voluntarism. In putting all emphasis on the human will, Duns Scotus departed

---

5. As already demonstrated by Sinnema, "The Discipline of Ethics in Early Reformed Orthodoxy," 10-44. See also Richard A. Muller, "Reformation, Orthodoxy, 'Christian Aristotelianism,' and the Eclecticism of Early Modern Philosophy," *Nederlands archief voor kerkgeschiedenis / Dutch Review of Church History* 81/3 (2001), 306-25.

6. Gregory, *Unintended Reformation*, 208.

7. Petrus Lombardus, *Sententiae in IV libris distinctae* 2.27.1, PL 192, 714. As we have seen in Chapters 1 and 2 Augustine is more balanced in his approach to 'pagan virtue' and human efforts to acquire the virtues than the final element of this phrase of Lombard's definition suggests.

8. Peter Abelard, *Dialogus inter philosophum, judaeum et christianum*, PL 178, 1651-2.

from his Aristotelian predecessors, but it would be incorrect to conclude that he and his followers, several Protestants included, did away with virtue entirely.⁹ The Reformers and especially post-Reformation theologians developed their ethics in relative continuity with the multifaceted tradition of medieval virtue ethics, either in an Aristotelian shape or in a Scotist approach or in a more Augustinian way. Contrary to what Gregory assumes, their ethical explorations are often part of their theological systems, just as we find in their medieval predecessors, as we will see. On the one hand, the Reformation included the ambition to reform theology based on the primacy of Scripture and to counter the fusion of revelation with worldly wisdom. On the other hand, it was clear that this should not lead to the entire abandonment of philosophy but rather to the re-establishment of its proper status as serving Christian doctrine.

In this chapter I will present a number of instances of how this is present in what is called Reformed orthodoxy or Reformed scholasticism—I use the terms interchangeably. The tradition of Reformed orthodox theology has often been explored, but until now scholarly attention has been paid almost exclusively to doctrine. As Luca Baschera observes in his overview, Reformed ethics in the era of Reformed orthodoxy is an almost completely untraveled terrain.¹⁰ Interestingly, Alasdair MacIntyre too observes that the revival of Aristotelian studies in the sixteenth century and their flourishing in Catholic as well as Protestant circles "is part of a history almost all of which still has to be written."¹¹ Yet, this does not prevent him from drawing far-reaching conclusions about the fragile coexistence of Aristotelianism in the moral sphere with a variety of Augustinian theologies and with increasingly anti-Aristotelian modes of theorizing. He speaks of "an ultimately unstable alliance of Calvinism and Aristotelianism," yet without referring to primary theological works.¹²

I will argue that this highly neglected tradition is precisely of great interest, not only because it importantly reveals the continuity of Protestant ethical understandings of the good, natural law, and the virtues, but also because its representatives developed their own understandings of these concepts, in the context of their theological concerns and in relation to new social and political orders in early modernity. Therefore, on the one hand, an investigation of this tradition may counter the dominant view of a breakdown of teleology and virtue ethics since the Reformation. On the other hand, this tradition may function as a valuable bridge between classical virtue ethics and modernity. For this purpose, I will sketch the contours of the way several Reformed scholastics adopted

---

9. Jean Porter, "Virtue Ethics in the Medieval Period," in Daniel C. Russell (ed.), *The Cambridge Companion to Virtue Ethics* (Cambridge: Cambridge University Press, 2013), 75–91.

10. Baschera, "Ethics in Reformed Orthodoxy," 519–20.

11. MacIntyre, *Whose Justice? Which Rationality*, 209.

12. Ibid., 225. Cf. 209: "no appeal to any agreed conception of the good for human beings, either at the level of practice or of theory, was now possible."

Aristotelian ethics in their philosophical and theological accounts of the moral life.

In this respect we can speak of 'Reformed Aristotelianism.' This means neither that all Reformed theologians that I present are Aristotelians, nor that those who can be regarded as 'Aristotelian' follow Aristotle without distinction. Rather Aristotle was regarded as the *artifex methodi* (master of method), the one who more than Plato or any other philosopher had established in his logic the rules of scientific arguing. This means that the use of the *corpus Aristotelicum*, the collection of Aristotle's works that had survived from Antiquity and through medieval manuscript transmission, was not static. The phenomenon of 'Aristotelianism' is to be understood in terms of modifications rather than representations of the original thought of 'the Philosopher.'[13] In this loose application of the term, 'Aristotelianism' includes both Catholic thinkers such as Thomas Aquinas, Cardinal Cajetan, and Francis Suarez, and a number of Lutheran and Reformed scholastics who all denied or modified tenets central to Aristotle's own thought but used Aristotelian philosophical categories as a stable epistemological and ontological framework. In this sense the term refers to a multi-varied tradition that started in the twelfth century and continued to the seventeenth century. The tradition of debate among Thomists, Scotists, nominalists, and Augustinians did not end with the Middle Ages, but continued through the Reformation and late Renaissance.[14] Muller concludes that "the object of the scholastic theologian or philosopher was, typically, not so much to be 'Aristotelian' as to be the formulator and mediator of a Christian philosophical model that both used and refused various elements of the classical tradition."[15] Similarly, Baschera comments with regard to the early Reformed theologian Peter Martyr Vermigli: "Vermigli, as did his Reformed contemporaries and their medieval predecessors, felt free to depart from Aristotle whenever this would prove necessary for the sake of truth. Vermigli's Aristotelianism was, therefore, as sincere as it was essentially eclectic."[16] Aristotle was part of a broader Christian epistemological and ontological framework that served the explanation of doctrinal and ethical issues.

This sincere but eclectic treatment of Aristotle holds for a number of Reformed theologians I will discuss. Therefore, rather than asking to what extent these authors are completely truthful to Aristotle, it is more appropriate and fruitful to approach the (Aristotelian) virtue ethical nature of their ethics from the answers they give to the three leading questions that I have distinguished in the introduction of this book: What is (the) morally good? What should we do? How do we know the good? Answers given in terms of the good life, the virtues and

---

13. Muller, "Reformation, Orthodoxy," 313.
14. Ibid., 314.
15. Ibid.
16. Luca Baschera, "Aristotle and Scholasticism," in Torrance Kirby, Emidio Campi and Frank A. James III (eds.), *A Companion to Peter Martyr Vermigli* (Leiden and Boston: Brill, 2009), 150–1.

human nature, respectively, form basic characteristics of virtue ethics, leaving much room for divergences but still providing sufficient continuity that justifies use of the denominator 'virtue ethics'. After introducing the field in a first section, I will follow these three questions in three sections but in a different order, starting with the epistemological question about how we know the morally good, since the answer to this question (in particular convictions about human nature, reason, natural law, and revelation) is foundational for ideas about the highest good and the good life as well as answers to the question of what we should do in terms of moral virtue.

Mapping the Field: Ethics in Reformed Scholasticism

Usually, the era of Reformed scholasticism is divided into three periods: early, high, and late Reformed scholasticism as different phases of using the scholastic method.[17] Since my focus is not on the scholastic method in systematic theology as such but on the way in which representatives of this tradition developed their ethics in relation to the virtue ethical framework as transmitted from medieval scholasticism, I focus on theologians that are of interest from this perspective.

The period of early Reformed scholasticism starts mid-sixteenth century and continues till the Synod of Dort (1618–19). In this period, ethics was treated not as a theological subject but as a philosophical discipline. Theologians of early Reformed orthodoxy differ in the extent to which philosophical ethics is based on classical philosophy, Aristotle in particular, on the one hand, and Scripture on the other. The period of high Reformed scholasticism dates from 1620 till 1700 and was marked by greater detail and definition in the theological system as well as by polemics on various fronts. Theologians of this period more regularly treated ethics as a theological discipline and made it part of their theological works, often consisting of several volumes. In the period of late Reformed scholasticism (1700–90), under the influence of the Enlightenment, the scholastic method of theology began to stagnate in favor of historical and exegetical approaches. Yet, in eighteenth-century Puritanism, the Christian life was still understood in terms of virtue. In this chapter I focus on early and high Reformed scholasticism.

As stated, the Reformation did not lead to the abandonment of Aristotelian ethics. This becomes immediately clear from the fact that the *Ethica Nicomachea* continued to function as the main textbook in the curricula of Lutheran and Reformed academies and universities. Although the dominant Aristotelian framework of sciences gradually came to be contested in the modern era, this did not affect the status of the Aristotelian model in both Catholic and Lutheran as well as Reformed universities and academies of the sixteenth and seventeenth

---

17. Willem J. van Asselt, T. Theo J. Pleizier, Pieter L. Rouwendal, and Maarten Wisse, *Introduction to Reformed Scholasticism*, trans. Albert Gootjes (Grand Rapids: Reformation Heritage Books, 2011).

centuries. Following the classical tripartite division of the *artes* into physics, logics, and ethics, courses in these fields followed in general an Aristotelian model, including the widespread practice of commenting on Aristotelian texts. The Renaissance brought not a removal of Aristotle, but a demand that better (Greek) texts should be used (in new editions of the *Ethica Nicomachea* Protestant theologians regularly cooperated with humanists), with an openness to other sources such as Platonism, Stoicism, and the Skeptical and Hermetic traditions.[18] As Dorothea Frede observes, the simple attribution of the decline of Aristotelian virtue ethics to the rebellion against Aristotelian metaphysics and physics in the early modern era is false: "Aristotle's ethics remained an integral part of the curriculum of the universities long after modern natural science had gone its own way."[19] This was precisely the case in Lutheran and Reformed universities and academies, where ethics was taught as a separate philosophical discipline in the *artes* program. Furthermore, the practice that grew out of the medieval tradition of commentaries on the *Nicomachean Ethics* continued not only in the Renaissance but also in these Protestant universities and academies.[20] Manfred Svensson lists no fewer than forty-six Lutheran and Reformed commentaries on the *Nicomachean Ethics* between 1529 and 1682! Not one generation of Protestant theologians passes without a new set of commentaries on Aristotle's *Ethics*. In short, the exposition of this work continued to form the backbone of moral education.[21]

This widespread practice of reading and commenting on Aristotle's ethics is contrary to the impression one gets from the position we find in the early views of the Reformers, Luther in particular. While Luther had lectured four times a week on Aristotle's *Ethics* in his first years at Wittenberg (1508–09), as soon as he started to lead the Reformation he advised to discard it completely, together with Aristotle's works on physics and metaphysics. According to Luther, Aristotle's "book on ethics is the worst of all books. It flatly opposes divine grace and all Christian virtues, and yet it is considered one of his best works. Away with such books! Keep them away from Christians."[22] Luther's abolishment of Aristotle and his proposed complete revision of the curriculum that follows from it is often taken as something that actually took place, but this was not the case. Aristotelianism continued to dominate the *artes* program. Although the *Ethica*

---

18. Muller, "Reformation, Orthodoxy," 307.
19. Frede, "The Historic Decline of Virtue Ethics," 128.
20. Muller, "Reformation, Orthodoxy," 309.
21. Manfred Svensson, "Aristotelian Practical Philosophy from Melanchthon to Eisenhart: Protestant Commentaries on the Nicomachean Ethics 1529-1682," *Reformation and Renaissance Review* 21/3 (2019), 218–38. A great number of original sources mentioned in this chapter can be found in the Post-Reformation Digital Library: www.prdl.org.
22. Martin Luther, "To the Christian Nobility," *LW* 44, 200–201 (*WA* 6, 457–8). Cf. his *Disputatio Heidelbergae habita* (1518), WA 1, 350–74 and his *Disputatio contra scholasticos theologos*, WA 1, 222–8.

Nicomachea disappeared from the curriculum for several years, Luther's colleague and successor, Philipp Melanchthon (1497-1560), who had the task of teaching ethics in Wittenberg, started to lecture again on Aristotle's ethics. The textbooks he developed for various disciplines including ethics were precisely what Luther had tried to abandon: compendia of Aristotle's works, albeit corrected and supplemented by the truths of biblical revelation. Melanchthon acknowledged the gap between the theology of Christ and Aristotelianism, but, based on the distinction between *Gesetz* and *Evangelium* (law and gospel), it was possible to see philosophy, including ethics, as "part of the divine law that is about civil morality (*partem legis divinae de civilibus moribus*)."[23] Melanchthon lectured at least eight times on Aristotle's *Ethics*, resulting in his commentary *In ethica Aristotelis commentarius* (Wittenberg, 1529) and extended *In primum, secundum, tertium, et quintum ethicorum commentarii* (Wittenberg, 1532). This work, republished in numerous editions, had an unparalleled influence. Melanchthon's own ethics, which notably grew out of his commentary on Aristotle, appeared in two forms: *Philosophiae moralis epitome* (1538) and *Ethicae doctrinae elementorum* (1550). In sum, Melanchthon believed that a Protestant reform of theological education should be grounded in the study of Aristotelian philosophy, including ethics. Since the use of Aristotle was properly based on the distinction between law and gospel, in fact Luther could not have anything against it.[24]

Theologians in Lutheran and Reformed universities and academies followed Melanchthon in treating ethics as a philosophical discipline, based on a reading of Aristotle's ethics and very often resulting in a published commentary. Just to mention some examples,[25] Otto Werdmüller (1513-52) published his *In libra ethicorum* (Basel, 1545), Jacobus Schegkius (1511-87) his *In X libros ethicorum annotationes* (Basel, 1550) and Andreas Hyperius (1511-64) delivered his lectures on the *Nicomachean Ethics* at the Marburg academy and published them in 1553 as *Ad X libros ethicorum scholia*. Peter Martyr Vermigli (1499-1562), former Augustinian monk and trained as an Aristotelian at the University of Padua, who became an important Reformed theologian, also delivered extensive lectures on the *Nicomachean Ethics* from 1554 to 1556 at the academy of Strasbourg. It was part of an 'extraordinary' program, which he combined with his work as professor of Old Testament. At the time he left Strasbourg for Zurich in 1556, his detailed commentary on Aristotle's *Ethics* was unfinished, but it was posthumously published as *In primum, secundum, et initium tertii libri ethicorum Aristotelis ad*

---

23. Philipp Melanchthon, *Enarrationes aliquod librorum ethicorum Aristotelis*, CR 16, 277-78.

24. Heinz Scheible, "Aristoteles und die Wittenberger Universitätsreform: Zum Quellenwert von Lutherbriefen," in Michael Bayer and Günther Wartenberg (eds.), *Humanismus und Wittenberger Reformation* (Fs. Helmar Junghans) (Leipzig: Evangelische Verlagsanstalt, 1997), 125-51; Sinnema, "Discipline of Ethics," 11-12.

25. See for the following overview: Sinnema, "Discipline of Ethics," 14-21, and Svensson, "Aristotelian Practical Philosophy."

Nicomachum commentarius in 1563. Hyperius's and Vermigli's commentaries were edited, republished, and provided with new comments by the Marburg Reformed philosopher Rudolphus Goclenius (1547-1628), who had also published his own ethical commentary as *Exercitationes ethicae* in 1592. All these commentaries contain concise treatments of Aristotle's ethics, taking him as a superior philosopher, yet correcting his views from (and harmonizing them with) Scripture as ultimate criterion of truth.

The practice of commenting on Aristotle's *Ethics* was common in other Protestant universities and academies as well. The statutes of the Geneva academy (1559), most likely written by Calvin, order that the professor of Greek shall explain a philosophical book on morality by either Aristotle, Plato, Plutarch, or a Christian philosopher. In the 1558 statutes of Heidelberg University, drawn up under the advice of Melanchthon and maintained when it went over to Calvinism three years later, a chair of ethics is listed among the five professors in the faculty of arts. Again, reference is made to a classical work of ethics, for instance Aristotle or Cicero. In later versions only Aristotle's works are mentioned as required textbooks. In this early phase of the university, a number of professors occupied the ethics position, Victorinus Strigelius (1524-69) being the most well-known. As many of his predecessors and contemporaries did, he too wrote a commentary on Aristotle's *Ethics*, which appeared posthumously in 1572 as *Aristotelis ad filium Nicomachum, de vita & moribus scripti libri X*. These teachings were so important that this university did not accept Ramus as Strigelius's successor because of his criticism of Aristotle (although Ramus's logic is not to be regarded as completely anti-Aristotelian; he rather broke with the exposition of Aristotle as the preferred way of teaching). Another famous Reformed theologian, Zacharias Ursinus, one of the authors of the Heidelberg Catechism, vigorously opposed Ramus's criticism.[26] In England, Samuel Heiland published his commentary on Aristotle's *Ethics* in London in 1581, followed by John Case in 1585. Similarly, at Leiden University, founded in 1575, ethics was taught at the faculty of arts too, though at first quite irregularly. Again, Aristotle's *Ethics* served as the main source, in particular as it was taught by Petrus Bertius, with some breaks, until he was finally dismissed in 1619 due to his Arminian sympathies. In that year Antonius Walaeus (1573-1639), a leading theologian at the Synod of Dort (1618-19) and member of the committee that drafted its Canons, joined the faculty and published his commentary on the *Nicomachean Ethics*: *Compendium ethicae Aristotelicae ad normam veritatis christianae revocatum* (Leiden, 1620). This book was the result of his lectures in ethics at the Middelburg Latin school and had great influence, since it became the official textbook for Latin schools. Walaeus considered the *Ethica Nicomachea* to be pedagogically more adequate than all other philosophical works on ethics and to offer the supreme method in

---

26. Donald Sinnema, "Aristotle and Early Reformed Orthodoxy: Moments of Accommodation and Antithesis," in Wendy Helleman (ed.), *Christianity and the Classics* (Lanham: University Press of America, 1990), 123-8.

addressing ethical issues. Yet, as in Vermigli's approach, errors in Aristotle's *Ethics* needed to be corrected "in accordance with the standard of Christian truth (*ad veritatis christianae normam*)."[27]

In sum, Reformed universities and academies until the seventeenth century taught ethics in the faculty of the arts as a *philosophical* discipline, taking Aristotle's *Nicomachean Ethics* as the most important textbook and ethical framework, and correcting it from Scripture where needed. This practice stands in great continuity with a broadly conceived Aristotelian tradition. The authors were not interested in doing full justice to Aristotle, but used Aristotle as the vehicle for transmitting a broader range of classical positions in moral philosophy and for developing their own positions. Moral philosophy is useful to theology, being traditionally understood by some authors as *ancilla theologiae* (handmaiden of theology) or *preambulum*, by others also as a point of contrast: through familiarity with moral philosophy one will be able to see what is distinctively Christian.[28]

Along with these commentaries on Aristotle's *Ethics*, Reformed (and Lutheran) theologians gradually developed their own (philosophical) ethics. Lambert Daneau (1530–95), working as lector of theology and assisting Theodore Beza at the Geneva academy, published the first independent Reformed ethics, titled *Ethices christianae libri tres*, in 1577. His ethics was part of a larger project in which he wanted to found all philosophical disciplines on Scripture rather than on classical works. At first sight, Daneau's approach of developing ethics solely from Scripture as the source of all knowledge is opposed to the trend of early Reformed ethics. Yet, it is important to notice that Daneau's ethics, though based on Scripture, is still to be regarded as a *philosophical* rather than as a theological discipline. In his approach to the sciences he simply follows the classical tripartite order of philosophical disciplines and publishes a *Physica christiana* (Lyon, 1576), a *Politice christiana* (Geneva, 1596), and an *Ethice christiana* (Geneva, 1577). As he states, "In the science of ethics, if we wish to think truly about the principles of our actions, we ought to philosophize from the Word of God (*ex Dei verbo philosophandum*)."[29] In book 1 of his ethics he offers an anthropological basis, with a clear influence of Aristotle and the Stoa but primarily based on the Word of God, in book 2 he treats the precepts of human moral action based on the Decalogue, and in book 3 he deals with the virtues and vices that correspond to the precepts of the Decalogue. As a whole his Christian ethics is a philosophical ethics, as

---

27. Antonius Walaeus, *Compendium ethicae Aristotelicae ad normam veritatis christianae revocatum* (Leiden: Elzevir, 1620), epistola dedicatoria 4 / Antonius de Waele, *A Compendium of Aristotelian Ethics Accommodated to the Standard of Christian Truth: Selections*, in Jill Kraye (ed.), *Cambridge Translations of Renaissance Philosophical Texts, Vol. 1: Moral Philosophy* (Cambridge: Cambridge University Press 1997), 122.

28. Svensson, "Aristotelian Practical Philosophy."

29. Lambert Daneau, *Ethices christianae libri tres* (Geneva: Eustathius Vignon, 1577) 1.14; trans. Sinnema, "Discipline of Ethics," 22.

Sinnema concludes, and "exhibits some similarities with and direct influences of Aristotle's *Nicomachean Ethics*, which he frequently cites."[30]

More in line with Melanchthon, Bartholomaeus Keckermann (1572/3–1609) treats ethics as a philosophical discipline in its own right in his *Systema ethicae* (1607).[31] This book was the product of his lectures in ethics at the Gymnasium of Danzig. Keckermann taught Hebrew and theology in Heidelberg and ended his teaching in his native town of Danzig. His ethics is largely Aristotelian in nature, but does not consist of a commentary on the ten books of the *Nicomachean Ethics*. Keckermann rather systematizes the content of Aristotle's work according to a logically determined method in his own system. He regards himself as the first to produce such a *systema ethicae*.[32] Another example of a Reformed philosophical ethics is Franco Burgersdijk's *Idea philosophiae moralis* (Leiden, 1623).

A different presentation can be found in those Reformed authors who treat ethics within major dogmatic works, not just in a single chapter among other *loci* on the Ten Commandments (*de lege*) but in a much more extensive way, namely, as a second part following the dogmatic first part of their work. In this approach ethics is explicitly treated as a *theological discipline*—theology being taken as a practical rather than a speculative discipline. Peter Ramus (1515–72) was the first who set the standard for this approach by defining theology as the doctrine of living well, and dividing his *Commentariorum de religione christiana* into two sections: one on faith and a second one on the actions originating from faith, but this did not yet result in a fully fledged ethical part. A good example of such a comprehensive work is by the German theologian Amandus Polanus (1561–1610), who published his *Syntagma theologiae christianae* (Frankfurt am Main, 1609), consisting of seven volumes on doctrine (the things to be believed, *credenda*) and three volumes on ethics (the things to do, *agenda*). Polanus treats ethics, including moral virtue, not from the perspective of the natural human being but exclusively as pertaining to the regenerate believer.[33]

---

30. Sinnema, "Discipline of Ethics," 23, whom I follow rather than Baschera, "Ethics in Reformed Orthodoxy," 531, who regards Daneau's work as "eminently theological." Strohm, *Ethik im frühen Calvinismus*, emphasizes the continuity between humanistic and Calvinistic understandings of morality and the use of Aristotelian as well as Stoic virtue ethical concepts in Daneau's work, on the one hand, and the way Daneau addresses the challenges of early modernity, with its widely felt sense of crisis of traditional authority, on the other.

31. Bartholomaeus Keckermann, *Systema ethicae tribus libris adornatum et publicis praelectionibus traditum in gymnasio Dantiscano* (Hanau: Antonius, 1607), republished in his *Opera omnia*, Vol. 2 (Geneva: Aubert, 1614), 251–376.

32. Keckermann, *Systema ethicae*, in *Opera omnia* 2, 376; Sinnema, "Discipline of Ethics," 32–3.

33. See Baschera, "Ethics in Reformed Orthodoxy," 521–7 for an exposition of Polanus's ethics.

Approaching ethics as a theological discipline within major dogmatic works was especially common in the era of high Reformed scholasticism of the seventeenth century, a period in which all-encompassing theological systems were developed. Other examples of this approach are Johannes Wolleb (1589–1629), *Christianae theologiae compendium* (Basel, 1626), Markus Friedrich Wendelin (1584–1652), *Compendium theologiae christianae* (Hanau, 1646), Peter van Maastricht (1630–1706), *Theoretico-practica theologia* (Amsterdam, 1682–7), and William Ames (1576–1633), *Medulla theologiae* (Franeker, 1627). In this last work, this English Puritan theologian, who worked as a professor in Franeker, treats ethics (called 'observance') as the second part of one single theological work after having dealt with faith. Yet, Ames's rejection of the direct use of Aristotle's ethics in theology does not mean that he did not use Aristotelian and Thomistic categories, as for instance in his book *De conscientia, et eius iure vel casibus* (Amsterdam, 1630). Another relevant example is the Zurich theologian Johann Heinrich Heidegger (1633–98). Before he moved from the chair of ethics to the chair of dogmatics, he had worked on a system of Christian ethics, which was posthumously published in 1711 as *Ethicae christianae prima elementa*, meant as a general introduction to Christian ethics for students of theology. His ethics is not part of a broader dogmatic work, but is no less theological in nature.[34] In addition, several authors published popular books on virtues and vices, such as Joseph Hall, *Character of Virtues and Vices* (London, 1609), Samuel Crook, *Ta diapheronta, or Divine Characters: In Two Parts* (London, 1658), Robert Fergusson, *A Sober Enquiry into the Nature, Measure and Principle of Moral Virtue* (1673), and James Owen, *Moderation Still a Virtue* (1704).

This overview reveals that Protestant ethics had developed in great continuity with medieval scholasticism, although the emphasis on biblical revelation with a number of authors as the main source and criterion makes a significant difference and varieties can be observed in the treatment of virtue and the virtues. In order to get a deeper impression of the content of their virtue ethics, in the remainder of this chapter I will investigate in more depth how several Reformed scholastic theologians with their various approaches understand the source of our knowledge of the good, the highest good and the good life, and the virtues successively. I will start with the Lutheran theologian Melanchthon, because he sets the stage for two approaches to ethics in Reformed orthodoxy: commentaries on Aristotle's *Ethics*, on the one hand—I will take Vermigli as an early example and Walaeus as a later—and philosophical ethics based on natural law, on the other—Keckerman will be taken as a prime example. In addition, Daneau forms a relevant contrast because he develops a philosophical ethics based on Scripture. Finally, I take Ames as exemplary of how a mainstream Reformed author of the seventeenth century treats (natural) law, the good, and the virtues in his comprehensive treatment of ethics as part of a single theological work.

---

34. Cf. Baschera, "Ethics in Reformed Orthodoxy," 540–5.

Knowing the Good: Natural Law and Revelation

How do we know the good? In a virtue ethical understanding, knowledge of the good is in one way or another grounded in human nature. This is why virtue ethics has often been closely related to natural law theory, which provides what Gregory calls 'an objective morality of the good'. A close look at the selected Reformed scholastics reveals that most of them indeed basically, though not exclusively, think in terms of natural law.

The importance of natural knowledge of the good becomes already clear from the fact that nearly all early Reformed scholastic theologians followed Melanchthon in teaching ethics as a philosophical discipline.[35] This choice is based on a distinction between law and gospel, as we have seen, and justified by reference to natural law as common ground and human nature as still resembling the image of God. Note that the argument for the validity of natural law is *theological* in nature. According to Melanchthon, as rational being and *imago Dei* the human being can understand the precepts of the *lex moralis* as part of the divine law.[36] Philosophical ethics, theologically understood as *usus civilis legis*, does not deal with salvation, and therefore philosophical ethics is sharply distinguished from Christian theology. On the other hand, this distinction does not imply that philosophical ethics and theology contradict each other. On the contrary, since natural law is based on divine law, Christian ethics cannot be in contradiction with what can be understood from natural law, for "the moral law is God's eternal and unchangeable wisdom and the rule of justice in God,"[37] and after the Fall every human being has knowledge of the moral law and therefore can distinguish "that which is right from that which is not right" and act morally.[38] The gospel is not contrary to the law but rather goes beyond it. Therefore, as in medieval scholastic thought, Aristotelian ethics and Christian theological ethics can coexist as non-competitive disciplines.

---

35. Sinnema, "Discipline of Ethics," 40: though an ethical dimension was always present in Reformed theology, "throughout the period of early orthodoxy, ethics as an academic discipline was considered to be philosophical. Before the seventeenth century there was no separate theological ethics."

36. Melanchthon, *Philosophiae moralis epitome*, CR 16, 23: "Nam lex divina hominum mentibus impressa est" and "quod ipsum tamen est lex naturae et pars legis divinae." Also: "Hoc [discrimen honestorum et turpium] est evidentissimum vestigium Dei in natura."

37. Melanchthon, *Ethicae doctrinae elementa*, CR 16, 168: "Lex moralis est aeterna et immota sapientia et regula iustitiae in Deo." Translation: Philipp Melanchthon: *The Elements of Ethical Doctrine: Book 1, Selections*, in Jill Kraye (ed.), *Cambridge Translations of Renaissance Philosophical Texts, Vol. 1: Moral Philosophy* (Cambridge: Cambridge University Press, 1997), 110.

38. Melanchthon, *Ethicae doctrinae elementa*, CR 16, 168 / *Elements of Ethical Doctrine*, 110.

Melanchthon defines moral philosophy as "that part of the divine law (*pars illa legis divinae*) which concerns itself with external actions."[39] It is

> the explication of the law of nature (*lex naturae*). It assembles, as far as reason is able to determine, demonstrations arranged in the order commonly used in the arts. Its conclusions consist of the definitions of the virtues or the precepts (*definitiones virtutum seu praecepta*) of the discipline which must be maintained amongst all men. These precepts agree with the Decalogue insofar as it deals with external discipline (*externa disciplina*).[40]

In a similar way, Keckermann develops ethics as practical philosophy which follows from principles of natural law, that is, moral precepts of what is right and just. Since natural law includes such moral principles, a natural morality is possible. The theological basis for this philosophical approach is that remnants (*reliquae*) of God's image in people remain after the Fall, which enables people to practice ethical, economic, and political virtues, without the special grace of the Spirit. Nevertheless, the Fall caused some defect in the *imago Dei*, with the result that all sciences including ethics in the end need to be completed from the Word of God.[41] However, since in Keckermann's approach philosophical ethics is sharply distinguished from theology and theology deals with spiritual virtues (inner life), ethics deals relatively independently with the moral virtues of the civic life (outer life). This division makes it possible to treat moral virtue, though being incomplete, as true virtue per se and truly good, even if it is not as good as spiritual virtue. Unbelievers may have moral virtues, which explains why among nonbelievers there are "many good and moral (*boni & honesti*) men."[42] Since moral philosophy has a relatively independent status, there is no need to correct Aristotle from the Bible, as commonly practiced in most commentaries on Aristotle's *Ethics* by Keckermann's contemporaries.

Yet, in the various commentaries on the *Ethica Nicomachea* too, ethics is conceived of as a philosophical discipline. According to Vermigli, "All knowledge is either revealed or acquired. In the first case it is theology, in the second philosophy."[43] Distinguishing true philosophy such as Aristotle's from corrupt philosophy such as that of the Epicurians, he states: "Since true philosophy derives

---

39. Melanchthon, *Philosophiae moralis epitome*, CR 16, 21.
40. Melanchthon, *Ethicae doctrinae elementa*, CR 16, 167 / *Elements of Ethical Doctrine*, 110.
41. Keckermann, *Systema ethicae*, in *Opera omnia* 2, 255 and 376; Sinnema, "Discipline of Ethics," 32–3.
42. Keckermann, *Systema ethicae*, in *Opera omnia* 2, 253 and 255; Sinnema, "Discipline of Ethics," 35–6.
43. Peter Martyr Vermigli, *In primum, secundum, et initium tertii libri ethicorum Aristotelis ad Nicomachum commentarius* (Zurich: Froschauer, 1563), 1 / Peter Martyr Vermigli, *Commentary on Aristotle's Nicomachean Ethics* (The Peter Martyr Vermigli Library

from the knowledge of created things, and from these propositions reaches many conclusions about justice and righteousness that God implanted naturally in human minds, it cannot therefore rightly be criticized: it is the work of God."[44] In this way, Vermigli acknowledges, on the one hand, the human being's natural ability to understand the good, and, on the other hand, that this ability is a divine gift. God "endowed our minds with light and planted the seeds from which the principles of all knowledge arose."[45] Yet, natural knowledge needs to be corrected from revelation. Grace relates to nature as restoration to creation: "The goal of philosophy is that we reach that beatitude or happiness that can be acquired in this life by human powers, while the goal of Christian devotion is that the image in which we are created in righteousness and holiness of truth be renewed in us."[46] Though the rationale and principles of both views are very different, philosophical ethics is worthwhile, because illumination from human nature both has its own limited right, and demonstrates, by comparison with Scripture, how revelation surpasses philosophy. In phrasing it this way Vermigli is more critical than Melanchthon.

Walaeus distinguishes between two different goods. One good, which has to be revealed to us, is supernatural and spiritual. The other good is natural and civic (*bonum naturale ac politicum*) and relates to "the life of man living in this world." "Through it he does exercise the virtues as well as the domestic and civic arts" and

> natural man has some residual freedom and capacity for attaining this good (*homini naturali aliquam adhuc libertatem et facultatem esse residuam*), as is attested by the arguments advanced by Aristotle, the example set by many praiseworthy pagans (*exempla multorum laudatorum Ethnicorum*) and even the Holy Scriptures, when speaking of the Pharisees.[47]

More than Melanchthon and Keckermann, Walaeus acknowledges that nature is weak in attaining this good, and therefore it has to be sought from God, who gives it by "special aid (*auxilium speciale*)."[48]

Quite different is Daneau's approach, since he tries to develop a *Christian* ethics, primarily based on Scripture: "the precepts of this so wholesome instruction cannot be drawn better or more safely or, I also add, more blessedly than from the Word of God himself, and especially from the part of it that is commonly called

---

9), ed. Emidio Campi and Joseph C. McLelland (Kirksville: Truman State University Press, 2006), 7.

44. Vermigli, *Ethicorum commentarius*, 7 / *Commentary*, 13.
45. Vermigli, *Ethicorum commentarius*, 1 / *Commentary*, 7.
46. Vermigli, *Ethicorum commentarius*, 8 / *Commentary*, 14.
47. Walaeus, *Compendium*, 137–8 / *Compendium of Aristotelian Ethics*, 128.
48. Ibid. Cf. *Compendium*, 141, where he speaks of *reliquiae imaginis Dei*.

the law of God or the Decalogue (*lex Dei sive Decalogus*)."[49] In Daneau's definition, ethics is about our external *and internal* holiness, that is, the reformation of our whole life, whereas Melanchthon's ethics was only concerned with external, civil life. Although Christian ethics shares with pagan philosophers a concern for teaching method, a desire for good order and decency, and a recognition of voluntary will, they differ because pagans draw precepts from the "corrupted and obscured light of human nature" rather than from revelation.[50] Although Daneau is much more negative about human nature than Melanchthon, Keckermann, and Vermigli, he shares with his contemporaries the view that the human being is created in the image of God and that remnants of the *imago Dei* have survived in the rational soul after the Fall. A general moral knowledge (*notitia generalis*) of the original righteousness, which was engrafted in Adam's mind, has survived in fallen man, which enables us to discern between good and evil (*rerum honestarum et turpium*) and to understand certain moral precepts.[51] Similarly, the will was not destroyed, but divine grace is needed to will what is *really* good. A natural disposition such as *synteresis*, understood as the disposition of the human mind by which we apprehend the basic principles of behavior, is acknowledged, but at the same time needs to be "reformed" (*restituenta*) since it has been corrupted by the Fall. Therefore, divine law is the final norm for moral action.[52] The Decalogue is related to natural law, but Daneau has no independent natural law: "This law of God is called natural, because before it became written down in human laws, it flourished in human minds."[53] The Ten Commandments suffice for his treatment of precepts and virtues of both the divine and the civil moral life, in which he nevertheless quotes a wide range of philosophical sources. In this way Daneau, unlike Melanchthon and Keckermann, intrinsically relates law to the gospel and nature to grace. Because of the corruption of human nature, human beings are unable to conform their actions to the law of God. Using the Aristotelian four causes, Daneau sees God as *causa efficiens* of moral action, though the human being too is an efficient cause, and identifies the *causa formalis* or form of moral action with "a new and outstanding quality, implanted in our souls by the Spirit of God . . . which consists of holiness and justice."[54]

The advantage of making moral action dependent on God and focusing on the need for regeneration may be that Daneau can relate grace and salvation intrinsically to 'the morality of the good' and the virtues. The disadvantage is that it becomes difficult to do justice to the morality of non-Christians who clearly are virtuous people and have a general moral knowledge. The solution Daneau finds,

---

49. Daneau, *Ethices christianae* 1.1, trans. Sinnema, "Discipline of ethics," 24 (slightly changed).
50. Daneau, *Ethices christianae* 1.2.
51. Ibid. 1.5 and 1.6.
52. Ibid. 1.14, 1.17; Baschera, "Ethics in Reformed Orthodoxy," 532–3.
53. Daneau, *Ethices christianae* 2.2; Sinnema, "Discipline of Ethics," 30.
54. Danaeu, *Ethices christianae* 1.18; Baschera, "Ethics in Reformed Orthodoxy," 534.

in accord with Calvin, is to relate the phenomenon of pagan virtues to divine grace (common grace) as well. For God is the author of all good, also in civil matters, including the actions of unbelievers which express the "civil good (*civiliter bona*)" as distinguished from the "truly good (*vere bona*)."[55] This enables Daneau to acknowledge that though unbelievers lack God's renewing grace, thanks to God's *general* grace God has raised up in every age distinguished persons who preserve human society by their moderation, justice, example, and precepts. "Indeed, God's Spirit is in unbelievers who live morally, but only to restrain the unbridled power and impulse of sin and our corrupt nature," so that it does not dominate, but the Spirit does not *renew* their mind and will.[56]

More than Daneau, Ames acknowledges the moral knowledge that natural law provides for the human being.[57] In *Conscience, Its Law and Cases* he divides law into divine and human, and divine law into natural law (*ius naturale*), which is the eternal law of God, and divine positive law (*ius positivum*), which is added to natural law by some special revelation of God, for instance precepts about the Sabbath. Ames defines natural law as "that which is apprehended to be fit to be done or avoided out of the naturall instinct of Naturall Light (*naturali instinctu luminis naturalis*), or that which is at least deduced from that natural light by evident consequence." It is called *natural* as it is "ingraffed and imprinted in the *nature* of man by the nature of God."[58] Ames identifies natural law also with the Decalogue and the Golden Rule as proclaimed by Jesus.[59]

According to Ames, human conscience—literally understood as *conscientia*, that is, 'to know together with'—is the instrument by which natural law is known by human beings: by means of God's gift of conscience—in line with what Albertus Magnus and Thomas Aquinas understood as 'an act of practical judgement'—the human being knows 'together with God' the divine judgments upon human actions.[60] Thus, conscience or συντήρησις (*synteresis*) is the natural disposition of the human mind by which it apprehends the general principles of

---

55. Danaeu, *Ethices christianae* 1.17, 1.18.

56. Ibid. 1.14; Sinnema, "Discipline of Ethics," 27.

57. Lee W. Gibbs, "The Puritan Natural Law Theory of William Ames," *Harvard Theological Review* 64 (1971), 37–57.

58. William Ames, *De conscientia et eius iure vel casibus libri quinque* (Amsterdam: Janssonium, 1630) 5.1.4 and 6 / *Conscience, with the Power and Cases Thereof* (London: Imprinted W. Christiaens, E. Griffin, J. Dawson, 1639), 160; cf. *De conscientia* 1.2.4 / *Conscience*, 5: the law "which is naturally written in the hearts of all men."

59. William Ames, *Medulla theologiae* (London: Robertum Allottum, 1627) 1.10.16 and 26 / William Ames, *The Marrow of Theology*, ed. John D. Eusden (Boston: Pilgrim Press, 1968), 111–12; Ames, *De conscientia* 5.1.20 / *Conscience*, 104–5.

60. Ames, *De conscientia* 1.2.1 / *Conscience*, 4: "a habit of the understanding by which wee doe assent unto the principles of morall actions, that is such actions as are our duty, because God hath willed, or commanded them."

natural law.⁶¹ Ames distinguishes between the *apprehension* of natural morality as a universal human intellectual trait, and the actual *application* of that knowledge toward the evaluation of specific actions. Although natural conscience is capable of the apprehension of moral principles in general form, the application of those principles is corrupted on a variety of levels by the effects of sin on our practical reasoning, which explains why *synteresis* can be hindered by sin from acting. Hence, Ames regularly points to the clarity of biblical moral instruction. He can even say that "there can be no other teaching of the virtues than theology which brings the whole revealed will of God to the directing of our reason, will, and life."⁶² Yet, this is not in contradiction with natural reason, for "the justice and usefulness of the things commanded . . . are in closest agreement with reason (*cum ratione maxime consentiunt*)," the will of God is "apprehended by reason (*a ratione apprehenditur*)," and moral acts need to be done "in deliberate reason (*ex deliberata ratione*)."⁶³ In sum, all human beings share a natural awareness of basic moral principles, because all persons, even the unregenerate, possess a conscience, but in the regenerate conscience is enhanced by biblical education and the effects of saving grace (which Ames calls "inlightened conscience"), which enables us to envision and strive for a fuller moral life.⁶⁴

The Highest Good and the Good Life

Do Reformed scholastic theologians adopt a eudaimonistic understanding of life, taking happiness or beatitude as the end of the virtuous life, as was stated in classical virtue ethics as well as in Augustine's Christian account of eudaimonism?

The ethics of several authors of early Reformed scholasticism indeed show eudaimonistic characteristics. This does not mean that Aristotle's definition of the highest good as *eudaimonia* is followed without distinction. In several commentaries on the *Nicomachean Ethics*, Aristotle's understanding of the highest good is corrected or supplemented, though this does not result in the abandonment of eudaimonism. Melanchthon corrects Aristotle's understanding of the end of life in stating that the *telos* of human life is not identified as happiness but as obedience to God,⁶⁵ which is to be understood as true happiness, for he states: "It is customary in philosophy to say that virtue is an end in itself and that it is not primarily desired for the sake of something else. But it would be more correct, even according to reason, to add a more powerful end, namely, that virtue is desired for the sake of

---

61. Ames, *De conscientia* 1.1.4 / *Conscience*, 2. Cf. *Marrow*, 1.10.26 / *Marrow*, 112.
62. Ames, *Medulla* 2.2.16-17 / *Marrow*, 226; Baschera, "Ethics in Reformed Orthodoxy," 528.
63. Ames, *Medulla* 2.1.19, 2.3.8 and 2.3.14 / *Marrow*, 221 and 233, respectively.
64. Ames, *De conscientia* 1.2.7 / *Conscience*, 5. Cf. Ames, *Medulla* 2.1.18 / *Marrow*, 221.
65. Melanchthon, *Enarratio libri II*, CR 16, 287-8.

God."⁶⁶ Melanchthon understands this in terms of primary and secondary end: "Virtue should be desired primarily for the sake of God, but subsequently also on account of present and eternal rewards," including "bodily goods."⁶⁷

Keckermann stays close to Aristotle's understanding of the good life. Although he distinguishes the relative highest good from the absolute highest good, that is, eternal salvation or *visio beatifica Dei*, he regards this as the domain of theology, not of philosophical ethics. Ethics is about the relative highest good, which pertains to the present life. Keckermann defines the relative highest good as civil good or happiness (*civilis felicitas hominis*).⁶⁸ He asserts that his view of the highest good "disagrees in nothing from the view of Aristotle," for whom civil happiness consists in the exercise of virtue.⁶⁹ Those theologians who condemn Aristotle's view of the highest good or happiness are wrong, because they confuse ethics and theology, the moral and the spiritual good. Although after the Fall this civil happiness is imperfect (*restricta beatitudo*) compared to eternal beatitude and although no one can find salvation by it, it can still serve to preserve human society and as such can be called *summum bonum*. For "something of perfection ought to be attributed to it, namely, with the standard of this life or of preserving human society in this life."⁷⁰

Vermigli too takes an eudaimonistic starting point. He differs from Plato and the Stoa in valuing the relative value of external goods, and from Epicurus because of his hedonistic understanding of *eudaimonia*. Vermigli translates *eudaimonia* as *felicitas* or *beatitudo* and identifies it with the Hebrew *ashre*.⁷¹ However, Vermigli redefines happiness more radically than Melachthon and Keckermann, identifying both commonalities and differences between the Aristotelian *eudaimonia* and the Christian *summum bonum*. Happiness is the end, but true happiness of this life consists in "our justification, remission of sins, and reception in glory."⁷² According to Vermigli, on the one hand, "in establishing that the function of men is happiness as shown through action, he [Aristotle] does not contradict Scripture." On the other hand, real happiness and blessedness "stem from the pure generosity of God," the justification of which Aristotle is not aware and which needs to be received through faith as "preeminent virtue."⁷³ Happiness depends on passively received justification (*iustificatio*), which is the source of a new ability to do the good (*regeneratio*). This does not mean that the virtues need not be exercised:

---

66. Melanchthon, *Ethicae doctrinae elementa*, CR 16, 170 / *Elements of Ethical Doctrine*, 115.
67. Ibid.
68. Keckermann, *Systema ethicae*, in *Opera omnia* 2, 251–3.
69. Ibid., 255; Sinnema, "Discipline of Ethics," 37.
70. Quote from Keckermann, *Systema ethicae*, in *Opera omnia* 2, 254; see also 2, 251–3; Sinnema, "Discipline of Ethics," 37.
71. Vermigli, *Ethicorum commentarius*, 75 / *Commentary*, 77–8.
72. Vermigli, *Ethicorum commentarius*, 91 / *Commentary*, 92.
73. Vermigli, *Ethicorum commentarius*, 200–201 / *Commentary*, 197–8.

"teaching custom and training" are means God gives us to use,[74] for happiness, in its workings if not in its source, is a matter of human activity.

Walaeus acknowledges the Aristotelian teleological structure of reflecting on the highest good as the end of human life: "What we call man's supreme good is the ultimate end of all human actions. It is also called beatitude and happiness (*felicitas*). The Greeks call it *eudaimonia* or *eupragia*."[75] Walaeus too corrects Aristotle's view and defines the highest good as the worship of God and our future happiness, for "virtue should not be desired for its own sake in such a way that it is not also desired for the sake of something else which is actually a greater good: that through it we may worship God and pave the way to future happiness."[76]

According to Daneau, the end of the good is to be found in the glory of God, as the *causa finalis* (the final cause or end) of moral action. In his view, this highest good can be attained only in the future life, whereas the 'pagans' wrongly seek it in well-being in this fallen life. From this it follows that the final good (*finis*) of all moral actions is found in what God commands in his Word. This means that moral actions should not only be to God's glory but also serve the neighbor. This *summum bonum* orders inferior secondary ends, which are related as means to the primary good.[77] Daneau's account, though teleological in nature, seems ambivalent with regard to eudaimonism, since obedience to God's commandments as such is regarded as decisive, suggesting a voluntaristic approach. Hence, he defines virtue as "the matching of our actions with God's law."[78] On the other hand, his focus on virtues as qualities of the actor and not only on precepts for moral actions means that his ethics is still eudaimonistic in nature. In his description of the *causa materialis* (material cause or content) of moral action he follows Aristotle's understanding of the soul as consisting of a rational and an irrational part, that is, the whole person, and Aristotle's distinction between moral and intellectual virtues.[79]

Ames describes his understanding of the good life as follows:

> Although it is within the compass of this life to live both happily and well, εὐζωία, living well, is more excellent than εὐδαιμονία, living happily. What chiefly and finally ought to be striven for is not happiness (*beatitudo*) which has to do with our own pleasure, but goodness (*bonum*) which looks to God's glory.[80]

Ames relates this ultimate end of the glory of God to a subordinate end of salvation and blessedness in the life of the regenerate believer, finally resulting in

---

74. Vermigli, *Ethicorum commentarius*, 225 / *Commentary*, 220.
75. Walaeus, *Compendium*, 15 / *Compendium of Aristotelian Ethics*, 123.
76. Walaeus, *Compendium*, 47 / *Compendium of Aristotelian Ethics*, 124.
77. Danaeus, *Ethices christianae* 1.2 and 1.17; Sinnema, "Discipline of Ethics," 24 and 28.
78. Danaeus, *Ethices christianae* 1.20; Sinnema, "Discipline of Ethics," 28.
79. Danaeus, *Ethices christianae* 1.16; Sinnema, "Discipline of Ethics," 27.
80. Ames, *Medulla* 1.1.8 / *Marrow*, 78.

the possession of "eternal life."[81] Living the good life is living to the glory of God. He understands the good in terms of the Augustinian *ordo amoris* and *bonum commune*:

> This is the order of love: God is first and chiefly to be loved and is, as it were, the formal reason of love towards our neighbor. After God, we are bound to love ourselves with the love of true blessedness (*veram beatitudinem*), for loving God with love of union, we love ourselves directly with that greatest love which looks forward to our spiritual blessedness. Secondarily, as it were, we ought to love others whom we would have to be partakers of the same good with us (*nobiscum participes esse volumus eiusdem boni*).[82]

In this way Ames includes a non-competitive eudaimonism in his Christian understanding of the good life as sanctification. Because he sees the good life as one, it is impossible to separate moral or civil good from the spiritual good. Therefore, the proper good includes moral and civil life: "moral virtues are the image of God in man (*imaginem Dei in homine*) and are thus, to a degree, theological virtues."[83]

The Virtues and Their Cultivation

In the early Reformed commentaries on and treatments of Aristotle, the virtues are considered the way to live the good life. Differences occur in how the virtues are defined and treated. Melanchthon adopts the Aristotelian definition of virtue as a habitus which inclines the will in conformity with reason and as a mean between two extremes.[84] According to Keckermann, moral virtues are a perfection of the will and the desires. He stays in line with Aristotle in his definition of moral virtue as "an active habit (*habitus*) arising from ongoing moral actions, suitably tempering and conforming the human will and desires to moderation for the sake of attaining civil good."[85] Furthermore, he fully accepts the Aristotelian 'mean' as the proper way to define virtue as to be found between two extremes, one of deficiency and one of excess. Interestingly, he distinguishes between guiding or universal means (justice and prudence), which are founded in the love of God (as general, non-Christian love), the neighbor and the self, on the one hand, and the guided or particular virtues, on the other. Keckermann orders these particular virtues not according to the Decalogue, but according to their object, namely love

---

81. Ames, *Medulla* 2.1.28 and 2.1.30 / *Marrow*, 222–3; Baschera, "Ethics in Reformed Orthodoxy," 527.
82. Ames, *Medulla* 2.16.13 / *Marrow*, 302.
83. Ames, *Medulla* 2.2.17 / *Marrow*, 226.
84. Melanchthon, *Enarratio libri II*, CR 16, 312 and 317–18.
85. Keckermann, *Systema ethicae*, in *Opera omnia* 2, 273; trans. Sinnema, "Discipline of Ethics," 39.

to the neighbor (e.g., generosity) and love to oneself (e.g., temperance) or love both to oneself and to the neighbor (e.g., truthfulness). On a lower level we find virtues that are said to be by analogy. These virtues are incomplete, conditional moral dispositions, classified as pertaining to oneself (shame), to the neighbor (sympathy), or both to oneself and to the neighbor (e.g., repentance).[86]

According to Vermigli, the philosophical virtues are acquired through habit, while theological virtues are inspired by the Holy Spirit. This corresponds with a difference in order:

> According to human reason, men should do righteous deeds before there is justification. But the order of divine sanctification is established far otherwise; first we believe, and afterwards are justified, and then the powers of our minds are restored by the Holy Spirit and by grace, and finally just and honest deeds follow.[87]

Vermigli agrees with Aristotle that the moral virtues are acquired through habit, which means that the human being does not possess virtues by nature but needs to acquire them by acting in a particular way. Moreover, virtues are qualities that make the one who possesses them 'good.' Furthermore, Vermigli sees the Aristotelian concept of virtue as a mean between two extremes as in line with Scripture, for instance, when Paul says that we should be wise in moderation (Rom. 12:3).[88] Also, he agrees with Aristotle that virtue can be acquired through habituation and that human goods are an activity of the soul in accordance with virtue, but limits this to the civil virtues. At the same time, as Baschera explains, Vermigli does not want to separate the civil virtues as part of a profane sphere from the spiritual or sanctified life and the theological virtues. Rather the virtue of faith by which we receive justification works as a renewal (*regeneratio*) of our entire life. Vermigli describes the virtues resulting from this *regeneratio* as inherent righteousness (*iustitia inhaerens*), which is distinguished from the imputed righteousness (*iustitia imputata*) by which the sinner is justified. Vermigli's interesting contribution is that he considers *iustitia inhaerens* in terms of an acquired *habitus* in the Aristotelian sense of the word, but in such a way that this habitus finds its source not in human activity but in *regeneratio* through the Spirit.[89] In this way, he incorporates Aristotelian habituation in sanctification.

In his treatment of the virtues, Walaeus follows the order of the *Nicomachean Ethics*—he examines Aristotle's ten ethical and five dianoethical virtues and corrects their material content from revelation.[90] Such correction is needed since

---

86. Keckermann, *Systema ethicae*, in *Opera omnia* 2, 294, 310–11 and 348; Sinnema, "Discipline of Ethics," 39.
87. Vermigli, *Ethicorum commentarius*, 8 / *Commentary*, 14.
88. Vermigli, *Ethicorum commentarius*, 307 and 367 / *Commentary*, 295 and 349.
89. Baschera, *Tugend und Rechtfertigung*, 155, 172–5.
90. Walaeus, *Compendium*, 139–253.

Aristotle had nothing to say about the gospel and the first table of the Decalogue, where the most outstanding virtues are contained; ignored some virtues from the second table, such as mercy (*misericordia*); and regarded some vices, such as revenge and carnal desire (*concupiscentia*), as virtues.[91]

In his discussion of virtue, Daneau distinguishes *heroic* or *divine* virtues that are rarely present among people as extraordinary gifts of God, such as the prudence of Salomon and the fortitude of Samson, and which cannot be possessed truly by unbelievers who only have a shadow of them, from *human* virtues which all persons may possess. These last virtues are found in two degrees: first, human virtue as a *perfect* habitus which is not the result of long practice, as in Aristotle's view, but is imparted by the Holy Spirit; only Christ had this perfect virtue, others attain it only in the future life; secondly, human virtue as an *imperfect* quality that struggles to resist a bad habit and can be found in believers, and also shadows of it in unbelievers.[92]

In contrast with the way ancient philosophers and medieval scholastics taught the virtues, Daneau derives his material description of the virtues from Scripture. Although "Scripture is not so precise in distinguishing virtues and vices that it does not often call the same virtue or vice by various names," Daneau prefers this to the scholastic attempt to systematize all human emotions and feelings, because it is ultimately impossible to grasp the feelings of the human soul entirely. Following Scripture means viewing the virtues and vices "insofar as they render what is due to God or to one's neighbor." They all serve and align with what God commands in the law with regard to himself and the neighbor. Therefore, the law is the rule for explaining all virtues.[93]

Ames too construes a system of virtues ordered from the two tables of the Decalogue and summarized by Christ in the double love commandment. The second table of the Decalogue is interpreted in terms of the virtues of justice and charity; the language of command, obligation, and obedience is harmoniously related to that of virtue, disposition, and perfection.[94] As in the Aristotelian and Thomist tradition, Ames defines virtue as "a condition or habit (*habitus*) by which the will is inclined to do well,"[95] and states that it is called a *habitus* "because it is in general a state of mind of various degrees of perfection. It is called a habit not only because one

---

91. Walaeus, *Compendium*, 10–11 / *Compendium of Aristotelian Ethics*, 123.
92. Danaeus, *Ethices christianae* 1.21-23; Sinnema, "Discipline of Ethics," 28–9.
93. Danaeus, *Ethices christianae* 1.24; Sinnema, "Discipline of Ethics," 29–30.
94. Ames, *Medulla* 2.16-2.21 / *Marrow*, 300–27.
95. Ames, *Medulla* 2.2.4 / *Marrow*, 224. cf. Daniel Westberg, "The Influence of Aquinas on Protestant Ethics," in Svensson and VanDrunen (eds.), *Aquinas among the Protestants*, 271: "Ames recognized something of the complementary aspects of the will and intellect, as they are related to goodness or truth, respectively. Perceiving this complementary function . . . could well have been the result of a fairly careful reading of the *Summa*, but Ames also resisted the intellectualist position (often associated with Aquinas) since it implied tendencies toward Pelagianism."

possesses it but also because it makes the subject behave in a certain manner, that is, it moves the faculty, which otherwise would not be moved, toward good."[96] Using the Aristotelian four causes, Ames defines virtuous acting as requiring

> a good efficient cause or beginning (*efficiens vel principium bonum*), that is, a well-disposed will working from true virtue. . . . Second, a good matter or object (*materia vel objectum bonum*), namely, something commanded by God. . . . Third, a good end (*finis bonus*)—or the glory of God and whatever redounds to his glory. . . . Fourth, a pattern or good standard (*forma . . . vel modus bonus*) is required. This is found when the act accords with the revealed will of God.[97]

Ames departs from Aristotle in at least three ways: (1) instead of taking the prudent man as the rule of virtue, the divine will is the sole rule, (2) although virtues may increase or decrease by frequent use of good or evil acts, good habits are also to be considered gifts "given by God and inspired by the Holy Spirit,"[98] which however does not exclude human agency, and (3) virtues are not to be defined as a mean between two extremes, since there can be no excess in virtues, but in conformity to their own standards.[99]

In sum, Ames does not hesitate to develop a reasonable account of virtue and the virtues, working in the broad Christian tradition of reinterpreting the cardinal virtues from revelation. The virtues are intrinsically related to each other in relationships of dependence of inferior virtues on superior ones, being in the end all expressions of the worship and glory of God.[100]

Conclusion

In contrast with MacIntyre's and Gregory's claims, our investigation has demonstrated that the ethics of Reformed scholasticism developed in great continuity with medieval scholasticism, its morality of the good, and the virtues making the good life possible. Aristotelian ethics continued to be the backbone of ethical education in Lutheran and Reformed universities and academies throughout the sixteenth century and continued to be an important point of reference in the Reformed scholastic works on ethics in the seventeenth century. At the same time, the emphasis on biblical revelation as the main source and criterion is distinctive in these Protestant accounts, but this does not result in "rival truth claims" and

---

96. Ames, *Medulla* 2.2.5 and 6 / *Marrow*, 224.
97. Ames, *Medulla* 2.3.3 and 7 / *Marrow*, 232–3.
98. Ames, *Medulla* 2.2.19 / *Marrow*, 227.
99. Ames, *Medulla* 2.2.35 and 39 / *Marrow*, 230–1; Baschera, "Ethics in Reformed Orthodoxy," 528–9.
100. Ames, *Medulla* 2.2.49 / *Marrow*, 232.

"bitter disagreements," as Gregory assumes. Rather God's commandments are seen as universal and as such in accord with natural law, although not all Reformed scholastic authors acknowledge natural law as a relatively independent source of moral understanding, alongside the gospel. Even in that case it is recognized that, thanks to divine grace, the *imago Dei*, though damaged through the Fall, remains in all human beings and enables them to distinguish good from evil.

Moreover, in none of the examined accounts is the eudaimonistic framework abandoned. As in Aquinas and other medieval scholastics, happiness, *beatitudo*, or the good life is defined from a perspective beyond earthly life. The aim is to live a good and virtuous life, either in the civil as distinguished from the spiritual life or rather in one undivided life of sanctification extending to all spheres of life. It must be observed that these views include potential tensions and imbalances, either by separating the theological (gospel) domain too sharply from the civil (law) sphere, or by overemphasizing the need for grace at the cost of human agency, habituation, and the full acknowledgment of non-Christian virtue. Yet, the examples of Reformed scholastics from the seventeenth century show that no radicalization of either of these positions comes to dominate. Ames's thoroughly theological ethics, for instance, does not follow Melanchthon's and Keckermann's separation of civil good from the spiritual good, but nevertheless includes a clear conception of natural law, virtue, and habituation in his account of Christian moral life.

As a whole, Reformed scholastics developed their virtue ethical core concepts in continuity with traditional understandings, without hesitating to construe their concepts according to their own theological views. Although in some respects they developed their ethics along modern paths it is implausible to say that these representatives of Protestant ethics decisively paved the way to a modern formal ethics. Rather this tradition is to be seen as a very relevant but highly neglected bridge between premodern and contemporary virtue ethics.

Chapter 5

CHARACTER FORMATION AS KIERKEGAARDIAN EDIFICATION

Several attempts have been made to open up a dialogue between Søren Kierkegaard and virtue ethics in general and Alasdair MacIntyre's contemporary account of virtue ethics in particular. Many of those who contributed to this dialogue criticized MacIntyre's portrayal of Kierkegaard as an advocate of an irrational "criterionless choice"[1] by outlining Kierkegaard's account of the nature of choice and rationality in the ethical sphere.[2] Others offered explorations of similarities and differences between both thinkers on various themes, for example, their valuation of modern ethics, their understanding of character formation and selfhood, and the status of moral rationality in relation to divine revelation.[3]

However, MacIntyre himself stays skeptical about the possibility of connecting Kierkegaardian existential ethics and Aristotelian-Thomistic virtue ethics.[4] In his concluding chapter to the volume *Kierkegaard after MacIntyre*, he points to two critical issues. First, although he admits that his initial portrayal of Kierkegaard was mistaken in several respects—he "ignored the complexity of the relationships

---

1. MacIntyre, *After Virtue*, 39 and 49.
2. For example, John J. Davenport, "The Meaning of Kierkegaard's Choice between the Aesthetic and the Ethical: A Response to MacIntyre," in John J. Davenport and Anthony Rudd (eds.), *Kierkegaard after MacIntyre: Essays on Freedom, Narrative, and Virtue* (Chicago and La Salle: Open Court, 2001), 75–112; Anthony Rudd, "Reason in Ethics: MacIntyre and Kierkegaard," in *Kierkegaard after MacIntyre*, 131–50.
3. Robert C. Roberts, "Existence, Emotion, and Virtue: Classical Themes in Kierkegaard," in Alastair Hannay and Gordon D. Marino (eds.), *The Cambridge Companion to Kierkegaard* (Cambridge: Cambridge University Press, 1998), 177–206; Gordon D. Marino, "The Place of Reason in Kierkegaard's Ethics," in *Kierkegaard after MacIntyre*, 113–28; Bruce Kirmmse, "Possibilities for Dialogue," in *Kierkegaard after MacIntyre*, 191–210; Norman Lillegard, "Thinking with Kierkegaard and MacIntyre about the Aesthetic, Virtue, and Narrative," in *Kierkegaard after MacIntyre*, 211–32; Edward F. Mooney, "The Perils of Polarity: Kierkegaard and MacIntyre in Search of Moral Truth," in *Kierkegaard after MacIntyre*, 233–64.
4. Alasdair MacIntyre, "Once More on Kierkegaard," in *Kierkegaard after MacIntyre*, 339–55.

between the choice of the ethical, the self that makes that choice, and the self that is constituted by that choice"[5]—MacIntyre still seems to insist that according to Kierkegaard the only way to make the transition from the aesthetic to the ethical (and from the ethical to the religious) is by way of a criterionless choice.[6] On the other hand, very interestingly, MacIntyre suggests that a different interpretation is possible as well, an interpretation in which the ethical continuity between the aesthetic (in a negative sense) and the ethical is acknowledged.

Hence, it is the second issue that creates the real gap between MacIntyre and Kierkegaard, a gap stemming from large differences between any Aristotelian-Thomistic position, on the one hand, and Kierkegaard's Protestant theological conceptions of revelation and faith as opposed to human reason and nature, on the other. Contrary to Kierkegaard, MacIntyre insists that, prior to and independently of revelation and of the gift of faith, we do have a conception of the human good that may adequately provide direction for our actions. Whereas in Aquinas' view grace presupposes and builds upon nature, in Kierkegaard's view there is no relationship between the moral and intellectual virtues, on the one hand, and theological virtues, on the other. Moreover, Kierkegaard presupposes a very different set of relationships between the will, reason, and the passions from those described by either Aristotle or Aquinas. According to MacIntyre, Kierkegaard has no place for rational choice (*prohairesis* or *electio*) as condition of how the virtues determine the character of our actions. His ethics is focused on "the categorical imperative of the will."[7] In conclusion, "The gap between an Aristotelian or Thomist ethics of the virtues and a Kierkegaardian ethics is just too great."[8]

In this chapter I will argue that Kierkegaard is to be located in the Augustinian tradition that is distinct from but not completely opposed to Aristotelianism, as we have seen. Although in Kierkegaard's thought the realities of the Christian drama of sin and salvation decisively criticize and transcend an Aristotelian moral theory based purely on 'human nature,' this criticism does not prevent him from speaking in a positive way about human nature, its teleology, and the virtues. From a Christian perspective such general features must be transformed profoundly, as I will show in an analysis of some of Kierkegaard's upbuilding discourses.

Yet, the question is if and in what respect Kierkegaard can be regarded as a 'virtue ethicist.'[9] The answer to this question depends on what we consider a proper definition of 'virtue ethics.' As Christine Swanton has demonstrated, definitions that identify virtue ethics with just one tradition, for instance Aristotelian

---

5. Ibid., 340.
6. Ibid., 341.
7. Ibid., 355.
8. Ibid., 353.
9. Robert C. Roberts, "Kierkegaard, Wittgenstein, and a Method of 'Virtue Ethics,'" in Martin J. Matuštík and Merold Westphal (eds.), *Kierkegaard in Post/Modernity* (Bloomington and Indianapolis: Indiana University Press, 1995), 48: "I am arguing . . . that Kierkegaard is pre-eminently a 'virtue ethicist.'"

eudaimonism, or a single exemplar, for instance Aristotle or Aquinas, do not suffice, since they would exclude other traditions and key figures that have a strong claim to be understood in virtue ethical terms.[10] Therefore, even if Kierkegaard would appear not to be very Aristotelian or Thomistic, it is still an open question whether Kierkegaard can be considered a 'virtue ethicist,' in the sense of the 'grammatical' understanding of virtue ethics I use in this book, and if so, what kind of virtue ethicist he may be. Or to phrase it more in line with the *constructive* aim of this book: What specific contribution may Kierkegaard, both as a modern philosopher and as a Protestant theologian, offer to an ethics of the good life under modern conditions?

In order to find answers to these questions, I will first shortly address MacIntyre's criticism of the ethical as a "criterionless choice" by pointing to Kierkegaard's teleologically structured anthropological framework that underlies all his writings. Next, I will investigate how Kierkegaard explicitly refers to Aristotelian (and non-Aristotelian) virtue ethical concepts. In a third section the language of perfection as related to the God relationship will be analyzed, particularly in Kierkegaard's upbuilding or edifying discourses. Formation appears to be understood in terms of edification. Finally, I will examine how virtue ethical 'grammar' functions in some of Kierkegaard's upbuilding discourses that deal with what apparently are virtues.

Kierkegaard's Teleological Conception of the Self

Let us start with a brief examination of MacIntyre's criticism of what he calls a "criterionless choice." In his contribution to the volume *Kierkegaard after MacIntyre*, MacIntyre first argues that *Either/Or* denies the possibility of mediation between the aesthetic and the ethical, which implies an exclusion of thought and reason and a fortiori of philosophy. There may be good ethical reasons to make the transition, but from the aesthetic point of view one has attitudes and beliefs that seem to disable the aesthete from evaluating and appreciating those views. One has to have already chosen oneself as an ethical subject in order to be able to appreciate those reasons. It can only retrospectively be understood as rationally justifiable, not prospectively.[11]

At the same time MacIntyre seems to agree with Peter J. Mehl, John J. Davenport, and Anthony Rudd[12] that Kierkegaard's anthropology entails a central teleological

---

10. Christine Swanton, "The Definition of Virtue Ethics," in Daniel C. Russell (ed.), *The Cambridge Companion to Virtue Ethics* (Cambridge: Cambridge University Press, 2013), 316-19.

11. MacIntyre, "Once More on Kierkegaard," 344.

12. Peter J. Mehl, "Kierkegaard and the Relativist Challenge to Practical Philosophy (with a New Postscript)," in *Kierkegaard after MacIntyre*, 2-38; Davenport, "The Meaning of Kierkegaard's Choice," and Rudd, "Reason in Ethics," respectively.

view of human nature and "that it does indeed follow from that view that there are good reasons for individuals to move from the aesthetic to the ethical and not merely good-reasons-from-the-standpoint-of-the-ethical."[13] Moreover, Norman Lillegard's contribution to the volume helps MacIntyre to discover a different possible interpretation of the nature of the aesthetic: suppose that the aesthetic personality can be viewed as one that is engaged in unacknowledged resistance to the ethical, "so that the aesthetic life requires a silent, but determined refusal of the ethical" and as such is already engaged with the ethical.[14] Whereas the dominant interpretation emphasizes the discontinuity between the aesthetic and the ethical, this strand of interpretation points to the continuities in the subtext.[15]

In my view, MacIntyre's intuition is right, but he is not able to conceptualize it properly because he limits himself to analyses of what Kierkegaard later calls "the aesthetic authorship" and doesn't take into account that an anthropological framework in which human nature is directed toward an ethical-religious *telos* underlies all Kierkegaard's works. In fact, this framework centers on what MacIntyre calls a conception of human-nature-as-it-could-be-if-it-realized-its-*telos*.[16] The teleologically structured anthropological view is not just a perspective within the ethical sphere, as presented in *Either/Or II*, but is part of Kierkegaard's anthropological framework that underlies all his elaborations of existential spheres and the figures that represent these spheres in the pseudonymous works, and culminates in the formula of the self in *The Sickness unto Death* and the way this formula functions in the topology of the various manifestations of despair. Thus, the various existential spheres and their individual expressions in *actuality* are to be distinguished from this anthropological framework as human *potentiality*. Mehl makes a similar claim by pointing to the distinction between "ethical reality" as the general *potential* of becoming and being a person, on the one hand, and the "subjectively actual" that refers to the *actual* or existential maintaining of this ethical reality by an individual in his concrete existence, on the other.[17] The former designates a potential that every individual possesses as a human being. It may be

---

13. MacIntyre, "Once More on Kierkegaard," 344.

14. Ibid., 348.

15. See for a different interpretation of the transition to the ethical life in Kierkegaard's thought, namely, from an 'internalist' understanding of practical reasons (Bernard Williams): Rob Compaijen, *Kierkegaard, MacIntyre, Williams, and the Internal Point of View* (London: Palgrave Macmillan, 2018).

16. MacIntyre, *After Virtue*, 40–1.

17. Mehl, "Kierkegaard and the Relativist Challenge to Practical Philosophy," 14. I take this as a more appropriate distinction than Davenport's between (1) the cognitive awareness of the objective authority of moral principles, a condition shared by both the aesthete and the ethicist, and (2) volitional identification which give one's actions personal significance, a condition only satisfied by the ethicist (Davenport, "Meaning of Kierkegaard's Choice," 82–3). *Either/Or II* is not so much about "the objective authority of moral principles" as about "ethical subjectivity" as a precondition for ethics.

characterized as a 'natural predisposition,' in a sense akin to a (Neo-)Aristotelian conception of human nature. Whereas the ethical in the latter sense may be conceived of as a stage or life sphere, the ethical in the former sense is not a stage but qualifies human nature as such. MacIntyre's interpretation ignores this distinction, resulting in his contradictory evaluations of the relationship between the aesthetic and the ethical.

A concept of the human being as a potentiality for development into a deeper self runs through Kierkegaard's oeuvre from *Either/Or* to *The Sickness unto Death*[18] and underlies the upbuilding works as well. In *Either/Or* this potentiality is described in terms of choice: the self chooses himself, not in his initial state of immediacy but in his "eternal validity."[19] In the 1844 upbuilding discourse 'To Need God is a Human Being's Highest Perfection' a similar distinction is made, but in a somewhat different setting. The discourse speaks of a "first self" that must develop into a "deeper self." The relation between these two 'selves' is portrayed as an inner struggle, a dialogue. Kierkegaard emphasizes the dynamics and development of the process of becoming oneself. In this upbuilding discourse he even uses the language of sickness and becoming healthy that is so characteristic of his later work: the deeper self is like a physician at the bedside of the sick, knowing that "this sickness is not unto death but unto life."[20] Whereas the first self is turned outward in seeking after the surrounding world as object of identification, the deeper self is aimed at turning the first self away from immediacy and externality

---

18. C. Stephen Evans speaks of "a teleological view of human nature" (*Kierkegaard's Ethic of Love: Divine Commands and Moral Obligations* (Oxford: Oxford University Press, 2004), 21) that is "fleshed out in a proper Aristotelian way with reference to capacities that are both universally human and distinctive in the way that humans exemplify them" (ibid., 19). Whereas other works, like *Fear and Trembling*, are more akin to a divine command ethics (although I don't think this book actually defends a divine command ethics, see my "The Irreducibility of Religious Faith: Kierkegaard on Civilization and the *Aqedah*," in Pieter Vos and Onno Zijlstra (eds.), *The Law of God: Exploring God and Civilization* (Leiden and Boston: Brill, 2014), 194–214), the Aristotelian view is present in the core idea of becoming oneself, for instance in Kierkegaard's *Concluding Unscientific Postscript*, where Johannes Climacus says that it is "every individual's task to become a whole person." See Søren Kierkegaard, *Concluding Unscientific Postscript*, ed. and trans. Howard V. Hong and Edna H. Hong (Princeton: Princeton University Press, 1992), 346 / *SKS* 7, 316.

19. Søren Kierkegaard, *Either/Or II*, ed. and trans. Howard V. Hong and Edna H. Hong (Princeton: Princeton University Press, 1987), 211 / *SKS* 3, 203. On the one hand, the idea of the absolute makes the self qualitatively different from how he existed before. On the other hand, choosing himself in his eternal validity does not mean that the self becomes someone other than he was before, but that he becomes himself, that is, that he chooses or, more correctly, receives himself as someone who existed before as this specific being who he is and no other (ibid., 177, 215 / *SKS* 3, 172–3, 206–7).

20. Søren Kierkegaard, *Eighteen Upbuilding Discourses*, ed. and trans. Howard V. Hong and Edna H. Hong (Princeton: Princeton University Press, 1990), 315 / *SKS* 5, 307.

to true self-knowledge.²¹ This does not mean that the conditions of the first self are completely worthless. In the end, when the first self submits to the deeper self, they are 'reconciled.'

Since becoming a free responsible person is a potentiality that belongs to each individual's natural capacity, *knowledge* of the human *telos* is a matter of each individual's self-reflexive relationship to him- or herself. Basically, the human potential of personhood that belongs to each individual's natural capacity is *itself* the normative standard by which to measure one's own existence. In order to acquire a true conception of oneself, one must be like a teacher in relation to oneself as a learner, as one of the discourses expresses it.²² In this sense, the ethical choice, as the affirmation of the task to actualize oneself as this definite individual, is not criterionless. It is an affirmation of oneself as a responsible human agent. The upbuilding discourse 'To Need God is a Human Being's Highest Perfection' expresses the central meaning of self-knowledge by emphasizing that the task is to know oneself not in relation to something else, but in relation to oneself.²³ To be sure, the discourse also directs the reader to the self 'before God,' which makes a significant difference. I will return to this after an examination of Kierkegaard's use of virtue ethical language in general.

The Vocabulary of Character and Virtue

Although Kierkegaard's anthropological scheme is teleologically structured, the vocabulary of 'self,' 'existence,' 'choice,' and 'subjectivity,' to which I referred in the preceding section, is apparently a modern one. What about virtue ethical concepts like 'character' and 'virtue'—how are they actually present in Kierkegaard's works?

Kierkegaard does indeed employ the term 'character.' Whereas 'subjectivity' functions in contrast with the interest of speculative philosophy, and 'individual' is defined in contrast with a life oriented to and by 'the crowd,' and 'self' designates the spiritual task of becoming oneself as opposed to being in anxiety or despair, and all these concepts are mainly directed toward modern phenomena, 'character' refers to a classical virtue ethical background. In *A Literary Review* it is used in contrast with the personality formation typical of the present age: "Morality is character; character is something engraved (χαρασσω); but the sea has no character, nor does the sand, nor abstract common sense, either, for character is inwardness."²⁴ Here, Kierkegaard refers to the etymology of the concept, which we also find in classical virtue ethical accounts. With Robert C. Roberts, Kierkegaard's concept

---

21. Ibid., 309 / *SKS* 5, 301.
22. Søren Kierkegaard, *Three Discourses on Imagined Occasions*, ed. and trans. Howard V. Hong and Edna H. Hong (Princeton: Princeton University Press, 1993), 60 / *SKS* 5, 434.
23. Kierkegaard, *Eighteen Upbuilding Discourses*, 313 / *SKS* 5, 305.
24. Søren Kierkegaard, *Two Ages*, ed. and trans. Howard V. Hong and Edna H. Hong (Princeton: Princeton University Press, 1978), 77–8 / *SKS* 8, 75.

of character may be described as "sustained dispositional ethical ... interest" or "commitment."[25]

Moreover, character is a matter of formation. In *The Book on Adler* Kierkegaard refers approvingly to the importance of character formation: "In antiquity the importance of a person's upbringing was valued very highly, and it was understood as a harmonious development of that which will carry the various gifts and talents and the disposition of the personality ethically in the direction of character."[26] This "ethical education of character," which requires much time and diligence, is replaced in modernity by an emphasis on "*instruction*" and the child is supposed to be able to bring up himself, which is "a great mistake."[27]

In the upbuilding discourses the term 'character' is absent, but as the quotation from *A Literary Review* indicates, 'inwardness,' which is frequently used in the discourses, functions more or less as its equivalent. Although this term is often contrasted with the outer world, its meaning is not limited to 'the private' or 'a turn inward' or a 'private interiority,' but means something like 'basic concern.' This becomes clear in the upbuilding discourse 'Strengthening in the Inner Being,' where Kierkegaard writes about a person to whom not just a concern for things in the world awakens, but "a concern about what meaning the world has for him and he for the world ... only then does the inner being announce its presence in this *concern*."[28]

Furthermore, inwardness as long-term and intensive concern is closely related to another concept: passion. In *A Literary Review* Kierkegaard speaks of an "essential passion" (*vaesentlige Lidenskab*),[29] which David J. Gouwens describes as "an extensive interest that shapes a person's life in great breadth."[30] Inwardness as intensive concern finds its counterpart in passion as extensive interest. This does not mean that every passion or emotion is capable of integrating personality into a moral character, only "essential passion" is. It is more than just an emotion, it is a uniting "idea" to which a person is passionately related, for instance a passion for justice, which encompasses a person's entire life as characterized by "seeking justice."[31] In short, both inwardness and essential passion are constitutive of Kierkegaard's concept of 'character.' The idea of an essential passion and commitment is similar to a (Neo-)Aristotelian idea of *telos*. Moreover, essential

---

25. Roberts, "Existence, Emotion, and Virtue," 180.
26. Søren Kierkegaard, *The Book on Adler*, ed. and trans. Howard V. Hong and Edna H. Hong (Princeton: Princeton University Press, 1998), 133 / SKS 15, 286.
27. Ibid.
28. Kierkegaard, *Eighteen Upbuilding Discourses*, 86 / SKS 5, 93. I agree with David J. Gouwens, *Kierkegaard as Religious Thinker* (Cambridge: Cambridge University Press, 1996), 97, that the juxtaposition of "inner being" and "concern" is central here.
29. Kierkegaard, *Two Ages*, 62 / SKS 8, 61.
30. Gouwens, *Kierkegaard as Religious Thinker*, 97.
31. Ibid.

passion as a 'uniting idea' is more 'rational' than MacIntyre presupposes in his criticism of Kierkegaard's supposed voluntaristic view of morality.

The same holds for Kierkegaard's treatment of continuity or stability of character. In *A Literary Review* Kierkegaard explains that whereas a person without character is an "unstable emptiness," a person with character has something to "dwell upon."[32] In the upbuilding discourses, Kierkegaard points to the importance of stability or constancy. In the discourse 'To Need God is a Human Being's Highest Perfection,' constancy is what the "deeper self" offers amid the changing reality and inconstancy of the "first self."[33] In a sense, the occasional discourse 'Purity of Heart' is dedicated to an exploration of constancy of character: purity of heart is to will one thing. Kierkegaard argues that only 'the good' is truly one. Only by taking on the essential character of the *object* of his willing (the good) can the self be pure in heart, that is, one. On the other hand, he can be one only when he *wills* the good. Interestingly, it is precisely this thought—purity of heart is to will one thing—which MacIntyre approvingly quotes and explicitly relates to the (Neo-)Aristotelian-Thomistic concept of 'integrity' or 'constancy,' that is, "singleness of purpose in a whole life."[34] In doing so, he in fact presupposes the teleological meaning of Kierkegaard's argument in this discourse.

All these elements reflect important features of the virtue ethical tradition, but for the most part rather implicitly. Thus, the question is: To what extent does Kierkegaard actually derive his concepts from Aristotle and other virtue ethical representatives?

Kierkegaard and Aristotle

From his Notebooks we know that Kierkegaard read the *Ethica Nicomachea* in 1842. In Notebook 13 we find a collection of interesting entries on Aristotle's *Ethics*,[35] which Kierkegaard apparently read both in German and Greek, but quickly and superficially, as Håvard Løkke convincingly argues, for "it did not make a great impression on Kierkegaard."[36] Løkke analyzes that Kierkegaard's

---

32. Kierkegaard, *Two Ages*, 54 / *SKS* 8, 54. See also Roberts, "Existence, Emotion, and Virtue," 180.

33. Kierkegaard, *Eighteen Upbuilding Discourses*, 314 / *SKS* 5, 306. Cf. Pieter Vos, "Self," in Steven Emmanuel, William McDonald, Jon Stewart (eds.), *Kierkegaard's Concepts* (Kierkegaard Research: Sources, Reception, and Resources 15.6) (Aldershot: Ashgate, 2015), 23–8.

34. MacIntyre, *After Virtue*, 203, as well as his *Whose Justice? Which Rationality?*, 165, and *Three Rival Versions of Moral Inquiry: Encyclopaedia, Genealogy, and Tradition* (Notre Dame: University of Notre Dame Press, 1990), 143.

35. *JN* 3, 385–6 / *SKS* 19, 387–9 (Not13:10-21).

36. Håvard Løkke, "*Nicomachean Ethics*: Ignorance and Relationships," in Jon Stewart and Katalin Nun (eds.), *Kierkegaard and the Greek World: Aristotle and Other Greek Authors*

notes, together with other instances in his works where he refers to Aristotle's ethics, are concerned with two themes: first, with how an agent's ignorance bears on the agent's act being voluntary or not; second, with the human being as social, especially in terms of friendship.

If I limit myself to the first theme, Kierkegaard correctly observes that Aristotle regards the voluntary as a wider category than προαίρεσις (*prohairesis*). However, it is striking, as Løkke demonstrates, that Kierkegaard translates the latter by 'intention' (*Forsæt*) instead of 'choice' or 'decision.' Løkke concludes that Kierkegaard did not discover that choice is a key notion in Aristotle's ethics.[37] This may be correct, but does not mean that Kierkegaard and Aristotle do not have much in common on this concept (although there are differences in how each thinker relates reason, will, and the passions), as Løkke himself admits.

Furthermore, in my view, Løkke's overall evaluation of Kierkegaard's treatment of Aristotle is too limited. For it is noteworthy that Kierkegaard is on Aristotle's side against Socrates and Plato in rejecting the view that we are entirely governed by reason. According to Kierkegaard, Aristotle dismisses their "idealistic view ... that all sin is ignorance." Nevertheless, Aristotle too "does not eliminate the difficulty, because he merely ends in a realistic counterposition."[38] Løkke interprets this realistic position in the sense that, according to Kierkegaard, Aristotle limits himself to concrete cases and situations, in particular that whether something happens or not depends on one's choice,[39] while, for Løkke, Kierkegaard fails to understand Aristotle's point that the choice is not merely directed to concrete actions, but to becoming a virtuous person, a good character. I think that this is a speculative interpretation of Kierkegaard's comments. In my interpretation, Kierkegaard regards Aristotle's realistic position as a better alternative to the intellectual psychology of Socrates and Plato, because Aristotle stresses the voluntary nature of sin, "such that something can be voluntary without being intended,"[40] as Kierkegaard remarks in the entry immediately preceding the one on Aristotle's counterposition to Socrates/Plato. At the same time, this is still not a solution, because in Aristotle's account the problem of sin is not *solved*.

(Kierkegaard Research: Sources, Reception and Resources 2.2) (Farnham and Burlington: Ashgate, 2008), 49.

37. Ibid., 53.

38. *JN* 3, 385–6 / *SKS* 19, 387–8 (Not13:15).

39. Løkke, "*Nicomachean Ethics*: Ignorance and Relationships," 54, who quotes Søren Kierkegaard, *Philosophical Fragments*, ed. and trans. Howard V. Hong and Edna H. Hong (Princeton: Princeton University Press, 1985), 17 note / *SKS* 4, 225, where the pseudonymous author Johannes Climacus dwells on Greek thought: "'The depraved person and the virtuous person presumably do not have the power over their moral condition, but in the beginning they have the power to become the one or the other, just as the person who throws a stone has power over it before he throws it but not when he has thrown it' (Aristotle)." This quote seems to refer to *EN* 1114a12–19.

40. *JN* 3, 386 / *SKS* 19, 388 (Not13:14).

Meanwhile, Kierkegaard's notes reveal that he was aware of some important virtue ethical presuppositions. First, he acknowledges the importance of the Aristotelian μεσότης or *mean* in the moral virtues, such as courage, temperance, generosity, and justice, and underlines its correctness, for desire and disinclination as the things with which the moral virtues struggle are neither good nor evil in themselves.[41] He also observes that the mean is not used in Aristotle's conception of the intellectual virtues, and mentions these virtues: τέχνη (practical knowledge), ἐπιστήμη (intellectual knowledge), σωφροσύνη (temperance), νοῦς (understanding), σοφία (wisdom), though it is a mistake to mention σωφροσύνη here instead of φρόνησις (prudence).[42] Secondly, Kierkegaard emphasizes that virtue is to be seen as an *attitude or acquired ability* (ἕξις), which brings continuity in one's acting.[43] Thirdly, notwithstanding Kierkegaard's wrong translation, he observes the centrality of προαίρεσις in Aristotle[44] and, contrary to MacIntyre's claim that I referred to in the introduction, the idea that our lives are morally formed by our previous deliberate choices is present in Kierkegaard's reading of Aristotle and arguably in his own thought as well, as I will illustrate later in my analysis of one of the upbuilding discourses. Fourthly, Kierkegaard is aware of the importance of the distinction between ποιεῖν (to make) and πραττεῖν (to do, to practice) in Aristotle, albeit that his interest is limited to how they function in poetry and art.[45] Fifthly, Kierkegaard understands the Aristotelian concept of *eudaimonia* or happiness as an activity that is desirable in itself.[46] Finally, Kierkegaard adopts the Aristotelian definition of motion (κίνησις) as a transition from possibility to actuality and this is a central point of departure for his thinking about freedom, the development of the self and actuality.[47]

Yet, it is indeed questionable whether these Aristotelian concepts really had a deep impact on Kierkegaard's thought. Kierkegaard also offers criticism of Aristotle, which reveals important differences between Aristotle and his own approach. In his notes of 1842, he criticizes Aristotle for his limited, aesthetic understanding of the human self as directed to happiness in the sense of intellectual contemplation. The contemplative life is understood in aesthetic terms and as isolation and not in terms of becoming spirit: "the happiness of the divine doesn't consist in contemplation but in eternal communication."[48] Surely, Løkke is right that Kierkegaard here posits something beyond Aristotle for which the latter should not be blamed. However, when Løkke describes Kierkegaard's criticism as being that "Aristotle's only fault in this regard is that he was born too late," such a qualification ignores

---

41. *JN* 3, 385–6 / *SKS* 19, 387–9 (Not13:11 and 19).
42. *JN* 3, 386 / *SKS* 19, 389 (Not13:19).
43. *JN* 3, 385 / *SKS* 19, 387 (Not13:11[a]).
44. *JN* 3, 385 / *SKS* 19, 387 (Not13:14).
45. *JN* 3, 386 / *SKS* 19, 388 (Not13:18).
46. *JN* 3, 387 / *SKS* 19, 389 (Not13:20).
47. *JN* 3, 393 / *SKS* 19, 396 (Not13:27).
48. *JN* 3, 387 / *SKS* 19, 389 (Not13:20).

that Kierkegaard here reveals how he envisions the relationship between Greek and Christian thought, namely that a philosopher like Aristotle may provide us with a valuable concept of virtue, formation, and its teleological structure, but that he "lacks the category needed to *complete* the movement."[49] Christian categories do not *oppose* or replace ancient categories, but indeed add something crucial to these categories and *transform* them in a profound way.

In a journal entry from 1949, Kierkegaard explains the difference in approach between a classical virtue ethical approach and his own Protestant view:

> Luther says, It is not good works that make a good man, but a good man who does good works, i.e., the man is what has become habitual, something more than all individual actions. And, indeed, according to Luther, one becomes a good man through faith. Thus, first comes faith. It is not through a virtuous life, good works, and the like, that one attains faith. No, it is faith that causes one truly to do good works.[50]

The main difference does not concern the formal description of virtue, for Aristotle too emphasizes that the good man is the one who has acquired good attitudes, which are more than individual actions. The point is that in Luther's Christian conception the source of the virtues differs: faith rather than what a human being himself accomplishes. This conviction is reflected in the famous remark in *The Sickness unto Death* that "the opposite of sin is not virtue, but faith,"[51] which is not intended as an entire disqualification of virtue, but as an acknowledgment of the difference in grammar and tradition between Antiquity and Christianity.[52] Kierkegaard indeed does not disqualify virtue, since in the quote about Luther he precisely refers to the crucial notion of the "habitual" in thinking the nature of good works following from faith. Notably, these works are not a matter of individual actions in response to what is received in faith, but by faith one is habituated in a particular way.

In sum, Kierkegaard concurs in many respects with Aristotle, but, as far as I can see, none of the Aristotelian concepts Kierkegaard mentions in his notes on the *Ethica Nicomachea* plays a decisive role in his works. There are only a few references to these concepts, such as the notion of the mean in *The Sickness unto Death*, which, however, he understands in a non-Aristotelian way as *ne quid nimis*, 'mediocrity,' and as such criticizes it.[53] Explicit references to Aristotelian concepts

---

49. *JN* 3, 387 / *SKS* 19, 389 (Not13:20) (emphasis mine).
50. *JN* 6, 373 / *SKS* 22, 369 (NB14:42).
51. Søren Kierkegaard, *The Sickness unto Death*, ed. and trans. Howard V. Hong and Edna H. Hong (Princeton: Princeton University Press, 1980), 82 / *SKS* 11, 196.
52. See Roberts, "Kierkegaard, Wittgenstein," 151.
53. Kierkegaard, *The Sickness unto Death*, 86-7 / *SKS* 11, 200. Cf. Rob Compaijen, "'Ne Quid Nimis' Kierkegaard en de deugd van de matigheid [Kierkegaard and the virtue of temperance]," *Tijdschrift voor Filosofie* 75/3 (2013), 455-85.

like *prohairesis, eudaimonia,* or *praxis* are absent, which does not imply that Kierkegaardian concepts like 'decision' or 'choice', 'eternal happiness' and 'existence' do not show commonality with these Aristotelian concepts. In conclusion, what we find in Kierkegaard's works are no more and no less than virtue ethical *traces*. I will illustrate this in my analysis of how some virtues and virtue ethical elements appear in his upbuilding works.

The Inverted Language of Perfection

Let us first observe the appearance of the word 'virtue' in the upbuilding discourses. It is not frequently used, but whenever Kierkegaard speaks about virtue it is in a positive way. The concept of virtue is appropriate to the purpose of upbuilding. In one of the discourses in 'The Gospel of Sufferings,' Kierkegaard speaks of "the road of virtue," which we cannot precisely locate but consists in "*how* it is walked."[54] Another discourse emphasizes: "It is true and always will be true that virtue is the highest sagacity"[55] and speaks of "the beautiful virtue of conciliatory spirit."[56] In the discourse 'Against Cowardliness' virtue is called a "sacred word."[57] Kierkegaard quotes Ludwig de Ponte saying that it is wretched "to have an abundance of intentions and a poverty of action, to be rich in truths and poor in virtues."[58] This utterance functions in an argument about the virtue of courage, meaning to act in the face of danger instead of avoiding action like a coward. In courageous action, the good is seen as "the goal," as "the truly great and noble," though it only takes on concrete meaning as something particular in relation to an individual's particularity.[59] Besides these clearly virtue ethical explications, Kierkegaard speaks of various vices that have to be conquered in the ethical task of becoming oneself, which includes overcoming oneself. In one's inner being there may be "the temptations of glory and temptations of fear and temptations of despondency, of pride and of defiance and of sensuality."[60] In these and several other instances, the language of virtue appears to be appropriate for the upbuilding task. Although virtue itself does not function as a core concept in the discourses but rather serves the upbuilding aim, Kierkegaard's use of it is in line with traditional virtue ethical language. Moreover, the upbuilding task itself can be regarded as a form of character cultivation in line with the virtue ethical tradition.

---

54. Søren Kierkegaard, *Upbuilding Discourses in Various Spirits*, ed. and trans. Howard V. Hong and Edna H. Hong (Princeton: Princeton University Press, 1993), 289 / *SKS* 8, 384.
55. Kierkegaard, *Eighteen Upbuilding Discourses*, 380 / *SKS* 5, 363.
56. Ibid., 380 / *SKS* 5, 364. Note that on the same page *duty* too functions in being dedicated to willing and practicing the good.
57. Ibid., 370 / *SKS* 5, 355.
58. Ibid., 350 / *SKS* 5, 337.
59. Ibid., 357–8 / *SKS* 5, 343–4.
60. Ibid., 320 / *SKS* 5, 311.

Another virtue ethical trace may be detected in how Kierkegaard applies the language of perfection (or excellence) in the discourses. Although this language is reminiscent of virtue ethics, one should be aware of the fact that perfection is not limited to the perfectibility of human nature in an Aristotelian sense, but is interpreted in the religious context of the relationship with God. In the discourse 'To Need God is a Human Being's Highest Perfection,' the self has to be turned away from the external in order to understand in profound self-knowledge that he is "not capable of anything at all."[61] Here, we find an example of what Kierkegaard calls "inverted dialectic" or "dialectic of reversal,"[62] which he employs in his upbuilding works to set out how in a Christian sense the positive is characterized by the negative and loss in the worldly sense is gain in a deeper sense, just as "the butterfly *gains* by losing the caterpillar's chrysalis."[63] Thus, perfection is paradoxically present in the acknowledgment of one's *in*capability. The highest a person can achieve is to become fully convinced that he himself is capable of nothing.[64] This 'annihilation' is the highest and most difficult thing of which a human being is capable. The self must "become nothing before God"[65] in order to rest in God "who is capable of all things."[66] Perfection includes the acknowledgment of one's "real self," and is interpreted as dependency on God. Kierkegaard wants to make his reader aware of the gift-like character of the self. In the end, it is not by one's own power that one becomes oneself, since one cannot create oneself.[67] In this sense, there is no true conception of the self without a corresponding conception of God.[68] The notion of 'annihilation before God' may sound rather extreme. I understand it as an attempt to emphasize the distinctive religious moment in which the self becomes aware of the fact that he is not able to realize himself by himself at all. To need God is precisely the real perfection of man.[69]

How is this theological perspective related to the philosophical-anthropological 'natural predisposition' we discovered previously? Interestingly, this discourse still presupposes that a person without the knowledge of dependency on God can still be a self with deep "roots in existence" and profound knowledge of its capabilities

---

61. Ibid., 319 / *SKS* 5, 310.
62. *JN* 4, 116, 292–3 / *SKS* 20, 194 and 292 (NB:194 and NB4:11).
63. Ibid., 292–3 / *SKS* 20, 292 (NB4:11).
64. Kierkegaard, *Eighteen Upbuilding Discourses*, 307 / *SKS* 5, 300.
65. Ibid., 369 / *SKS* 5, 354.
66. Ibid., 318 / *SKS* 5, 309–10. See also *The Sickness unto Death*, 71 / *SKS* 11, 185.
67. See Kierkegaard, *Either/Or II*, 215 / *SKS* 3, 207.
68. Kierkegaard, *Two Ages*, 63 / *SKS* 5, 437; *The Sickness unto Death*, 40, 79, 113–14 / *SKS* 11, 155, 193, 225–6; Søren Kierkegaard, *Practice in Christianity*, ed. and trans. Howard V. Hong and Edna H. Hong (Princeton: Princeton University Press, 1991), 160 / *SKS* 12, 163–4. See Vos, "Self," 23–8.
69. See Kierkegaard, *Eighteen Upbuilding Discourses*, 312 / *SKS* 5, 304: "If, however, this view, that to need God is man's highest perfection, makes it more difficult, it does this only because it wants to view man according to his perfection and bring him to view himself in this way."

and talents which he develops "as much as possible in conformity with his given situation."[70] These natural capabilities are acknowledged; however, from a religious upbuilding perspective, such self-knowledge and self-realization is incomplete and may even be a delusion, since one knows oneself in relation to "something else," that is, one's capabilities or talents, instead of knowing oneself in relation to oneself and to God. Hence, the emphasis is put on the inverted conception of perfection as incapability before God, who at the same time makes all things possible.[71]

Notwithstanding this radical transformation, the natural is thus somehow presupposed. That the former does not exclude the latter becomes also clear in the discourse 'To Preserve One's Soul in Patience': "Let us praise what is truly praiseworthy, the glory of human nature . . . let us pray that we might be granted the grace to perfect this glory gloriously in a more beautiful and more unambiguous way."[72] On the one hand, human nature is valued, in this case because of its remarkable strength in the moment of danger or sickness. On the other hand, grace is needed to endure spiritual dangers. Although Kierkegaard uses the language of perfection, he does not adopt a Thomistic model of *gratia perficit naturam*, since this model would be too harmonious, but an Augustinian-Protestant model of radical transformation.[73]

In conclusion, Kierkegaard does not avoid references to natural morality. In one of the Christian discourses of 'The Gospel of Sufferings,' he refers to the "moral order of things" that is "easily grasped" and "universally accepted."[74] All kinds of earthly ends or goods and related means belong to this order. On the other hand, Kierkegaard speaks of the "infinitely superior" end of "eternal happiness."[75] This good "beyond all measure"[76] is decisive, which points to a radical transformation of nature by grace, a "profound change" of what "natural man" wishes or desires.[77] I think that 'transformation' is indeed an adequate description of how Christian

---

70. Ibid., 313 / *SKS* 5, 304.
71. Ibid., 313–14 / *SKS* 5, 305–6.
72. Ibid., 182 / *SKS* 5, 186.
73. Note that Kierkegaard did not show any serious interest in Aquinas' theology, nor in his philosophy. In his time Hegelians were the only people that seemed to sympathize with Aquinas. As a consequence, in Kierkegaard's perception, Aquinas was under the verdict of being an 'objective thinker.' See Benjamín Olivares Bøgeskov, "Thomas Aquinas: Kierkegaard's View Based on Scattered and Uncertain Sources," in Jon Stewart (ed.), *Kierkegaard and the Patristic and Medieval Traditions* (Kierkegaard Research: Sources, Reception and Resources 4) (Farnham and Burlington: Ashgate, 2008), 183–206.
74. Kierkegaard, *Upbuilding Discourses in Various Spirits*, 312 / *SKS* 8, 404–5.
75. Ibid.
76. Ibid.
77. Ibid., 250 / *SKS* 8, 349. See also ibid., 141 / *SKS* 8, 239, where Kierkegaard distinguishes between an eternal understanding in which "the means and the end are one and the same," and the temporal, mundane understanding in which "the end is considered more important than the means."

conceptions of faith and grace relate to natural virtuousness in Kierkegaard's thought. Transformation implies more than just the perfection or completion of nature, but less than the complete replacement of nature by grace.

The Grammar of Virtue

In Kierkegaard's treatment of specific classical and Christian virtues in the upbuilding works we detect similar patterns. Courage, for instance, presupposes that there is some resistance. As in the traditional description, courage is the proper attitude for facing danger and for overcoming anxiety. Kierkegaard uses the metaphor of a rider on a horse. The rider is the courageous one that subdues what is base and shying in him.[78] On the other hand, courage is understood within a Christian framework of meaning, namely as an attitude that is related to suffering rather than to fighting. The notion that courage is marked by voluntary and avoidable suffering reflects a Christian conceptualization of this virtue. The prime example is not the warrior, as in the Greek conception, but the martyr who is willing to suffer for the good.

Another important virtue in the upbuilding works is patience. Whereas "courage goes freely into the suffering that could be avoided . . . patience makes itself free in the unavoidable suffering."[79] Patience perfectly illustrates what virtue is "a category of freedom" making literally "a virtue of necessity," of what is defined as necessity, namely, the unavoidable.[80] Again Kierkegaard distinguishes between a natural and a Christian conception of patience. In a natural sense patience is beneficial in order to achieve something in life—the expectation, the fulfillment is so to say bound up with temporality. In this case, patience is directed to an external condition, to something that is gained by virtue of patience. The goal is external and patience functions as a means to gain the desired goal.[81] Religiously speaking, patience is required in order to gain and preserve one's soul; moreover, gaining one's soul *is* precisely gaining patience. Finally, patience is defined in terms derived from the Christian tradition. Patience is not just about giving each person and each thing the time they need or waiting for the fulfillment of a wish, but real patience "leaves its expectancy up to God."[82]

From this perspective it is understandable that an Aristotelian virtue like magnanimity is not seen as a virtue, because of the assumption that it is important that you have much to give. Rather than magnanimity, it is the Christian virtue of mercy that comes to the fore.[83] For mercifulness consists not in *what* one gives but

---

78. Ibid., 118 / *SKS* 8, 119.
79. Ibid., 119 / *SKS* 8, 220.
80. Ibid., 119 / *SKS* 8, 221.
81. Kierkegaard, *Eighteen Upbuilding Discourses*, 161–2 / *SKS* 5, 161–2.
82. Ibid., 221 / *SKS* 5, 220.
83. Ibid., 362 / *SKS* 5, 348.

in *how* one gives.[84] Finally, the discourses show important traces of the trio: faith, hope, and love.[85] Although these virtues are not employed in a Thomistic way as infused gifts, they function in keeping a person in the decision to be with the good; as such they are treated by Kierkegaard, like Aquinas, as virtues of the will.

In this way, various virtues are described in language that reflects elements of a long and multifaceted history of virtue ethics, but without making very explicit references to this tradition. Kierkegaard does not "cobble together a compromise table of virtues comprising both classical and Christian entries," as Bruce Kirmmse rightly observes.[86] A coherent eudaimonistic and virtue ethical framework of cardinal and theological virtues is absent. Therefore, the proper approach is to examine whether an essential *grammar* of virtue is present in Kierkegaard's treatment of those qualities we usually call virtues.[87] Following Roberts's Wittgensteinian approach, 'grammar' in this case means "some kind of internal conceptual order that the virtue possesses."[88] 'Grammar' also points to the distinctiveness of a particular language of virtue and the virtues, bringing out "those distinctive concepts in terms of which an exemplifier of these virtues 'sees the world.'"[89] Kierkegaard's treatment of the virtues in the upbuilding works displays at least four grammatical rules that may be regarded as constitutive of the grammar of virtue he uses.

A first grammatical rule is that virtues are not simply described as dispositions to perform actions that follow ethical rules, but rather as *encompassing attitudes of a person* as moral character. In Kierkegaard's description of patience, for instance, a kind of circularity functions that is akin to Aristotelian descriptions and underscores that virtue is such an encompassing attribute characterizing a person. The development of a patient character and the development of the virtue of patience are one and the same. Patience is envisioned as a character trait:

> "It [the good seed] grows in patience." In these words, the condition and the conditioned are again inseparable, and these words themselves suggest duplexity and unity. The person who grows in patience does indeed grow and develop. What is it that grows in him? It is patience. Consequently, patience grows in him,

---

84. Søren Kierkegaard, *Works of Love*, ed. and trans. Howard V. Hong and Edna H. Hong (Princeton: Princeton University Press, 1995), 327 / SKS 9, 323.

85. For instance, Kierkegaard, *Upbuilding Discourses in Various Spirits*, 100–101 / SKS 8, 204–5.

86. Kirmmse, "Kierkegaard and MacIntyre," 198.

87. In her analysis of Kierkegaard's discourses and other works Sylvia Walsh, *Kierkegaard and Religion: Personality, Character, and Virtue* (Cambridge: Cambridge University Press, 2018), 74–107, highlights similar features to the ones I do, but she comes to the opposite conclusion: Kierkegaard "largely adopts a negative stance toward virtue in his authorship" (106). Walsh can only arrive at this conclusion because she limits herself to Kierkegaard's ambivalent use of the *language* of virtue and neglects the underlying *grammar* of virtue.

88. Roberts, "Kierkegaard, Wittgenstein," 154.

89. Ibid., 155.

and how does it grow? Through patience. If the person who gains himself will just be patient, he will surely grow in patience.[90]

A second grammatical rule concerns the *complex psychology of virtue*, in which one virtue is in one way or another *related to other virtues*. In order to be courageous, one has to be prudent as well. It may also require perseverance, hope, and other virtues. This aspect is traditionally expressed in the so-called doctrine of 'the unity of the virtues.' Kierkegaard does not offer an account of such doctrine, but in his treatment of the virtue of meekness or 'gentle courage' he demonstrates that this virtue is at least compounded of other virtues:

> There is courage (*Mod*), which bravely defies dangers; there is high-mindedness (*Høimod*), which proudly lifts itself above grievances; there is patience (*Taalmod*), which patiently bears sufferings; but the gentle courage (*sagte Mod*) that carries the heavy burden lightly is still the most wonderful compound.[91]

In "gentle courage" or meekness the strength of courage and the endurance of patience are combined. Moreover, the virtues find their unity in their directedness toward the good. The pursuit of this goal requires other virtues, for instance love, self-control, and resoluteness.[92] More importantly, those qualities that can be considered virtues are ordered according to the *ordo amoris*, the command to love the neighbor as rooted in the love of God (*genitivus subjectivus* and *objectivus*). The virtue of love is the virtue that unites all the virtues, as Kierkegaard demonstrates in *Works of Love*.

A third grammatical rule is that the virtues are qualities which not just are to the benefit of the one who acquires them but also *contribute to the common good*. Kierkegaard describes three theological virtues as "goods of the spirit," which are characterized as "communication" or "communion (*Meddelelse*),"[93] that is, as essentially directed to a *bonum commune*. By having faith, love, and hope one does not take away something from others, but acquires something in which all others can participate and benefit:

> The one who seeks or possesses these goods does not therefore do well only for himself but does a good deed for all; he is working for all, his striving to acquire these goods is in itself immediately enriching for others. . . . This is the humanity of spiritual goods in contrast to the inhumanity of earthly goods.

---

90. Kierkegaard, *Eighteen Upbuilding Discourses*, 169 / SKS 5, 168.
91. Kierkegaard, *Upbuilding Discourses in Various Spirits*, 239–40 / SKS 8, 339.
92. Kierkegaard, *Eighteen Upbuilding Discourses*, 361 / SKS 5, 347: "It is certainly true that the good, the truly great and noble, is different for different people, but resolution, which is the true acknowledgement, is still the same. This is a very upbuilding thought."
93. Søren Kierkegaard, *Christian Discourses*, ed. and trans. Howard V. Hong and Edna H. Hong (Princeton: Princeton University Press, 1997), 116–17 / SKS 10, 127–8.

What is humanity (*Menneskelighed*)? Human likeness (*menneskelige Lighed*) or equality (*Ligelighed*).⁹⁴

The communion of the spiritual goods extends to humanity as a whole, it is all-encompassing, as this is an essential part of the Christian faith. Kierkegaard describes these spiritual goods as what I have called 'non-competitive' and as opposed to "earthly goods" like wealth or possession, which are always competitive in nature, for what is mine is not yours and vice versa, even if I give some of it to you.

A fourth element belonging to the grammar of virtue is that a *broad range of human capacities* such as knowledge, emotion, will, and imagination are involved.⁹⁵ In my view, this applies to Kierkegaard's treatment of the virtuous qualities, although not without reserve: in the end the will seems to be decisive. In 'Purity of Heart' the relationship between feeling, knowledge, and will becomes clear. In relation to the good, the starting point is "immediate feeling," which is "the vital force" in which "is life," but this feeling "must 'be kept'" in order not to lead to double-mindedness. It must "not be left to its own devices, but . . . be entrusted to the power of something higher that keeps it."⁹⁶ It needs "knowledge of the good," which provides a clear understanding of one's situation. However, knowledge and understanding can also deteriorate into double-mindedness, as soon as they call you away from actuality for the sake of obtaining an observer's point of view. Knowledge or understanding must "penetrate time," in a "deliberation" that will not lead to knowledge from the "distance of eternity" but to a real understanding of oneself in actuality.⁹⁷ Therefore, ultimately the will is needed as the most decisive capacity in one's dedication to the good. It even seems that the will completely overrules knowledge and reason: it is double-mindedness to think that not "the will is the mover but that it itself is to be moved . . . and supported by reasons, considerations, the advice of others, experiences, and rules of conduct."⁹⁸ Yet, this is only one part of the story. As Roberts has pointed out, the upbuilding discourses repeatedly instruct the reader how to *think* about a particular situation. The key to gaining freedom from all kinds of care, for instance, is not to change one's physical or social circumstances, but to change one's way of thinking about a situation.⁹⁹ It is the "power of thought" that can take away "the thought of possession."¹⁰⁰ Consciousness, that is, a particular way of thinking, is a decisive condition in an

---

94. Kierkegaard, *Christian Discourses*, 117 / SKS 10, 128.
95. Roberts, "Kierkegaard, Wittgenstein," 154–5.
96. Kierkegaard, *Upbuilding Discourses in Various Spirits*, 72 / SKS 8, 179.
97. Ibid., 73–4 / SKS 8, 180–1.
98. Ibid., 75 / SKS 8, 182.
99. Roberts, "Existence, Emotion, and Virtue," 190–1.
100. Kierkegaard, *Christian Discourses*, 26 / SKS 10, 38.

upbuilding process in which one also comes to know oneself.[101] Thus, religious thoughts are the basis for a configuration of emotional responses. These patterns of response may become stable dispositions of the personality.

As a whole, the discourses show an ambiguous evaluation of thought and reason, including what we may call 'prudence' or 'practical wisdom' in the sense of *phronesis*. Reason can be used both positively and negatively. On the one hand, (religious) thought and understanding definitely have a positive function in how to respond to the vicissitudes of life. On the other hand, reason can operate as *Klogthed*, meaning 'shrewdness,' 'calculating smartness,' 'sophisticated reasoning,' which makes one avoid real dedication to the good and real resoluteness over against those vicissitudes. One must do away with all such calculation, shrewdness, and probability, in order to will the good only "because it is the good."[102] In this respect the Augustinian and Protestant emphasis on the will is indeed prevalent over the acknowledgment of human rational powers. Although Kierkegaard thus gives his own particular ordering of the human capacities, he does employ what I have called a 'grammar of virtue.'

Conclusion

In conclusion, in Kierkegaard's upbuilding discourses the virtues serve the aim of upbuilding or edification, that is, serve to make the reader aware of him- or herself as existing 'before God.' One element of the upbuilding aim is that virtues like patience, meekness, love, and courage become part of the reader's mind and attitude. At the same time, upbuilding or edification itself can be seen as aimed at the formation of the self before God, as a cultivation of character. The upbuilding is directed toward the *telos* of selfhood and as such functions in a teleologically structured anthropological view that in the end is theological in nature. As MacIntyre himself suggests in his later reflections, what separates him from Kierkegaard is not the lack of teleology, but the different conceptions of reason, deliberate choice, and the relationship between the natural and the theological. Whereas MacIntyre considers revelation to be essentially in line with ethical reason and the theological virtues to be *additional* to the natural virtues, in Kierkegaard's Augustinian-Protestant view the necessity of radical *transformation* is pivotal, yet not in such a way that the natural capacities of human nature are completely ruled

---

101. Kierkegaard, *Eighteen Upbuilding Discourses*, 314 / *SKS* 5, 306. See also the theme 'What Meaning and What Joy There Are in the *Thought* of Following Christ' (Kierkegaard, *Upbuilding Discourses in Various Spirits*, 218 / *SKS* 8, 320, italics mine) and the title '*Thoughts* that Wound from Behind—for Upbuilding' (Kierkegaard, *Christian Discourses*, 161 / *SKS* 10, 169, italics mine).

102. Kierkegaard, *Eighteen Upbuilding Discourses*, 380 / *SKS* 5, 364.

out. On this point Kierkegaard is firmly rooted in Lutheranism and even shows an affinity with Calvin.[103]

Although my analysis confirms that Kierkegaard's conception of the will and his overall moral psychology differ from Aristotle's and Aquinas', Kierkegaard's depictions of virtue and the virtues in the upbuilding discourses demonstrate that virtue ethics in a broader sense is present. In several respects, Kierkegaard's treatment of the virtues is akin to both classical and Christian virtue ethical accounts. We can detect a 'grammar of virtue' which underlines personal character formation, interrelatedness of the virtues, relatedness to the common good, and the functions of will, emotion, and reason.

Does this all make Kierkegaard into a "virtue ethicist," as Roberts and others claim? As said, the answer depends on how virtue ethics is defined. Following the grammatical approach as proposed in the Introduction of this book, we can say that, in the first place, Kierkegaard's anthropology entails a teleological view of human nature, albeit not primarily defined in eudaimonistic terms but rather in (modern) terms of becoming oneself. Moreover, his theological understanding of ethics does not rule out a concept of natural morality which is the ground of moral knowledge. Finally, he explicitly and implicitly, though not exclusively, refers to the virtues in outlining the (Christian) moral life. On the basis of these 'grammatical' criteria, Kierkegaard could be regarded as a virtue ethicist. However, in the sense of a preeminent representative of the ethical theory that most consider to be virtue ethics par excellence, that is, Aristotelianism and Thomism, Kierkegaard cannot be regarded as a virtue ethicist. His explicit references to this particular tradition and his explorations of virtue and the virtues are too limited for such a characterization. In this respect it is more appropriate to say that there are clearly *virtue ethical traces* in his work and that his thought, rather than being a form of virtue ethics (as, for example, this is the case in Reformed scholasticism), fruitfully contributes to an actual virtue ethics.

This can be explained from Kierkegaard's primary ethical aim. His central aim is not to offer an ethics or a fully fledged ethical theory, but to put to the fore the ethical meaning of what we may call 'the first-person perspective.' Kierkegaard's ethical project, so to say, can be regarded as shifting back the focus from ethical theory or particular moral issues to the irreducible moral individuality. It is concerned with what it means to be a human being, to be a responsible individual agent. Kierkegaard focuses on the precondition of ethics, on ethical subjectivity, and uses various ethical concepts, such as command, virtue, the good, duty, and natural morality, that help him to meet this aim. In this way, Kierkegaard adopts in his works both modern deontological principles, as well as virtue ethical and teleological concepts, without coinciding entirely with one of these approaches.

---

103. Though Calvin's direct influence on Kierkegaard is rather limited, as is demonstrated by David Yoon-Jung Kim, "Kierkegaard and the Question of the Law's Third Use," in Jon Stewart (ed.), *Kierkegaard and the Renaissance and Modern Traditions* (Kierkegaard Research: Sources, Reception and Resources 5.2) (Farnham: Ashgate, 2009), 81–110.

On the other hand, this 'first-person perspective' and focus on ethical subjectivity brings him close to the central concern of Neo-Aristotelian virtue ethics, namely its focus on the human agent as the bearer of moral qualities rather than on right moral actions or universal ethical principles.

There is one more aspect in Kierkegaard's work which is relevant to thinking through virtue ethics from a Protestant theological perspective: his account of the imitation of Christ as the ultimate and paradoxical expression of becoming a true self, that is, an other-directed, loving self, which is the subject of the next chapter.

Chapter 6

PUTTING ON CHRIST

Throughout the history of virtue ethics, the meaning of prime exemplars in the cultivation of the virtues has been pivotal. Moral exemplarity is not only an indispensable part of philosophical virtue ethics extending from Aristotle's *Nicomachean Ethics* to the recent work of Linda Zagzebski,[1] but also part of a long theological virtue ethical tradition, in which the exemplarity of Christ and the saints has been emphasized. The aim is to acquire the virtues of the exemplar by emulation or zeal (ζῆλος), as the desire and the attempt to acquire the exemplary virtues of the exemplar which one does not yet possess.[2] It is this important aspect of virtue ethics to which we turn in this chapter.

From the outset one could ask, however, whether acquiring the virtues through imitation of the examples of Christ and the saints is ever really possible. It is telling that historically exceptional exemplars like saints and martyrs, though portrayed as exemplary, actually did not function as examples for ordinary people. In a historical survey Robert Bartlett notes that "despite this ever-repeated invocation of the exemplary function of hagiography, in practice saints were more often seen as powerful patrons to be prayed to rather than models to be emulated, as wonderworkers rather than as examples."[3] In fact, the meaning of the saints as moral models was very limited—only the saints took the saints as models. A huge distance remained between the sanctity of the saints and the everyday life of ordinary people. In Protestantism the saints even lost their vicarious role and although in theory they were still considered as valuable moral exemplars, in practice their role seems to be almost completely diminished. Others argue that emulating the saints as models is not desirable at all.[4]

---

1. See, for instance, *EN* 1107a2; Linda Zagzebski, *Exemplarist Moral Theory* (Oxford: Oxford University Press, 2017).

2. Aristotle, *Retorica* 1388a32, describes ζῆλος as a painful though noble emotion about lacking the good you admire in exemplary exemplars, which motivates to acquire the same good. Emulation is sharply distinguished from jealousy or envy (φθόνος), which is the desire to take the good away from the other.

3. Robert Bartlett, *Why Can the Dead Do Such Great Things? Saints and Worshippers from the Martyrs to the Reformation* (Princeton: Princeton University Press, 2013), 511.

4. One of the most strong defenses of the claim against saints as exemplars is Susan Wolf's classic article "Moral Saints," *The Journal of Philosophy* 79/8 (1982), 419–39. I will

Furthermore, imitation of a model has been criticized as non-authentic behavior or hypocrisy. For 'putting on virtue' assumes that one 'acts the part' of the person one wants to become, pretending to live a life one actually does not really live. Therefore, in modernity, authenticity is emphasized over imitation of exemplars, as Jennifer Herdt observes in her seminal study *Putting on Virtue*. She traces this modern view back to early Protestantism and to Martin Luther in particular. Luther considered the attempt to act virtuously by imitation of saints as hypocritical, not because it is a betrayal of the authentic self but because acquiring virtue falsely assumes that human beings are capable of moral agency by their own efforts. Instead, we should rely solely on God's grace and be transformed by him from within.[5]

Standing in this tradition, several Protestant thinkers nevertheless emphasized the importance of discipleship, *Nachfolge* or *imitatio Christi*, thereby at least suggesting that following Christ as an exemplar in one way or another is possible. To give but a few examples, although Christ should not be reduced to a mere exemplar, the very notion of following Christ is not absent in Luther's work. Calvin, more boldly, states that "Christ . . . is set before us as a model (*exemplum*), the image (*forma*) of which our lives should express."[6] Centuries later, Kierkegaard reemphasizes the imitation of Christ as a critique of established Christianity that takes divine grace in vain. Christ is considered the paradigm or exemplar (*Paradigmet, Forbilledet*) that manifests the ideal Christian existence and requires imitation.[7] Similarly, Bonhoeffer emphasizes the lowliness of Christ as paradigm to be followed as an antidote to cheap grace,[8] but also speaks of the conformation (*Gleichgestalltung*) to the form and image of Christ.[9] One of the most important recent advocates of the exemplary meaning of Christ is Hauerwas, who considers *imitatio Christi* the way to "learn to locate our lives within God's life, within the journey that comprises his kingdom."[10] Thus, if the notion of imitation of exemplars is in any case present in Protestantism, couldn't it be found in the notion of following Christ as the paradigm and exemplar of the Christian life?

However, if Christ may function in this way as exemplar to be imitated, the same problem as with the saints reappears. For what Christ seems to represent is *not* ordinary life, but an exceptional life marked by self-sacrifice, neighborly love, and holiness. How could he actually become an exemplar to be imitated by ordinary people? Hence Tom Wright remarks in his popular book *Virtue*

elaborate on the exemplary meaning of the saints in Chapter 8.

5. Herdt, *Putting on Virtue*, Ch. 6.
6. *Inst.* 4.6.3 (trans. Henry Beveridge).
7. Kierkegaard, *Practice in Christianity*, 233–57 / *SKS* 12, 7–253.
8. Dietrich Bonhoeffer, *Discipleship* (Dietrich Bonhoeffer Works 4) (Minneapolis: Fortress Press, 2001) / *DBW* 4.
9. Dietrich Bonhoeffer, *Ethics* (Dietrich Bonhoeffer Works 6) (Minneapolis: Fortress Press, 2001), 93 / *DBW* 6, 80.
10. Stanley Hauerwas, *The Peaceable Kingdom: A Primer in Christian Ethics* (Notre Dame: University of Notre Dame Press, [1983] 1986), 75.

Reborn that holding up Jesus as an example of how to live a moral life, "with his astonishing blend of wisdom, gentleness, shrewdness, dry humor, patience with blundering followers, courage in confronting evil, self-control in innumerable situations of temptation,"[11] is facing us with an ideal completely beyond our reach. This points to the age-old question of how the gap between Christ's exceptionality and everyday life can be bridged when we take him as moral exemplar. How can ordinary people ever succeed in 'applying' his exemplarity in everyday life? Should one not abandon the whole idea of imitation of Christ as hypocrisy and blameworthy human effort?

In trying to find an answer to these questions, in this chapter I investigate what kind of exemplarity may be implied in a Protestant understanding of *imitatio*, discipleship, or following Christ—I use these terms as interchangeable though each term may include different nuances. I pretend neither to provide an all-encompassing account of such a Protestant view, nor that it is the only possible Protestant account of *imitatio Christi*, but I draw important insights from at least some pivotal Protestant theologians from the Reformation until our time—Luther, Calvin, Kierkegaard, and Bonhoeffer, in particular. First, I will argue that from a Protestant view the starting point cannot be to take up immediately the task of imitation of Christ as a human effort to bridge the gap between the exceptional exemplar and the follower. Rather, it belongs to the heart of the Reformation that we are fundamentally in need of redemption and re-direction, the central aim of Luther's doctrine of justification, which, however, also has a distinctive ethical meaning. Next I will argue that this view does not exclude human agency. I will point to new approaches of Luther and Calvin in which the gift of grace is understood in terms of a double participation in Christ: a receptive grace and an active partaking. In a third section it will be argued that from this perspective following Christ is primarily to be understood as becoming part of the new life of Christ, which is related to ordinary life. As I will demonstrate in the final sections, following Kierkegaard and Bonhoeffer, imitation is not a matter of emulating an extraordinary exemplar, but a striving that is rooted in Christ's lowliness, which causes imitation to be in principle a possibility for each individual. The task is not to copy the exemplar but to resemble him in one's own particular life. In this sense, imitation is a putting on of Christ that is not hypocrisy but an authentic re-presentation in which the self 'realizes itself.'

The Need for Other-Directedness

The verdict on imitation as a human effort that is in fact hypocrisy is deeply rooted in the theology of the Reformation. Herdt analyzes that in Luther's view we can neither become righteous before God nor become participants in divine

---

11. Tom Wright, *Virtue Reborn* (London: Society for Promoting Christian Knowledge, 2010), 109.

activity through imitating Christ. Rather than trying to foster virtue by actively practicing neighborly love, the starting point should be radical passivity, in which we relinquish any reliance on our own activity and put our trust solely in God.[12] Imitating Christ's charity and humility will lead to hypocrisy and false piety, just as much as going on pilgrimages, venerating saints' relics, exercising rote prayer, and buying indulgences.[13] As a consequence, Luther seems to reject any notion of Christ as external exemplar. For to hold up Christ as exemplar is to "imagine Christ as an innocent and private person who is holy and righteous only for Himself."[14] What restores to us the image of God is not our successful imitation of Christ, but a marriage that unities otherwise alienated parties. Through faith the soul and Christ are married and exchange attributes: Christ takes human sin and bears God's wrath, while the believing soul can glory in whatever Christ has as though it were its own. This 'marriage' is not a union of like with like, of copy assimilating with original, but a union in which God accepts us in our complete difference from him, not just in that we are finite creatures (as in Aquinas' view), but in that we are sinful.

In her evaluation Herdt criticizes what she calls Luther's "hyper-Augustinianism." Luther's insistence that prideful human agency is to be displaced by the indwelling Christ who is to renew the sinner from inside out is not understandable in terms of gradual human transformation and habituation. "How is a passive, displaced agency to be gradually transformed? How can *we* be habituated except through *our own* action? What we find in Luther is an exaggerated insistence on passivity arising out of a competitive understanding of human and divine agency."[15]

Although Herdt acknowledges that in principle Calvin could restore the trust in habituation since he more than Luther emphasizes the gradual process of sanctification and the possibility of the transformation of character through action, in her view, he shares with Luther an underlying instability. For both want the believer to rely solely on what Christ has accomplished for us *extra nos*, "but they cannot be confident that this external work of Christ is indeed *for us* apart from some consciousness on our part."[16] Whereas Luther's concern is to avoid deceptive external works, Calvin's concern is that external appearances properly show forth inner faith, since given the prominence of the doctrine of predestination the pertinent question becomes whether one belongs to the elect or not. This makes the believer permanently look for a sign of the works of God within the self in order to become sure about his or her election.

In my view, Herdt's analysis of the Reformers' theology is profound but one-sided. I propose a different reading which is surprisingly interesting with regard to

---

12. Herdt, *Putting on Virtue*, 174.
13. *LW* 31, 345 / *WA* 7, 50.
14. *LW* 26, 287 / *WA* 40.1, 448: "non debemus ergo fingere Christum innocentem et privatam personam . . . quae pro se tantum sit sancta et iusta"; Herdt, *Putting on Virtue*, 177.
15. Herdt, *Putting on Virtue*, 188.
16. Ibid., 199.

the understanding and development of any virtue ethics. Herdt puts all emphasis on the competing relation between divine and human agency. In doing so she rightly points to Luther's and Calvin's verdict on human agency in justification, but ignores that their criticism of human self-sufficient virtuousness and habituation reaches beyond the point of valuing divine over human agency. To be sure, Luther and Calvin criticize the virtues acquired by one's own effort as worthless *coram Deo*. In Luther's view, in the end such virtues cover vices and people who only practice outward virtues are hypocrites,[17] and according to Calvin, virtuousness of natural man does not make man righteous before God, as we have seen in Chapter 3.[18] True virtues are not an intrinsic part of human beings and do not exist as *habitus* of human nature, but are divine gifts.

The question is: Why would it be so important to emphasize this need for God's grace from the start, which is so profound in Luther's and Calvin's thought? My answer is that it is not only because as sinful beings we are fundamentally in need of a merciful God and dependent on justification *extra nos*, as Herdt rightly emphasizes, but also because it has a fundamentally ethical meaning in line with Augustine: God's redemptive acting is the only way to free the self from natural self-centeredness or self-serving love. What is at stake here is beyond a simple valuation of divine over human agency, it is about the need of radically opening up the self, as closed in itself (*incurvatus in se*), by God as the 'transcendent other.' In Luther's *Large Catechism*, the ongoing argument is that God offers not only his grace as justification, but also himself as the good gift of pure love to the believer in which the believer comes to participate.[19] It is in the concrete encounter with God who reveals himself as self-giving love that we become partakers of his unselfish love, bringing this love into existence in our lives.[20] In a double movement, the believer is not only *freed from* the need to achieve virtue that will merit salvation

---

17. For example, *LW* 25, 151 / *WA* 56, 171.

18. *Inst.* 2.3.4. Similarly, in Luther's works we find serious criticism of virtuous aspirations of human nature *coram Deo*. Since a gradual development from a sinful into a virtuous human being is impossible, and a Christian rather has to benefit from a continuous return to grace, Luther calls almost the whole of Aristotle's *Ethica* the worst enemy of grace (*pessima est gratiae inimica*, *WA* 1, 226). On the other hand, Luther gives the virtues their place within the larger context in which divine grace is preeminent. Moreover—and again parallel to Calvin—*in civil life* one does become a doer on the basis of good deeds, "just as one becomes a lutenist by often playing the lute, as Aristotle says" (*WA* 40.1, 401 / *LW* 26, 256), which implies that virtues as traits of character can be developed over time through habitual behavior. Such a philosophical perspective is justified, but has to be distinguished from the theological. See Meilaender, *Theory and Practice of Virtue*, 100–26.

19. Martin Luther, "Large Catechism," in *The Book of Concord*, ed. T. G. Tappert (Philadelphia: Fortress Press, 1959), 357–462 / *WA* 30.1, 125–7.

20. Simo Peura, "What God Gives Man Receives: Luther on Salvation," in Carl E. Braaten and Robert W. Jenson (eds.), *Union with Christ: The New Finnish Interpretation of Luther* (Grand Rapids: Eerdmans, 1998), 76–95. Note that Luther presupposes that unselfish love is

and exercises of habituation in virtue that could demonstrate human righteousness, but also *freed to* "'put on' his neighbor and so to conduct himself toward him as if he himself were in the other's place."[21] As a consequence, good deeds are no longer self-directed (including justification of the self before God) but unselfish and other-centered. Luther even says that "love is the highest virtue (*charitas summa virtus est*)."[22]

In sum, since no human being really wants God's will naturally, to receive virtue as gift means first of all to be *dispossessed* from natural inclinations that are basically self-directed. Secondly, this self-dispossession makes it possible to become radically *open* to the other human being, including the enemy. From this Protestant view a particular interpretation of the virtues is possible that is relevant to the development of virtue ethics in general. Virtues are to be understood not as first person virtues (perfection of the natural in the self), but as second person or interpersonal virtues (unselfishly directed to the other), enabling the self "to relate to the other person precisely because 'my' self-will is no longer obstructing 'my' perception of the other person."[23]

In my view, this interpretation reflects Paul's description of the virtues as "fruit of the Spirit" (Gal. 5:22). The fruit of the Spirit corresponds to a crucifixion of the flesh with its passions and desires (Gal. 5:24) and its excesses (Gal. 5:19-21), on the one hand, and consists in particular in other-directed virtues such as love, peace, goodness, and gentleness, on the other. Living in the Spirit means walking in the Spirit, and this means to serve the other. Therefore, the text ends in the ethical exhortation not to become conceited, provoking one another or envying one another (Gal. 5:26). The work of the Spirit is that we are transformed from inside out into the image of Christ, in order to become really *free* to God and the other. One is freed *from* securing one's own existential ground and freed *to* receive the good life as a true gift, which makes it possible to share it as a common good and to give to others, as the true destination of human life.[24]

Participation as Receptivity and Activity

In a next step, I want to demonstrate that the Reformers' use of the concepts of 'Christ present in faith' and 'participation' does not exclude but includes human

---

already written as natural law in the hearts of all human beings, asking to trust in God alone as the source of all goodness. I leave this aspect out of my argument.
21. *LW* 31, 371 / *WA* 7, 69.
22. *LW* 27, 58 / *WA* 40.2, 72.
23. Jochen Smidt, "Critical Virtue Ethics," *Religious Inquiries* 3/5 (2014), 40.
24. This paragraph is taken from Pieter Vos, "Setting Free and Bringing to Purpose: The Work of the Spirit in Cultivating the Virtues," in Gijsbert van den Brink, Eveline van Staalduine-Sulman, and Maarten Wisse (eds.), *The Spirit Is Moving: New Pathways in Pneumatology* (Leiden and Boston: Brill, 2019), 303.

activity. Although Herdt refers to new interpretations of Luther by Mannermaa and others in terms of Christ not only offering forgiveness but also being present in the believer,[25] she does not acknowledge that this interpretation implies a different relation between divine and human agency.[26] In my view, participation in Christ includes not only a competitive but also a *non*-competitive account of divine and human agency that is beyond the question whether the effected renewal is Christ's or one's own. The declared righteousness and the effected renewal *are not* one's own since they are only present in union with Christ, but at the same time they *are* one's own since not only is Christ's righteousness declared *to* the believer but also is Christ really present *in* the believer. The point is that the person of the believer can no longer be seen as separated from the person of Christ.[27] Yet this does not exclude the agency of the believer, as Luther states for instance in his *Lectures on the Galatians*: "Christians do not become righteous by doing righteous works, but once they have been justified by faith in Christ, they do righteous works."[28]

25. Especially what is known as 'the Finnish Luther research,' for example, Tuomo Mannermaa, *Christ Present in Faith: Luther's View of Justification*, ed. Kirsi Stjerna (Minneapolis: Fortress, 2005); Braaten and Jenson, *Union with Christ*; Herdt, *Putting on Virtue*, 390.

26. This is not to say that Herdt's account is without nuance on this point, but in the end "either Luther stresses that all Christian activity is in fact the activity of the indwelling Christ, to which the human person is passive. Or he emphasizes human activity at the expense of slipping back into the contractual language of the via moderna" (*Putting on Virtue*, 186).

27. The core of the argument of the Finnish Luther school is that Christ's presence in the believer does not leave God outward to the person but concerns a "communion of being between God and man" or a "communication of attributes" (Mannermaa, "Justification and *Theosis* in Lutheran-Orthodox Perspective," in Braaten and Jenson, *Union with Christ*, 27, 32). I take this as a more promising interpretation than that of Meilaender, who continues interpreting Luther in terms of a "tension between a virtue which we can claim as our possession . . . and a virtue which must be continually reestablished by divine grace" (*Theory and Practice of Virtue*, 122). Herdt, *Putting on Virtue*, 188, refers to Mannermaa's conclusion that "according to Luther, the modus of the existence of a Christian is always *passio* (*Gewirktwerden*): a person is neither inwardly nor outwardly active; one experiences only what God affects in oneself" (39), but this quote is part of a description of the "nihilizing work" of the agony of the Cross, through which one must pass and which, "of course, does not imply a total annihilation. It refers only to the destruction of the person's constant effort to make himself god and to justify himself" (ibid.). And Simo Peura, "Christ as Favor and Gift," in *Union with Christ*, 44, explicitly speaks of human agency: "The good deeds of the Christian are good 'fruits' provided by gift [the gift of Christ constituting the Christian's internal good]."

28. *LW* 26, 256 / *WA* 40.1, 402.

Elsewhere Luther speaks of cooperation with Christ's justice in which we follow the example of Christ and become conformed to his image.[29]

With regard to Calvin, similar new interpretations in the so-called 'new approach to Calvin' clarify how participation is a central aspect of his theology emerging from a soteriology that affirms union of God and humanity in creation and redemption.[30] In this approach the emphasis on redemption is related to living a life of active gratitude in union with Christ. As J. Todd Billings has demonstrated, central to Calvin's account of the moral life is the *duplex gratia*: in the first grace of God's justification believers participate by imputation in Christ's righteousness, in the second grace of sanctification the believers actually become partakers in Christ's righteousness and begin "the slow process of transformation."[31] This not only includes human agency, but also opens up the possibilities of fostering a Christ-like character in imitation and cultivating pertinent virtues.

Another way to understand the relation between divine agency and human agency in the cultivation of the virtues is in terms of condition and action respectively. This is exemplarily expressed in the biblical exhortation "be fervent in spirit" (Rom. 12:11), which most likely refers to the Holy Spirit. Although we cannot guarantee the flame of the Spirit's presence, and although we can only seek the Spirit and ask him to intervene (receptivity), this does not mean that there is nothing to do (activity). In one and the same verse, it is stated that our action is "to serve the Lord." This suggests that we can develop the virtues of love, hope, joy, patience, hospitality, and peace (Rom. 12:9-18) by our engagement in intentional, regular acts of service. Paul calls us to practice all kinds of acts that belong to these virtues and to cultivate them, like abhorring evil, distributing to the needs of others, blessing one's persecutors, not repaying evil by evil, feeding who is hungry, even the enemy, and many other things. As David Horner and David Turner say: "In service we use our abilities and resources to become the hands and feet of Christ to promote the good of others." At the same time, "It is the fervency of the Spirit, as the prior condition, that gives these practical acts of service their meaning and energy."[32]

To summarize the argument so far, in Luther's and Calvin's theologies of grace, human agency is both excluded and included. Dispossession and the breakdown of human agency is needed because justification is solely based upon divine grace in Christ and, as I interpret it from an ethical perspective, because human self-directedness needs to be broken down in order to become really open to the other as neighbor. On the other hand, human agency is included because the

---

29. For example, Luther, "Sermo de duplici iustitia," in Martin Luther, *Studienausgabe*, Vol. 1 (Berlin: Evangelische Verlagsanstalt, 1979), 223–4.

30. In particular Billings, *Calvin, Participation, and the Gift*.

31. Ibid., 107.

32. David Horner and David Turner, "Zeal," in Michael W. Austin and R. Douglas Geivett (eds.), *Being Good: Christian Virtues for Everyday Life* (Grand Rapids: Eerdmans, 2012), 101. This paragraph is taken from Vos, "Setting Free and Bringing to Purpose," 304.

human being partakes fully in the new life which, though not yet fully realized, is manifesting itself already in the old life by virtue of the life-giving Spirit of Christ. In conclusion, participation can be understood as a particular way of relating to Christ as exceptional exemplar, namely, as characterized by a dialectics of receptivity and activity. On the one hand, receiving the exceptional redeemer as a gift imputed to the believer is a form of participation in which the receiver does not contribute but nevertheless shares in the goodness of the one who gives. On the other hand, participation also includes active partaking: in union with Christ the believer is empowered to live a life of active gratitude in daily life.

What does this all mean for understanding Christ as moral exemplar? The implication of the line of thought so far is that Christ as exemplar to be followed is to be seen as part of the broader Christological and soteriological framework. Imitation of Christ is only valuable as part of the overarching concept of participation and union with Christ. An important reason is that Christ should not be *reduced* to a mere example to be followed, which would make Christ only an external model or an ideal among others. A second reason is that it is not primarily the follower that has to bridge the distance to Christ as a high moral ideal, but God who not only redeems the sinner but also gives himself as a gift. In this line of thought Bonhoeffer states: "Jesus calls to discipleship, not as a teacher and a role model, but as the Christ, the Son of God."[33] Within the framework of participation in Christ, imitation of Christ as exemplar receives its proper place, which is not a limited place. In the view of the Reformers, imitation is an intrinsic part of the union with Christ. In his commentary on 1 Jn 2:6, Calvin relates the union with Christ strongly to imitation and vice versa: John "calls us also to Christ, to imitate Him (*ut eius simus imitatores*). Yet he does not simply exhort us to the imitation of Christ, but, from the union we have with Him, proves we should be like Him. He says that a likeness (*similitudo*) in life and actions will prove that we abide in Christ."[34] Union with Christ includes imitation of Christ, which includes human agency.

Imitation of Christ in Ordinary Life

In the Protestant theological approach presented so far, imitation of Christ does not consist in the human effort to emulate Christ as moral ideal, but is the active side of participation in the new life as already established by Christ. In this section

---

33. Bonhoeffer, *Discipleship*, 57 / *DBW* 4, 45.

34. John Calvin, *The Gospel according to St. John 11-21 and the First Epistle of John* (Calvin's Commentaries 5) (Grand Rapids: Eerdmans [1959] 1995), 247. Jimmy Agan, "Departing from—and Recovering—Tradition: John Calvin and the Imitation of Christ," *Journal of the Evangelical Theological Society* 56/4 (2013), 801–14, lists many more instances in Calvin's works to make this point.

I will demonstrate that this starting point makes it possible to relate the imitation of Christ to ordinary life. Again I depart from Luther.

Luther does not think of *imitatio Christi* in the way St. Francis of Assisi or Thomas a Kempis do. Francis became a mendicant monk and tried to live in poverty, following Christ's commandment to the young man in Mt. 19:21 literally: "If you would be perfect, go, sell what you possess and give it to the poor, and you will have treasure in heaven; and come, follow me." This command asks for total obedience and radical discipleship. Yet, according to Luther, Francis and his brothers did not understand Christ's command properly.[35] From our perspective it may be hard to understand Luther's severe criticism of Franciscan poverty, since we tend to consider St. Francis as prime example of saintliness, but Luther's argument is that, in fact, Francis did not really leave everything, since he still had to live and he could even live securely on the goods of others. As Oswald Bayer explains Luther's view, we cannot exist without having, that is, without having space, air, a place, a body, and time. Therefore, the question is what it means to follow Christ in space and time, being a Christian in the world.

Importantly, Luther does not oppose evangelical discipleship against Pauline household duties (*Haustafeln*, Col. 3:18–4:1; Eph. 5:21–6:9) and wants to avoid the dilemma of homeless discipleship or a home without discipleship. His solution consists of differentiating obedience to the first table of the Decalogue ("I am the Lord your God. You shall have no other gods before me") from obedience to the second table.

> In the call to discipleship Christ speaks of leaving and selling everything for the sake of the first table, the public profession of faith. . . . The things that you rightfully have and possess for this life according to the second table are to be joyfully renounced for the sake of the first table, that is, for the sake of eternal life. However, outside of the matter of the first table and the profession of God all things are to be sought after, preserved, defended and administered. For we are required to obey the second table, that is, to care for the body and this life according to the divine and natural right, nurturing, protecting and managing it.[36]

In this way Luther develops an understanding of discipleship as a difficult dialectic of letting go of everything and keeping everything. Discipleship is not opposed to ordinary life, but has to take place in ordinary life. Luther reinterprets the three

---

35. As Luther states in an interesting series of theses prepared for a disputation which took place at the university of Wittenberg on May 9, 1539, entitled *Die Zirkulardisputation über das Recht des Widerstands gegen den Kaiser (Matth. 19:21) (De tribus hierarchiis: ecclesiastica, politica, oeconomica et quod Papa sub nulla istarum sit, sed omnium publicus hostis*, WA 39.2, 34–91). I follow Oswald Bayer's illuminating reading of this treatise in his *Freedom in Response: Lutheran Ethics: Sources and Controversies*, trans. Jeffrey F. Cayzer (Oxford: Oxford University Press, 2007), 119–37.

36. WA 39.2, 40, trans. Bayer, *Freedom in Response*, 133.

classical monastic vows of poverty, chastity, and obedience as to be lived out in the spheres of ordinary life, in the spheres of property and work; sexuality and family; and social and political justice, respectively.[37]

Following this view of discipleship as applied to 'the household of the world,' I think two important conclusions can be drawn about the nature of the imitation of Christ. A first implication of this view is that Christ is to be followed in the paradoxical sense of irrevocably becoming part of the new life he establishes and to perform this in ordinary life, which expresses itself in an ethics of neighborly love. Jesus's call to follow him is a call to discover in the present time the features of the new life pointing forward to the coming kingdom by sharing already in his life. As Bonhoeffer states, following Christ is not an "interesting but potentially revocable lifestyle" or a "supplement, completion, or perfection" of one's past,[38] but it brings the follower in an irrevocable situation. Bonhoeffer shows how in the Gospels this irrevocability and the need to obey in discipleship are ethical in nature, consisting of neighborly love.[39] Discipleship includes an indispensable ethical responsibility to discover what the new order means in the entanglements of life with all its relationships. Imitation of Christ means to be for others what Christ is for us. As Luther says, each should become as it were a Christ to the other.[40]

Secondly, this view implies that following Christ does not mean to copy his deeds literally. We are not to follow literally what he did in terms of specific deeds—this would make him an idol or a deadly principle—but to follow his obedient love in our own situations as Christ obediently loved in his.[41] Therefore, Kierkegaard distinguishes imitation from copying Christ. He considers it a mistake in the Middle Ages that asceticism was taken as the absolute *telos* and that people copied (*copierede*)—for instance in the conformity sought in the appearance of the stigmata—Christ rather than imitated (*efterfulgte*) him.[42] Imitation should not become a perverted mimicking (*Efterabelse*).[43] Similarly, in his book *Nachfolge* Bonhoeffer nowhere adopts the language of copying Christ's deeds. In *Ethics* he too writes that becoming like Christ is not a form of mimicking, a repeating of his form, but that Christ's form manifests itself in people.[44] This is also why Wright, as quoted in the introduction, denies that all we need is the good example of Jesus. For Jesus "doesn't go about saying, 'This is how it's done; copy me.' He says, 'God's kingdom is coming; take up your cross and follow me.'" We indeed encounter Jesus's humility and other virtues. "But these are not 'examples of how to do it.'

---

37. Bayer, *Freedom in Response*, 125–6.
38. Bonhoeffer, *Discipleship*, 73 / DBW 4, 64.
39. Bonhoeffer, *Discipleship*, 76 / DBW 4, 67.
40. LW 31, 367 / WA 7, 66.
41. James Gustafson, *Christ and the Moral Life* (Louisville: John Knox, [1968] 2009), 152–3.
42. JN 4, 227 / SKS 20, 227 (NB2:227) and JN 8, 184 / SKS 24, 186 (N22:151).
43. JN 8, 175 / SKS 24, 178 (NB22:144).
44. Bonhoeffer, *Ethics*, 96 / DBW 6, 83.

They are indications that a new way of being human has been launched upon the world."[45] In the words of Gene Outka, we can only "follow at a distance."[46]

In this sense, Jesus can be perceived as exemplar to be followed, but because he is still heterogeneous to ordinary human beings—as Calvin notes, "the Lord did many things which he did not intend as examples for us"[47]—we should not copy him, but follow him in neighborly love. As Calvin writes in his commentary on 2 Cor. 8:9: "Having mentioned love he [Paul] now refers to Christ as the perfect and unique pattern of it . . . for it must be clear to everyone that by Christ's example we are incited to beneficence so that we should not spare ourselves when our brethren require our help."[48] Imitating Christ as moral exemplar means most of all to love the neighbor as he did.

Imitation as Ethical Requirement

In the view developed so far, it is not yet clear how habituation takes place in imitation. 'Putting on virtue' as gradual transformation seems still under the verdict of hypocrisy. At this point Kierkegaard's view is interesting, because he does not align hypocrisy to imitation and resemblance of Christ but considers the *abandonment* of imitation in the Protestantism of his time to be hypocrisy. Precisely on this point, Kierkegaard was a main source for Bonhoeffer's account of discipleship as opposed to cheap grace.[49] As a Lutheran Kierkegaard considers grace the center of the Christian faith, but Christ is also the example (*Forbilledet, Exemplet*) to be followed in imitation (*Efterfølgelse*): "we are to resemble (*ligne*) him, not merely profit from him,"[50] as Kierkegaard writes in his notebooks. "Protestantism has more or less reached the point at which Xt [Christ] is no longer the ideal, the Exemplar (to which every individual must relate himself, honestly admitting how it is with him), but an idea."[51] Not imitation but the reversal of the

---

45. Wright, *Virtue Reborn*, 110, 112.

46. Gene Outka, "Following at a Distance: Ethics and the Identity of Jesus," in Garrett Green (ed.), *Scriptural Authority and Narrative Interpretation* (Philadelphia: Fortress Press, 1987), 148-9; the expression is derived from Graham Greene's novel *The Power and the Glory*.

47. *Inst.* 4.19.29.

48. John Calvin, *The Second Epistle of Paul the Apostle to the Corinthians and the Epistles to Timothy, Titus and Philemon* (Calvin's Commentaries 10) (Grand Rapids: Eerdmans, [1964] 1991), 110-11.

49. In writing *Discipleship* Bonhoeffer was greatly influenced by the anthology *Der Einzelne und die Kirche: Über Luther und den Protestantismus* (Berlin: Wolff, 1934), with selections from Kierkegaard's works, see, for example, Bonhoeffer, *Discipleship*, 39, 47-8, 53, 59, 62, 137, 287 / *DBW* 4, 23, 34-5, 40, 47, 50, 140, 303.

50. *JN* 4, 212 / *SKS* 20, 213 (NB2:182).

51. *JN* 8, 390 / *SKS* 24, 385 (NB24:105).

requirement of imitation is hypocrisy. "The more I look at it, the more it seems to me that Protestantism (however true the Lutheran position might be)—that Protestantism's hypocrisy is the rlly [really] aggravated and calculated hypocrisy."[52]

Since from Luther's perspective imitation of an external example may be seen as hypocrisy, the question is why according to Kierkegaard Protestantism's *neglect* of the imitation of Christ is hypocrisy. The obvious reason is that nineteenth century's established 'Christendom' is far removed from the original ideal. Note that Kierkegaard uses the term 'ideal' not in the general sense of a moral ideal but to designate that Christ decisively manifests the Christian existence as normative for all who call themselves Christians. In *Practice in Christianity* (under the pseudonym Anti-Climacus) Kierkegaard states that being a Christian means to become contemporary with Christ. Although Christ is also confessed in his loftiness as the Son of God, the criterion for being a Christian is *contemporaneity* with Christ and one can only become contemporary with Christ-in-time, that is, Christ in his lowliness. The problem of established 'Christendom' is that it assumes that it has overcome this state of lowliness and has become a triumphant church.[53] Imitation means to follow Christ in his lowliness and implies suffering, self-denial, dying from oneself and the world, humiliation, and even the risk of persecution.[54] In emphasizing suffering and cross-bearing in this way, Kierkegaard presents imitation in opposition to the hypocrisy of the Christian culture of his time. Not trying to become like Christ, but presuming that one can be a Christian without expressing these features is hypocrisy. Imitation must be emphasized again, "at least dialectically,"[55] that is, that imitation is demanded of everyone and that by humbly admitting that one does not meet the ideal one can rely on grace.

A second reason why getting rid of imitation is hypocrisy concerns the way it is justified, by saying that it would be presumptuous to follow Christ. In his notebooks Kierkegaard explains:

> Generally what presents itself as the extraordinary (*Overordentlige*) does not want to have imitation, replication. The extraordinary wants to be admired.... But Christ demands imitation;... he is ... the prototype oriented to the universally human, of which everyone is capable. Now human craftiness comes in again; we invert getting out of imitation, as if this were humility, and invert wanting to imitate Christ, as if this were presumption, as if he (generally like the extraordinary) would be angry about it, offended by it. O, human hypocrisy.[56]

---

52. *JN* 8, 520 / *SKS* 24, 509 (NB25:92).
53. Kierkegaard, *Practice in Christianity*, 237 / *SKS* 12, 230.
54. Ibid., 213 / *SKS* 12, 209. Similar accents in Bonhoeffer: "Just as Christ is only Christ as one who suffers and is rejected, so a disciple is a disciple only in suffering and being rejected, thereby participating in crucifixion" (*Discipleship*, 85 / *DBW* 4, 78).
55. *JN* 8, 399 / *SKS* 24, 394 (NB24:115).
56. Søren Kierkegaard, *Journals and Papers*, Vol. 2 (Bloomington: Indiana University Press, 1967), no. 1939 / *SKS* 27, 629; papir 507.

The hypocrisy is that people present it as a matter of humility not to pretend to wanting to become like Christ, meanwhile making the Christian life as easy and cheap as possible.

Thirdly, in abandoning imitation Christ is misunderstood as an extraordinary person, which reveals an esthetic understanding of exemplarity. Kierkegaard distinguishes between the *extraordinary*, as an esthetic category, asking for admiration, and the *example*, as an ethical category, demanding imitation.[57] "In aesthetic fashion, he [the exemplar] is made into someone extraordinary; people admire and admire him—in order to get rid of him ethically."[58] This does not mean that admiration does not have any value, "but ethically, admiration must in fact immediately be converted into action tending toward imitation."[59] Thus, "in ethics, there is no extraordinary; viewed ethically, the extraordinary is the norm, is what all of us must do."[60]

The term 'ethical' has two connotations that are important, because they precisely indicate how the follower is to be related to the example. First, the ethical is related "to the universally human, of which everyone is capable."[61] An ethical understanding of Christ means that he is not only understood in his complete difference from human beings as redeemer and God's eternal gift but also as the lowly servant, who has become the lowliest of all people. Precisely because of his lowliness Christ is the exemplar that can be imitated by every human being, including the "otherwise lowliest person."[62] On the other hand, since Christ became the lowliest of all, there is no excuse *not* to imitate Christ. For imitating Christ in his lowliness means that the life of imitation does not consist in imitating Christ's loftiness—if this would be possible at all—or in exceptional excellences that generally are admired, but precisely in his lowliness. Therefore, imitation necessarily implies suffering, suffering in the specific sense of becoming a lowly servant like Christ. The remarkable outcome of Kierkegaard's severe insistence on the imitation of Christ's example is that it is not an extraordinary ideal but an ethical requirement for everyone.

This brings us back to the core question of this chapter: How can the exceptional Christ be an example to everyone? This can be clarified from the second connotation of 'the ethical,' namely that imagining Christ as example is at the same time a demand on me: I should be as the example is. "An imitator *is* or strives *to be* what he admires, and an admirer keeps himself personally detached, consciously or unconsciously does not discover that what is admired involves a claim upon him, to be or at least to strive to be what is admired."[63] Christ shows in an ideal way what

---

57. *Practice in Christianity*, 237–8 / *SKS* 12, 230–2.
58. *JN* 8, 276 / *SKS* 24, 276–7 (NB23:144).
59. *JN* 8, 277 / *SKS* 24, 277 (NB23:144).
60. *JN* 8, 381 / *SKS* 24, 377 (NB24:91).
61. Kierkegaard, *Journals and Papers*, Vol. 2, no. 1939 / *SKS* 27, 629 (papir 507).
62. *Practice in Christianity*, 238 / *SKS* 12, 232.
63. Ibid., 241 / *SKS* 12, 234.

it means to exist as human being over and against God, which is in Kierkegaard's view the ultimate way of becoming oneself, that is, a self resting in God: "in Christ is it true that God is man's goal and criterion."[64] Since Christ in an ideal sense has showed what it means to be a human being before God, Christ is the moral exemplar who shows the ideal self of the human being. Therefore, what counts is not to copy Christ's particular actions, but to realize the authentically Christian existence in my own life, existing in the way he existed. As Rob Compaijen argues, if I would understand the *imitatio Christi* as literally imitating him, then this would be a sign that I do not really want 'to be myself'; literally imitating Christ would violate my existence as this concrete, particular individual. In confrontation with Christ's ideal outside myself it is my own ideal self that should become manifest in my factual existence. The imitation of Christ is at the same time the realization of the ethical task of 'becoming oneself.' The content of this authentic existence is again ethical in nature: it consists of neighborly love, as Christ is exemplary precisely in his unselfishness and love.[65] Because Christ as example or ideal is immediately related to this ethical task, other exemplars, such as disciples and apostles, saints, and martyrs ("witnesses of the truth"), may be relevant as well: "If I know a man whom I must esteem because of his unselfishness, self-sacrifice, magnanimity, etc., then I am not to admire but am supposed to be like him,"[66] that is, to exist as he exists and to love as he loves.

In Kierkegaard's account of the virtue of love the relation between imitation as putting on Christ, becoming a self, and love of the neighbor becomes clear. Although imitation of Christ requires self-renunciation, it is the love of the neighbor which at the same time includes self-love. For love makes it possible to overcome any competing relationship between love of the self and love of the neighbor. In love, the love of the neighbor and love of the self are intrinsically related, since the commandment is: "You shall love your neighbor *as yourself*" (Mt. 22:39). Relating neighborly love to self-love points neither to a precondition of self-love nor to a comparison between the two. The common explanation that we need to love ourselves *before* we can love the other is not what is at stake in this commandment.

Kierkegaard explains this in his book *Works of Love*. If the commandment to love the neighbor as yourself is properly understood, it also says "the opposite": you shall love yourself "in the right way." "To love yourself in the right way and

---

64. Kierkegaard, *Sickness unto Death*, 114 / *SKS* 11, 226.

65. Rob Compaijen, "Authenticity and Imitation: On the Role of Moral Exemplarity in Anti-Climacus' Ethics," in Heiko Schulz, Jon Stewart, and Karl Verstrynge (eds.), *Kierkegaard Studies Yearbook 2011* (Berlin: De Gruyter, 2011), 341–63.

66. *Practice in Christianity*, 242 / *SKS* 12, p. 235. Kierkegaard calls martyrs and saints "derived exemplars." However, "Instead of letting them remain as exemplars, they were transformed into intercessors who prayed for a person" (*JN* 8, 168 / *SKS* 24, 170 (NB 22:128)).

to love the neighbor correspond perfectly to one another; fundamentally they are one and the same thing." The commandment can be interpreted as follows:

> When the Law *as yourself* has wrested from you the self-love that Christianity sadly enough must presuppose to be in every human being, then you have actually learned to love yourself. The Law is therefore: You shall love yourself in the same way as you love your neighbor when you love him as yourself.[67]

This last sentence means that 'to love yourself in the right way' is nothing other than to love (the neighbor). The implication is that self-renunciation does not require self-annihilation. Self-renunciation means that you renounce egotistic love, a wrongly directed love, in order to make space for 'true love,' including a love of the self that is no longer selfish. Renunciation points to a transformation of the self, a profound transformation by *agapè* in the imitation of Christ. To put it slightly differently, the more (neighborly) love you possess the more you *truly* love yourself. From a Christian perspective the love of the self cannot be separated from love of the neighbor. Kierkegaard, the thinker who preeminently explores the task of 'becoming oneself' as a 'single individual,' identifies this becoming oneself precisely *as* love, which is the core of the *imitatio Christi*.

'Putting on Christ' as Habituation

Finally, the question is *how* in imitation a Christ-like character can be cultivated in which Christ's love and righteousness (and other virtues) are resembled. Or to put it differently, how may habituation take place in the view of imitation developed so far?

Part of Herdt's critical argument is that Luther replaces one sort of hypocrisy—the act of putting on virtue—for another: 'putting on Christ.' In Luther's forensic conception of justification, we exchange roles (we are "clothed in" Christ, while he takes on our clothes as sinner). Thus, Christian righteousness is a kind of pretense making Christians, as Herdt puts it, nothing other than "saved hypocrites."[68] According to Herdt, in the end Luther wrongly characterizes the Christian as basically passive: a person is neither inwardly nor outwardly active but experiences only what God affects in him or her.[69] Even if faith transforms from inside out, it should be acknowledged that transformation also takes place from outside in and includes habituation and our emulative activity.[70]

---

67. Kierkegaard, *Works of Love*, 22–3 / *SKS* 9, 30.
68. Herdt, *Putting on Virtue*, 179, with reference to Luther, *WA* 40.1, 443, 448, 452 / *LW* 26, 284, 288, 290.
69. Herdt, *Putting on Virtue*, 188.
70. Ibid., 195.

Since I think human agency is not excluded from Luther's view of the Christian life, as argued above, I think that in principle habituation and emulation can be valued from his perspective. However, I agree with Herdt that the 'how' of imitation and habituation is developed insufficiently in Luther's (and Calvin's) work. Therefore, I finally turn once more to Kierkegaard's treatment of imitation, which is indeed developed in terms of a process of habituation and formation of the moral self but is also in accord with the view of imitation developed so far.

Interestingly, Kierkegaard does not limit 'putting on Christ' to divine acting in justification and sanctification, but precisely extends the metaphor to imitation, as he explains in one of his notebooks: putting on Christ means to appropriate Christ's merits in the atonement "*and* to seek to resemble him." In Kierkegaard's view of putting on Christ a habituation from outside in is implied: it "is a substantial expression for making something inward."[71] The metaphor of 'putting on' even absorbs the notion of imitation, however, not with the effect that the human self and human activity are reduced to just putting on clothes:

> It is not said [in the image of putting on] that you should strive to imitate Xt [Christ] (when that sort of thing is said, it indirectly implies that the two nevertheless remain essentially unlike)—no, you are to put him on, attire yourself in him . . . as when a person resembles another almost to the point of being indistinguishable from him, not merely striving to imitate him, but *reproducing* him. Xt [Christ] *gives* you his clothing (satisfaction) and then requires that you are to *reproduce* Him.[72]

It seems to me that in this explanation of 'putting on Christ,' a particular and quite unique form of *emulation* is implied. It differs from other conceptions of emulation, since the aim is not to increase oneself in order to become as lofty as the exceptional exemplar, but to become as lowly as he is, as we have seen. Moreover, putting on Christ does not mean that Christ takes over my own agency, with the consequence that I almost disappear. As we have seen, Christ's exemplarity always includes an ethical requirement, the task of becoming a self, that is, of realizing what is exemplary in the exemplar in one's own particular existence. Now, in the fragment quoted, it almost seems that Kierkegaard falls back on the language of replication and copying of the example. However, the Danish word used here, *gjengiver*, has the connotation of 're-presenting' and 'giving back.' So, the surprising outcome is that it is rather the example that almost disappears in the 're-production' or 're-presentation' and not the human self. 'Putting on Christ,' like 'eating his Word,' is "the strongest expression of appropriation."[73] One becomes as it were a Christ.

---

71. *JN* 6, 396 / *SKS* 22, 391 (NB14:80).
72. Ibid.
73. *JN* 6, 396 / *SKS* 22, 391 (NB14:80).

Furthermore, Kierkegaard's explanation points to an interesting conception of *habituation* which extends from external imitation and imagination to internal appropriation and re-presentation. Although in *Practice in Christianity* imitation is emphasized in opposition to admiration and imagination, it is at the same time described as a process of habituation that includes moments of admiration, imagination, responding, taking responsibility, and actualization. Admiration is a relevant starting point but it should not be the endpoint, because imitation means that one strives to *be* what one admires. Kierkegaard pays much attention to how admiration and imagination can go astray. Admiration can result into envy.[74] "Admiration . . . is just as dubious a fire as the fire of erotic love, which in the turn of the hand can be changed into exactly the opposite, to hate, jealousy, etc."[75] Judas is an example of admiration that turned into the opposite. A deeper form of admiration is shown by Nicodemus, who risks getting to know something of the one he admires. He tries to relate to the admired, but in the end "he wished to keep himself personally detached."[76] One can also stay personally detached by making imitation into something conditional: "if it were made necessary, I would be willing to die for it."[77] This is an inadequate kind of imagination, since it is without any consequences for the present existence.

Adequate imagination brings the example in relation to one's own actual existence. According to Kierkegaard, in a sense it means gradually to forget as it were the example and to concentrate on the self, as he explains by the example of a general magnanimous exemplar: "When I am aware of the other person, this unselfish, magnanimous person, I promptly begin to say to myself: Are you such as he is? I forget him completely in my self-concentration . . . but, no, forgotten him I have not, but for me he has become a requirement upon my life."[78] Whereas in the admiration of an extraordinary example, "I vanish more and more, losing myself in what I admire," in the ethical relation of imitation "the other person vanishes more and more as he is assimilated into me or as I take him as one takes medicine, swallow him—but please note, because he is indeed a *requirement* upon me to give (*give*) him back in replica (*i Gjengivelsen*, in reproduction), and I am the one who becomes larger and larger by becoming more and more to resemble him."[79]

In conclusion, although Kierkegaard comes close to the idea of replication, he uses it in a different sense than copying the example. The agency of the imitator is fully involved in a process in which he does not disappear but becomes more and more a self which reproduces or presents Christ in the singularity of his own life.

---

74. *Practice in Christianity*, 241 / *SKS* 12, 234.
75. Ibid., 246 / *SKS* 12, 239.
76. Ibid., 247 / *SKS* 12, 240.
77. Ibid., 251 / *SKS* 12, 243.
78. Ibid., 242 / *SKS* 12, 235–6.
79. Ibid., 242–3 / *SKS* 12, 236.

Conclusion

The Protestant account of the imitation of Christ presented in this chapter makes it possible to bridge the gap between Christ's exceptional exemplarity and the ordinary life of the imitator. It is Christ himself who makes the imitator participate in the new life he established, in which imitation is the active side on the human part in union with Christ. As Bonhoeffer states, "Since we have been formed in the image (*Bild*) of Christ, we can live following his example (*Vorbild*). On this basis, we are now actually able to do those deeds, and in the simplicity of discipleship, to live life in the likeness of Christ."[80] This includes the cultivation of the virtues, which are no longer understood as first person virtues (perfection of the natural in the self) but as second person or interpersonal virtues (unselfishly directed to the other). Furthermore, imitation takes place in ordinary life, where Christ is not to be copied but to be resembled in the particular relations and responsibilities of ordinary life, ethically expressed in the virtue of neighborly love. Imitation of Christ is possible because it is not an attempt to emulate the exceptional example of Christ but to become as lowly as he is and because it always includes the ethical demand on the self to 'become oneself' in relation to the exemplar. Therefore, 'putting on Christ' is neither hypocritical pretending nor pretentious replication, but a particular kind of imitation and habituation in which Christ is as it were re-presented. The individual becomes so to say a Christ, a Christ to the neighbor, while remaining within the particularities of his or her particular life.

---

80. Bonhoeffer, *Discipleship*, 287 / *DBW* 4, 303.

Chapter 7

THE FRAILTY OF HUMAN VIRTUE

Given the Protestant view that cultivation of the virtues is closely related to the activity of Christ and that it is characterized as resembling Christ's lowliness, as has been pointed out in the previous chapter, is any growth in the virtuous life possible? If moral growth is possible, what may be the nature of this growth, given the reality of evil which is so manifestly acknowledged in Protestant views?

In an Aristotelian virtue ethics, growth in virtue is basically conceived of as developing, empowering, and perfecting what is already given in nature. The presupposition is that human desire and human reason naturally are aimed at the good, though education and upbringing are the necessary conditions for developing natural inclination in a proper direction: "nature gives us the capacity to acquire them [the virtues], and completion comes through habituation."[1] The virtues of character do not arise in us *by nature*, but "virtue of character (ἦθος) is a result of habituation (ἔθος)."[2] The aim is to develop from a condition in which one does the right things for the wrong reason (because it is required) toward the embodiment of true virtue in which one does the right things for the right reason (out of a settled character).[3] What education and upbringing contribute is nothing other than developing, empowering, and perfecting what is already given in nature, that is, what reason and desire by nature already are aimed at, understanding and wanting the good. The only problem is that some objects look as if they are goods but in fact are not. The task of upbringing is to teach how to recognize those things that are only seemingly good. With the help of good educators who teach us what the right activities are and with the good examples of those who are preeminently virtuous, it is in principle possible to acquire the virtues. In the classical scheme of the human faculties of reason, desire, and will, the faculty of human reason is decisive. If human flourishing does not succeed, this is basically due to a lack of knowledge (or a lack of basic necessary external goods and circumstances, as we have seen in Chapter 2): one lacks a correct view on reality and as a consequence one does not succeed in directing the passions properly.

---

1. *EN* 1103a25–27. Quotes from Aristotle, *Nicomachean Ethics*, Cambridge Texts in the History of Philosophy, trans. Roger Crisp (Cambridge: Cambridge University Press, 2000).
2. *EN* 1103a15–18.
3. *EN* 1103a24–1103b2; 110621–23.

This presupposition is fundamentally challenged in Christianity. The Christian view too states that in order to attain a good life knowledge of the good is needed, that one needs to want the good, and that in this sense the will follows reason. However, evil is not just explained in terms of a lack of knowledge of the good, but also as a lack of the will: although one knows the good, one nevertheless chooses not to do it (Rom. 7). The problem is not so much a lack of knowledge as a lack of good will. This is not a matter of tragic external circumstances but of human guilt before God, who created the human being as prepared for the good. Augustine phrased how this fundamentally changes the whole scheme: the human will is able to want things for which there are no good reasons and that do not have good effects on our well-being. Evil is not just a matter of bad luck or a lack of reason or reflective desire, but of a wrong will.[4] Good and evil are not external realities but belong primarily to the interior space, the realm of the will. In Augustine's view, based on a Pauline understanding, the human will has the ability to want those things for which there are no good reasons and that do not have good effects on our well-being. We can willingly oppose the good, and evil can intermingle with the good we desire by nature.

What is at stake here is not just the discovery of the human will as a third faculty, but the question how the good life and the virtues can be acquired given the experience of an internally divided human will. In a Christian account of the virtues, the fact that we can willingly oppose the good is to be acknowledged. Therefore, what is needed is not just formation of what is already present in human nature, but a radical transformation from an external source: divine grace. As has been pointed out, the theological anthropology and the theology of sin and grace of the Reformers and Reformed scholastic theologians as well as Kierkegaard can to a great extent be regarded as a continuation of this Augustinian line of thought.

In this chapter I want to look for the potential of this view rather than taking it as a weakness or an obstacle in a Protestant account of virtue ethics. In this respect three other phenomena relative to acquiring and practicing the virtues are relevant as well. In the first place, we may observe that in real-life exemplary virtues regularly appear to exist alongside deep-seated vices. Think for instance of Martin Luther King, who was exemplary in his commitment to justice and civil friendship, his forgiveness of his enemies, his prudence in his work for social justice, his self-restraint, his perseverance, and his courage to the point of martyrdom, but who nevertheless saw himself and was seen by others as a person whose character was flawed in important ways. This concerns not some incidental acts but patterns of activities that should be regarded as vices, such as repeated extramarital intercourse and mistreatment of women, which apparently coexisted with his exemplary virtues.[5] This case of what Jean Porter calls "the flawed saint" seems to be in contradiction with the classical thesis of the unity of the virtues,

---

4. Augustine, *Confessiones* 8.22–27.
5. Jean Porter, "Virtue and Sin: The Connection of the Virtues and the Case of the Flawed Saint," *The Journal of Religion* 75/4 (1995), 521–3.

which holds that anyone who possesses one of the cardinal virtues in the full sense, necessarily possesses all of them.[6] Secondly, if we consider less exemplary people, we see that most of them have neither moral virtues nor moral vices but rather what Christian Miller calls "mixed traits."[7] As situationism claims, based on empirical research, most people do not possess the robust character traits we call virtues, that is, cross-situationally consistent character traits. Rather, their moral behavior and decisions are largely motivated by situational variables.[8] Finally, Jochen Smidt speaks of human frailty with regard to the virtues, that is, the propensity of virtues to transform into vices. The famous Stanford prison experiment and the Milgram experiment[9] demonstrated people's propensity to fall prey to manipulation and put into question any optimistic belief in the goodness and moral capacity of human beings.[10]

---

6. Ibid.

7. Christian B. Miller, "The Mixed Trait Model of Character Traits and the Moral Domains of Resource Distribution and Theft," in Christian B. Miller, R. Michael Furr, Angela Knobel, and William Fleeson (eds.), *Character: New Directions from Philosophy, Psychology, and Theology* (Oxford: Oxford University Press, 2015), 164-91; Christian B. Miller, *The Character Gap* concludes from his investigation of important psychological experiments: "Here is the predicament that most of us seem to be in. We are not virtuous people. We simply do not have characters that are good enough to qualify as honest, compassionate, wise, courageous, and the like. We are not vicious people either—dishonest, callous, foolish, cowardly, and so forth. Rather, we have a mixed character with some good sides and some bad sides" (169).

8. Gobal Speenivasan, "The Situationist Critique of Virtue Ethics," in Russell (ed.), *The Cambridge Companion to Virtue Ethics*, 290-314.

9. In the Stanford prison experiment, conducted by Philip Zimbardo in 1971, volunteer college students were assigned to be either 'prison guards' or 'prisoners.' It turned out that many students embraced their assigned roles, that some 'guards' enforced authoritarian measures and ultimately subjected some 'prisoners' to psychological torture, while many 'prisoners' passively accepted psychological abuse and actively harassed other 'prisoners' who tried to stop it. In the Milgram experiment, conducted by psychologist Stanley Milgram in 1961, participants operated as a 'teacher' doing a test with a 'student.' If the 'student' answered a question wrong during the experiment, the 'teacher' had to 'shock' the student with electric shocks, whose intensity increased with every new wrong answer. If the 'teacher' asked the experimenter to stop because of the pain he observed in the 'student,' the experimenter made the 'teacher' continue the test by emphasizing that he, the experimenter, took all responsibility. Because of the higher authority of the experimenter, a significant number of 'teachers' continued the experiment, even if 'students' were 'shocked' to the maximum.

10. Smidt, "Critical Virtue Ethics," 36-7. With regard to the Milgram experiment and other experiments, Miller, *Character Gap*, 93 concludes: "Most of us have characters, which, when put to the test, lead us to obey people we see as legitimate figures. Our desires to

In sum, we have at least four ways in which the frailty of our virtues becomes apparent: (1) we can willingly do things for which there are no good reasons, which relativizes the power of reason, (2) virtues can exist along with deep-seated vices in one (virtuous) person, which contradicts the classical thesis of the unity of the virtues, (3) due to (extreme) situational factors even the virtues themselves can quite easily transform into real vices, which challenges the idea of stability of character, and (4) due to other (less extreme) factors most people have neither virtues nor vices but rather mixed character traits, which relativizes the human ability to become a virtuous character.

In this chapter, I will not address these issues in detail, but approach the frailty of human virtue, which these features reveal, more generally from an Augustinian and a Protestant perspective on sin and moral growth in the Christian life. The potential weakness of the Augustinian-Protestant tradition, namely that the possibilities of human nature to acquire and cultivate virtue are seen as limited, may turn out to be its strength: by asserting that even 'the most holy' and morally exceptional person before God is still a sinner dependent on God's grace we may be able to do justice to human frailty and moral flaws and open up a transcending perspective. First of all, the issue of the flawed saint as a challenge to the thesis of the unity of the virtues will be taken up. I will argue that a Thomistic account of the thesis does not suffice because the problems of human frailty remain unresolved, whereas Augustine's interpretation does prove adequate. Augustine's realistic approach is basically adopted in the theological views of the Reformers. Next, the question is how the insistence on human sinfulness and grace in Protestant accounts of the moral life relates to a virtue ethical understanding of the moral life in terms of growth and cultivation of the virtues. I will argue that taking into account Protestant theological conceptions results in an articulation of moral growth in which moral excellence is possible, though imperfection is still part of one's character. Finally, the virtue of humility will be presented as a paradoxical virtuous way to acknowledge that one does not have the virtues, at least not in their fullness.

Challenging the Thesis of the Unity of the Virtues

What does the thesis of the unity of the virtues entail? Basically, the thesis is about the internal connection of the (cardinal) virtues. Following Socrates's arguments, Plato's *Protagoras* contends that the separate virtues of justice, temperance, courage, and practical wisdom (and piety, mentioned here but dropped from the list in the *Republic*) are somehow one and the same thing. The virtues are all instances of practical wisdom. From this thesis of the unity of the virtues it follows that if we possess one virtue, we possess them all or if we lack one virtue, we lack

obey can become so strong in certain situations that we will intentionally kill an innocent person."

them all.[11] Although the thesis is more present in Plato than in Aristotle, Aristotle too discusses its basic elements. While Aristotle does not agree with Socrates that the virtues are all instances of practical wisdom, he agrees that virtue cannot exist without practical wisdom. Although, according to Aristotle, it is possible to possess some virtues before others, one can only be called good without qualification if one possesses practical wisdom.[12] In the ancient conception the unity of the virtues has to do with the relation of each individual virtue to the overall good of one's life: being courageous, for instance, means that acting courageously, while done for its own sake, also is part of the overall good of one's life as a whole; understanding this is part of grasping what courage is.[13]

Therefore, an appropriate way to understand the thesis of the unity of the virtues is to start with one cardinal virtue and investigate how this virtue presupposes the other three cardinal virtues. Justice, for instance, is the virtue of dealing properly and fairly with others, giving each one his or her due. This virtue includes knowledge about what is just but also doing what is just. Practical wisdom (prudence), as the disposition to make right moral judgments, includes both knowing what is just and doing what is just in a given situation. If this is correct, in addition one needs courage and temperance to choose what is most importantly just in the face of all kinds of distracting fears (courage) and desires (temperance). Similarly, each of the other cardinal virtues can be described as intrinsically related to the others. Courage, for instance, is not just the ability to act in the face of danger, for this may be rashness if one is not acting in pursuit of what is truly good and right (justice). True courage also requires practical wisdom to judge which risks are worth running for which ends, that is, in light of the good of one's life as a whole. It is in need of temperance, so that one's risk-taking will not be vitiated in the service of unworthy desires.

The thesis of the unity of the virtues is held not only in ancient philosophy but also in Christian thought. Augustine, for instance, frequently speaks of the four cardinal virtues as intrinsically connected, though this is mostly not defended explicitly as it is presupposed in the course of his argument. In his Letter 167 he speaks of the *inseparabilitas virtutum*[14] and in *De Trinitate* he says that the virtues cannot be separated, since all four have a fixed place in the human soul.[15] Aquinas too defends the thesis of the unity of the virtues or, as he calls it, the connection of the virtues.[16] Following Aristotle rather than Socrates, he states that the moral virtues are not just intellectual but qualify the basic human passions and desires or appetites that provide the immediate impetus for human action: temperance

11. Plato, *Protagoras* 329c–334c; 349b–360e.
12. *EN* 1144b14–1145a2.
13. Annas, *The Morality of Happiness*, 75.
14. *Ep.* 167.4, *PL* 33, 735.
15. Augustine, *De Trinitate* 6.4.6. See for an overview of Augustine's remarks on the unity of the virtues: Bovendeert, *Kardinale deugden gekerstend*, 98–9.
16. *ST* I-II 65.

qualifies the capacity for sensual desire; courage or fortitude the capacity for irascible passions; and justice the rational appetite, which Aquinas defines as the will. Prudence, as the intellectual capacity to discern and choose what is good, right, and just in accordance with one's overall desires, can only develop in someone who indeed has these qualified passions and desires. Prudence is the capacity to discern the kinds of actions that instantiate the good desires that are qualified by the moral virtues. The cardinal virtues are connected because neither the moral virtues nor prudence can be operative without the other.[17]

As we have seen, the thesis of the connection of the virtues seems to be in contradiction with reality, at least as we understand it nowadays. Obviously, there are people who are not prudent but nonetheless kind or fair. Movies and real-life experiences show us courageous but bad people. We meet people who cheat on their income taxes but are still faithful friends and family members. However, not all of these examples contradict the thesis of the unity of the virtues. As Jean Porter demonstrates, according to Aquinas—the same case could be made for the Greek understanding—the seeming courage of the bad person is not the same quality as the courage of the one who is just, temperate, and prudent. The courage of the bank robber is not similar to the courage of the good soldier in battle. Since the conception of a virtue is always linked to a conception of the good and worthwhile in human life, the courage of the bank robber cannot count as real virtue. Without a conception of the good, one lacks the context within which one can determine which dangers are worth risking for which goods. Prudence is precisely the ability to discern which specific act or course of activity would fulfill the ideals of good conduct as part of the overall good of a life. From this perspective the good qualities of a bad person, like courage, are only virtues in a very imperfect sense. The thesis of the connection of the virtues implies that only those people are fully virtuous who combine an understanding of what it means to live a humanly good life with the settled desires and sensibilities that correspond to that understanding.[18]

The thesis of the connection of the virtues can be maintained with regard to the 'courageous robber,' but how about the 'flawed saint'? Aquinas' account of the connection of the virtues allows for the phenomenon of a flawed saint only up to a certain point. In the case of a saint, we need to speak of a qualitatively different set of capacities, the theological virtues, by which one attains the end that transcends the natural *telos*, namely union with God.[19] Yet, the language of grace is also moral language, since the infused virtues do have practical significance transforming the personality in various ways and making the moral virtues expressions of *caritas*: "All the moral virtues are infused together with charity. . . . It is therefore clear that the moral virtues are connected, not only through prudence, but also because of charity."[20] According to Aquinas, the infused virtue of charity is inconsistent with

---

17. *ST* I-II 57.5; 58.2 and 3; 65.1; Porter, "Virtue and Sin," 524–25.
18. Porter, "Virtue and Sin," 525–28.
19. *ST* I-II 5.5; 62.1; 109.5; Porter, "Virtue and Sin," 534.
20. *ST* I-II 65.3; Porter, "Virtue and Sin," 535.

serious, that is, mortal, sins. One mortal sin would destroy the infused virtues, since it is a free turning away from the final end of the union with God,[21] whereby the very principle of the life of grace would be destroyed: "Mortal sin is incompatible with divinely infused virtue, especially if this be considered in its perfect state. But actual sin, even mortal, is compatible with humanly acquired virtue."[22] This allows moral flaws in 'a saint' only to a limited extent. Though Aquinas acknowledges that it is possible to act contrary to an acquired virtue without thereby immediately losing it, this does not include *patterns* of bad activities, that is, real vices as in King's case. In his case real and even heroic virtues informed by aims and ideals that are good (commitment to justice, forgiveness, and civic friendship) are combined with equally real vices, particularly through repeated—and regretted—extramarital affairs. Aquinas would indeed regard King's vices as mortal sins. Therefore, in this view, a person whose life is marked by such deep moral struggle and real vices cannot count as a person of virtue.[23]

The central point of the thesis of the connection of the virtues is not that the virtuous person is perfect, but the integral connection between prudence and the moral virtues as well as the connection to the good. Therefore, the thesis can allow a flawed saint, yet, only if the moral flaws are not too serious. Porter observes that in this respect the case of King is problematic, not so much because of the repeated extramarital affairs but rather because of a certain callousness toward his spouse and other partners. In the end this flaw seems to distort the operations of the practical intellect, the will, and the passions. Yet, King's passion for justice, his forbearance, and concern for others are beyond question. It would be unsatisfactory to deny his virtue in this regard because of his flaws in other domains. On the other hand, it would also be unsatisfactory to reject the thesis of the connection of the virtues, since the connection between the moral virtues, on the one hand, and intellectual virtue, on the other hand, is convincing. According to Porter, this dilemma reveals why we experience difficulties in understanding the combination of weakness and heroism in King's case.[24] In the end, Porter concludes that Aquinas was wrong in saying that the life of charity is inconsistent with serious sin. The relation of sin and the life of grace is more complex than Aquinas can recognize.[25] At this point, Porter's argument ends, leaving the problem quite unsolved.

Moral Flaws, Vices, and the Unity of the Virtues

In my view, the way Augustine relates the interconnection of the virtues to the continuation of sin is more promising than Aquinas' view. This can be explained

---

21. *ST* I-II 87.4.
22. *ST* I-II 63.2 ad 2.
23. Porter, "Virtue and Sin," 529 and 537.
24. Ibid., 528–32.
25. Ibid., 538.

from Augustine's Letter 167 which he wrote to Jerome in the year 415, consulting this biblical translator and exegete on the statement made in Jas 2:10—namely that whoever keeps the whole law but offends in one point becomes guilty of all. Augustine explains that he has difficulties with understanding this biblical statement and immediately relates this to the problem of the unity of the virtues: "Does a person who has one virtue really have them all, and does a person who lacks one really have none? If this is true, that statement of James is confirmed."[26]

Augustine raises similar questions to those addressed in the previous section. For instance, he refers to the rebel Lucius Sergius Catilina (108–62 BC), who was courageous but was neither just nor temperate. From the thesis of the unity of the virtues it follows that such an apparent case of courage that occurs in isolation from the other virtues is not really an instance of courage at all.[27] However, as Langan demonstrates, Augustine's argument also takes a different track than what we have seen until now. Augustine points to a different problem of the unity thesis; namely, that it makes moral formation perplexing and conversion from vice to virtue implausibly difficult. If we have either all the virtues or none, the consequence is that one must acquire all the virtues at once.[28] Thus, Augustine is especially worried by the perfectionist attitude implied in the doctrine of the unity of the virtues. How could we then understand the clearly virtuous behavior of one who is still morally imperfect?[29]

Here we discover Augustine's break with Stoicism. According to the Stoa, at least in how Augustine understands it, a gap exists between the imperfect person without any virtues and the sage who possesses the virtues perfectly. The only way to move from the former to the latter is by a spontaneous and immediate transformation.[30] In contrast, Augustine defends that it is possible to grow into

---

26. *Ep.* 167.4. In this section I quote from Augustine, *Letters* II/3: *Letters 156–210* (The Works of Saint Augustine: A Translation for the 21st Century), trans. Roland Teske, ed. Boniface Ramsey (New York: New City Press, 2004), 94–104. In my explanation I roughly follow John P. Langan, "Augustine on the Unity and the Interconnection of the Virtues," *Harvard Theological Review* 72/1-2 (1979), 81–95.

27. *Ep.* 167.7.

28. As we already have seen in Chapter 2, Augustine is not so much in dialogue with Aristotle and the Peripatetics, who acknowledge that the virtues need to be acquired gradually, as with the Stoics and the Neo-Platonists. At the same time, Augustine's worry applies to Aristotle as well; since in an Aristotelian view it is still presupposed that there can only be growth in virtue if one gradually acquires *all* the virtues.

29. Langan, "Augustine on the Unity of the Virtues," 86–9.

30. Cf. Cochran, *Protestant Virtue and Stoic Ethics*, 60: "Because the Stoics embrace a strong commitment to the unity of the virtues and believe that only virtue is a good, they tend toward an understanding of the virtues as acquired through a marked experience of transformation akin to a conversion." Basically, the Stoics regard both virtue and vice as 'all-or-nothing propositions.'

virtue, by advancing from darkness into light, through habituation gradually proceeding from vice to virtue.[31]

It is this point of view, in which it is assumed that a person can have a virtue and a vice at the same time, that enables Augustine to avoid the unacceptable consequences of the thesis of the interconnection of the virtues without giving up this interconnection altogether. By allowing the coexistence of contrary dispositions, virtue and vice, it is still possible to accept that the virtues all remain bound together but also that this does not exclude the presence in the individual human person of sins and vices. As Langan demonstrates, Augustine qualifies the interconnection thesis from the identification thesis, that is, the virtues being various expressions of one quality, love. The moral life of the Christian is understood as the progressive development of *caritas*, which is the one entity that underlies the activity of all the virtues and which no one can possess fully and perfectly in this life.[32] According to Augustine, what is decisive is whom we love: not our self-love (*amor sui*) but only the love of God (*amor Dei*) enables us to choose virtuous actions for their own sake. Therefore, he starts not with natural human capacities suggesting how these may be best balanced and developed, as in classical virtue ethics, but with love as the real source of the virtues. Christian virtue is fundamentally responsive—responsive to the grace that converts us from self-love to love of God. Virtue must be connected to Christ and is always related to the need for conversion, since in this life virtue remains imperfect and our loves remain divided.[33]

Augustine summarizes his argument in his letter to Jerome as follows:

> Virtue is the love by which one loves what should be loved. This is greater in some, less in others, and not at all in still others, but it is not so perfect in anyone that it cannot be increased in him as long as he lives. But as long as it can be increased, then of course that which is less than it ought to be comes from a vice (*ex vitio est*). Because of that vice *there is not a righteous person on earth who will do good and not sin* (Eccl. 7:21). Because of that vice *no living being will be righteous in the sight of God.* (Ps. 143:2)[34]

It is because of this 'vice,' this falling short of the good that could be present in our virtuous activity, that each of us is a sinner (which also explains why Jas 2:10 is correct). A realistic account of sin, in combination with a gradualist notion of virtue that is identified with *caritas*, makes it possible to maintain the thesis of the interconnection of the virtues without resulting in the objectionable conclusion that all human persons lack all the virtues.

---

31. *Ep.* 167.13.
32. Langan, "Augustine on the Unity of the Virtues," 90.
33. Herdt, *Putting on Virtue*, 45–7.
34. *Ep.* 167.15; *PL* 33, 739.

From this Augustinian view, it is possible to explain the phenomenon of the flawed saint, in whom *caritas* is more present than in most of us, but is still not perfect. In some respect it may even be (almost) absent, as the example of King exemplifies, but it is still possible to grow until God completes it in the life to come. As Augustine says:

> We can correctly say, 'Greater love is found in this person than in that one,' and 'Some love is found in this person and none in that,' . . . and we can say of a single person that he has greater chastity than patience and greater chastity today than yesterday if he is making progress, and that as yet he has no continence, but does have no small amount of mercy.[35]

In this way, it is possible to do justice to the fact that real virtues may exist alongside flaws, even deep-seated vices. It is also possible to do justice to the fact that most people embody mixed traits, that is, are more or less virtuous in some respects and more or less vicious in others. Since we can grow in love, as properly directed to God, our mixed character traits, moral flaws, or deep-seated vices are not a static given which makes any growth impossible. On the contrary, as pilgrims on the way and thanks to God's loving grace we can still make progress.

Moral Growth and Sanctification

Notwithstanding dissimilarities in their theological account of virtue and the virtues, the Reformers share with Augustine the view that the standard of the moral life is not to be found in the human being but in Christ, that virtues are not to be seen as referring only to themselves, and that the proper direction of the virtues is determined by divine grace and conversion. Let us look more closely at some Protestant accounts of the moral life. How does the insistence on human sinfulness and grace in traditional Protestant accounts relate to an understanding of the moral life in terms of growth in virtue? What are the implications for the phenomena of moral flaws and mixed character traits?

As we have seen in the previous chapter, unity with Christ in sanctification is an appropriate starting point for thinking through the virtuous life from a Protestant perspective. In his early study *Character and the Christian Life* (1975), Stanley Hauerwas already took up the Protestant doctrine of sanctification as the point of departure for developing an ethics of character as the way to understand the unity and continuity of the moral self. The doctrine of sanctification in the theology of Calvin, Wesley, and Edwards provides him with a basis for constructing a positive relation between sanctification and an ethics of character without falling into the pitfall of 'work righteousness'.[36] This gives space to moral growth, not in the sense

---

35. *Ep.* 167.14.
36. Hauerwas, *Character and the Christian Life*, 187.

of becoming morally better and better, but as a continued working out of the reality of Christ in the life of the believer. More recently, Elizabeth Agnew Cochran stated that in the view of the Reformers moral growth is gradual, not linear as in an Aristotelian and Thomistic understanding. It starts from the gift of Christ's complete and perfect righteousness received in justification. Therefore, the moral life requires a continual return to one's conversion to God.[37] As we have seen in the previous chapter, in Calvin's concept of *duplex gratia*, participation includes both *imputation* of Christ's righteousness and the active *partaking* in this righteousness in sanctification. By participation in the second grace of sanctification the believer becomes a partaker in Christ's righteousness and begins "the slow process of moral transformation," as Todd Billings points out.[38]

As Hauerwas observed in his early work, change of the person is an essential element in the doctrine of sanctification as developed in Protestantism. The emphasis on the person and personal renewal expresses that sanctification is not accomplished by doing certain prescribed acts, but these acts should flow from a deeper source that concerns the way we are.[39] For Calvin, sanctification or repentance is a turning of life to God, requiring a transformation of the heart, so that the outward life is in full correspondence with this renewed heart.[40] This concerns a change in the total direction of our lives, which includes all our actions, dispositions, and beliefs.[41]

The doctrine of sanctification, the emphasis on the change of the 'person' and the transformation of the 'heart' and its integrity are good starting points, but according to Hauerwas the Reformers and later Protestant theologians lacked the instruments to think through the actual meaning of these concepts in the life of the believer. The doctrine of sanctification clearly expresses that a real change takes place in the believer, but it is less clear how this change takes shape and how it will be effective in terms of moral growth. Therefore, Hauerwas tries to overcome the inability in Calvinistic and Methodist accounts of the Christian life, with their emphasis on divine commands, to characterize the human side of the union with Christ and to understand the nature of the self that is graced, by interpreting sanctification in terms of the formation of character.[42] In his later works, Hauerwas considers justification and sanctification to be secondary terms and situates the self more concretely in the narrative of God as revealed in the life, the death, and the resurrection of Christ and in the context of the formative community of the church.[43]

---

37. Cochran, *Protestant Virtue and Stoic Ethics*, 114.
38. Billings, *Calvin, Participation, and the Gift*, 107.
39. Hauerwas, *Character and the Christian Life*, 196.
40. *Inst.* 3.3.6.
41. Hauerwas, *Character and the Christian Life*, 197, 201–2.
42. Ibid., 193–4.
43. See, for example, Hauerwas, *The Peaceable Kingdom*, 94–5.

I agree that although traditional Protestant ethics offers a good starting point in terms of justification and sanctification, the concepts of character, narrative, and community need in addition to be spelled out in order to understand the nature of the self that is graced. However, as has become clear from Chapter 4, other than what Hauerwas assumes, the need to cultivate the virtues as part of the Christian character has already been present in Protestant theology, Reformed (and Lutheran) scholasticism in particular. Moreover, Hauerwas's Neo-Aristotelian approach shows some weaknesses when it comes to the serious challenges of the apparent human frailty in acquiring the virtues.

This can be clarified by two basic metaphors which Gilbert Meilaender distinguishes: 'journey' and 'dialogue.' 'Dialogue,' or probably more adequate, 'dialectics,' takes the Christian life as a back-and-forth between the two voices with which God speaks: the accusing voice of the law and the accepting voice of the gospel. 'Journey,' on the other hand, implies a process in which people gradually and graciously are transformed by the pilgrimage to which they have been called. Journey is "the process by which God graciously transforms a sinner into a saint, as a pilgrimage (always empowered by grace) toward fellowship with God."[44] According to Hauerwas, the metaphor of journey is and should be the primary one,[45] whereas Meilaender from his Lutheran perspective defends that the two metaphors should be kept in tension because a one-sided emphasis on journey and pilgrimage would cause doubt and distress when we see little progress, or may cause overconfidence when we concentrate on the progress toward the goal of pilgrimage.[46] In my view, Meilaender is right, and this is highly relevant with regard to the issue of the frailty of human virtue.[47] The question is how to understand the nature of moral growth in the Christian life, given the persistent propensity to moral flaws. With regard to this question it is worthwhile to return to the view of the Reformers once more.

Progress without Perfection

Luther's view of the Christian moral life can be explained from his famous description of the believer as *simul iustus et peccator*. An illuminating way to understand this phrase is by pointing to the distinction between grace and gift,

---

44. Gilbert C. Meilaender, "The Place of Ethics in the Theological Task," *Currents in Theology and Mission* 6 (1979), 200.

45. Hauerwas, *Character and the Christian Life*, xxvii.

46. Meilaender, "The Place of Ethics," 210; Hauerwas, *Character and the Christian Life*, xxix.

47. See for a more extended discussion of Hauerwas's and Meilaender's positions: Pieter Vos, "Calvinists among the Virtues: Reformed Theological Contributions to Contemporary Virtue Ethics," *Studies in Christian Ethics* 28/2 (2015), 206–8.

as developed by Luther in his 1521 response to Latomus.[48] Grace affects our forensic status before God, while the gift transforms our characters. Grace is "an outward good, God's favor, the opposite of wrath,"[49] which affects us as whole persons. Through grace we are completely justified before God, despite our sinfulness. The gift, in contrast, gradually cleanses us of sin: "faith is the gift and inward good which purges the sin to which it is opposed."[50] This gift of faith is infused, which works to transform us from within, though this working is not yet finished: "Everything is forgiven through grace, but as yet not everything is healed through the gift. The gift has been infused, the leaven has been added to the mixture."[51] In this way Luther emphasizes the continuation of a gradual transformation (journey): "he does not want us to halt in what has been received, but rather to draw near from day to day so that we may be fully transformed into Christ."[52] At the same time, Luther holds the two aspects of *simul iustus et peccator* together (dialogue), in what Wilfred Joest calls the *Totalaspekt* and the *Partialaspekt*. On the one hand, the sinner is totally justified before God through Christ's righteousness. On the other hand, the believer is partially justified/ partially a sinner, moving gradually toward the goal already anticipated in its completion by God's judgment.[53]

In Calvin's account the notions of journey and dialogue seem to be in balance, since it is not just the dialogue of the accusing voice of the law and the saving voice of God's grace that characterizes the Christian moral life, but 'participation in Christ' also points to the unity of the believer with Christ and the empowering of the Spirit to live a life of active gratitude. Here the language of growth is indeed present: "restoration does not take place in one moment or one day or one year,"[54] God renews the minds of the believers throughout their lives. As Todd Billings concludes, one side of double grace is that "by the Spirit, believers are also engrafted on to Christ—receiving him as nourishment for gradual transformation

---

48. Herdt, *Putting on Virtue*, 184-6. Though Herdt interprets Luther's view as a far-reaching displacement of human agency by the indwelling Christ, as we have seen in Chapter 6, she acknowledges that the elements of gradual progress and habituation are nevertheless present in Luther, referring to Luther's response to Latomus. Here I follow her latter train of thought.

49. *WA* 8, 106 / *LW* 32, 227.

50. Ibid.

51. *WA* 8, 107 / *LW* 32, 229.

52. *WA* 8, 111 / *LW* 32, 235.

53. Wilfried Joest, *Gesetz und Freiheit: Das Problem des tertius usus legis bei Luther und die neutestamentische Parainese* (Göttingen: Vandenhoeck & Ruprecht, [1951] 1968), 278-80. See Herdt, *Putting on Virtue*, 185.

54. *Inst.* 2.3.9.

and growth."55 In *Institutes* 3.6.5 it is surprisingly the metaphor of journey, of pilgrimage, in which both enduring flaws and progress are held together.

> But seeing that, in this earthly prison of the body, no man is supplied with strength sufficient to hasten in his course with due alacrity, while the greater number are so oppressed with weakness, that hesitating, and halting, and even crawling on the ground, they make little progress, let every one of us go as far as his humble ability enables him, and prosecute the journey once begun. No one will travel so badly as not daily to make some degree of progress. This, therefore, let us never cease to do, that we may daily advance in the way of the Lord; and let us not despair because of the slender measure of success. How little soever the success may correspond with our wish, our labour is not lost when today is better than yesterday, provided with true singleness of mind we keep our aim, and aspire to the goal, not speaking flattering things to ourselves, nor indulging our vices, but making it our constant endeavour to become better, until we attain to goodness itself. If during the whole course of our life we seek and follow, we shall at length attain it, when relieved from the infirmity of flesh we are admitted to full fellowship with God.56

On the one hand, Calvin speaks of "little progress" and states that there is no one who is not far removed from "evangelical perfection." Calvin does not advocate perfectionism: "I do not so strictly demand evangelical perfection that I would not acknowledge as a Christian one who has not attained it. For thus all of us would be excluded from the church."57 On the other hand, perfection is precisely to be set "before our eye as the end at which we ought constantly aim." It is the eschatological goal toward which we travel, not just as something which lies ahead but as a goal that guides us on the journey. As he elsewhere states (contra the Anabaptists): "We are purged by his sanctification in such a way that we are besieged by many vices and much weakness as long as we are encumbered with our body. Thus it comes about that, far removed from perfection, we must move steadily forward, and though entangled in vices, daily fight against them."58 Similarly, the Westminster Larger Catechism says about sanctification that it "is neither equal in all, nor in this life perfect in any, but growing up to perfection."59

More explicitly, Reformed scholastics understand gradual habituation and the persistence of moral flaws in terms of virtue. Peter Martyr Vermigli states that "men cannot be blessed by themselves alone (*per seipsos non posse beatos esse*)

---

55. Billings, *Calvin, Participation, and the Gift*, 108; cf. *Inst.* 3.14.4; 4.17.1.
56. *Inst.* 3.6.5 (trans. Henry Beveridge).
57. *Inst.* 3.6.5.
58. *Inst.* 3.3.14.
59. "Westminster Larger Catechism," in *The Constitution of the Presbyterian Church in the United States of America* (Philadelphia: Office of the General Assembly, 1954), Q 77.

since their nature was flawed from the beginning."⁶⁰ On the other hand, "when we have been restored and reborn, however, we cooperate with the grace and spirit of God and acquire the habits of the virtues by which we are repaired and made better every day. For this reason Paul urged the Philippians to work out their own salvation" (Phil. 2:12).⁶¹ Interestingly, Vermigli includes the possibility of sudden transformation in his understanding of the virtues. Concerning fortitude, for instance, "it is certainly not always true that it is acquired by those who experience danger and become used to being unafraid. There have been many to whom it was given suddenly, like the martyrs who possessed extreme constancy; these were formerly so weak that they were unwilling to endure the slightest suffering."⁶²

William Ames implicitly affirms the thesis of the unity of the virtues, understanding the cardinal virtues as "four conditions necessarily required in the disposition that deserves the name of virtue."⁶³ Of these four conditions, justice "orders and constitutes virtue," prudence "directs it and frees it from error," fortitude "strengthens it against misfortune," and temperance "makes it pure and defends it against all allurements."⁶⁴ He interprets these cardinal virtues from Scripture and sees them explained almost by name in 2 Pet. 1:5-6:

> *Add to faith virtue* (i.e., justice or a universal rightness), *to virtue knowledge* (or prudence rightly directing all your ways), *to prudence continence* (the temperance by which you can resist the allurement of all pleasures which attract and draw men from the right way), *to continence patience* (fortitude with which you may outlast any hardship for righteousness' sake).⁶⁵

According to Ames, there can be no such thing as degree in real virtue: "There is no virtue which at least in application does not extend itself to all things contained within the compass of its object. He is not temperate who is moderate in one lust but indulges in others." On the other hand, "in respect of the *subject* a particular virtue may be stronger in one person than in another, either because of apter natural disposition, or more frequent use, or more perfect judgement of reason, or finally because of a greater gift of God."⁶⁶ The virtues can increase by daily use and exercise: "To the extent that the acts of virtue, or contrary vices, are more intent, more frequent, and more continual, they bring about either an increase or

---

60. Vermigli, *In primum, secundum, et initium tertii libri ethicorum Aristotelis ad Nicomachum commentarius*, 227 and Vermigli, *Commentary on Aristotle's Nicomachean Ethics*, 222.
61. Vermigli, *Ethicorum commentarius*, 353 / *Commentary*, 337.
62. Vermigli, *Ethicorum commentarius*, 309 / *Commentary*, 297.
63. Ames, *Medulla theologiae*, 2.2.25 / Ames, *The Marrow of Theology*, 228.
64. Ames, *Medulla* 2.2.32 / *Marrow*, 229–30.
65. Ames, *Medulla* 2.2.33 / *Marrow*, 230.
66. Ames, *Medulla* 2.2.41 / *Marrow*, 231.

diminution of virtue."⁶⁷ Interpreted in this way, the unity of the cardinal virtues can be acknowledged without requiring that a virtuous person needs to possess all the virtues. In doing so, like Vermigli, he shows some leniency in understanding virtues in terms of habituation and grace, which in a sense concurs with the situationist observation that our virtuous activity is situation dependent.

In addition, Reformed theology has something in particular to help spell out the nature of growth in the virtuous life given the persistence of moral flaws and vices: the very notion of 'reform.' This means that rather than by progress toward perfection virtue is marked by reform, in the sense that individual virtue follows a pattern of repetition and renewal rather than quantitative or linear growth. Growth is neither a matter of natural development nor something that is achieved once and for all. It rather demands reform, a continuous renewal. This notion is also present in Karl Barth's understanding of the Christian life. In his seemingly critical evaluation of virtue ethics and his preference for a command ethics, growth in the Christian life is possible so long as we acknowledge that such growth is marked by "repetition and renewal."⁶⁸ As Barth states: "The principle of necessary repetition and renewal, and not the law of stability, is the law of the spiritual growth and continuity of our life."⁶⁹ As a consequence, a Reformed concept of *semper reformanda* acknowledges development of the human subject and growth in the Christian life, but in a moderate sense. On the one hand, the process of renewal in the moral life is never finished—sanctification is eschatological. On the other hand, the moral life is conceived of as more than just a dialectics between response and failure of response to divine commands, namely as a continuous renewal or a renewing in continuity from God's side.

The Paradoxical Virtue of Humility

The insistence on human frailty and the persistence of sin in the moral life in the Christian tradition is not only something that is seen as opposed to the virtues and the virtuous life. Human frailty also finds a paradoxical expression in a particular virtue: humility. As André Comte-Sponville says: "Humility is a humble virtue, so much that it even doubts its own virtuousness: to pride oneself on one's own humility is to lack it."⁷⁰

In Antiquity, humility could not be regarded as a virtue. In Christianity, humility is the virtue that prevents the virtues from becoming vehicles of pride. According to Augustine, the virtues of Christian character are forms of Christian love, which

---

67. Ames, *Medulla* 2.2.44 / *Marrow*, 231.

68. Werpehowski, *Karl Barth and Christian Ethics*, 33; Nolan, *Reformed Virtue after Barth*, 7–8.

69. Karl Barth, *Church Dogmatics*, Vol. II/2, ed. G. W. Bromiley and T. F. Torrance (Edinburgh: T&T Clark, 1957), 647.

70. Comte-Sponville, *A Short Treatise on the Virtues*, 140.

is love for God. Virtue is nothing else but perfect love of God.[71] The opposite is love of the self, which is basically pride. In Augustine's view we cannot underestimate the human inclination to *superbia*: even when honorable virtues are only related to themselves and are sought for no other end, even then they are puffed up and inflated with pride. They are reckoned vices rather than virtues, because they are forms of love their possessor has for himself rather than for God.[72] The point is that virtues never have only reference to themselves. Humility is the virtue that qualifies human activity and guarantees that virtue is not simply a mask worn by *superbia*.

Thus, humility is the opposite of pride. However, we should immediately acknowledge that it can also be a form of pride, for instance, if it is used in a calculated way in order to procure advancement in honor or power. It can be a form of resentment, as Nietzsche demonstrates: humility that is essentially motivated by the desire to topple people who are stronger than the weak one who hides himself behind humility. Humility can also be confused with low self-esteem, a lack of confidence in one's own abilities, resulting in complete passivity. However, none of this can count as part of humility as a *virtue*, that is, as an excellent quality of the soul. Rather, envy, resentment, ruthless ambition, invidious comparison, low self-esteem, and rejoicing in the downfall of others are the opposite of humility.

According to Comte-Sponville, humility is not the same as the vice which Aristotle calls *micropsuchia*, lowliness, that is, forsaking one's true worth, to the point of not allowing oneself to undertake any higher action (*abjectio*).[73] Humility is not ignorance about what one is, but rather acknowledgment of what one is not: it is the virtue of the human being who knows that he or she is not God. Hence, humility is not incompatible with greatness, achievement, and excellence. Moses was great in leadership and yet Scripture describes him as being more meek or humble than anyone else (Num. 12:3). As said, the opposite of humility is not human greatness or excellence, but pride. According to Aquinas, pride is the desire to become like God by one's own powers: "Pride denotes immoderate desire of one's own excellence, a desire that is not in accord with right reason."[74] Pinsent explains the various manifestations of pride that Aquinas has in mind as being against right reason: (1) ascribing an excellence to oneself that one does not possess, (2) thinking that one has acquired for oneself some excellence that one has received as a gift, (3) thinking that some excellence that one has received as a gift is due to one's own merits, and (4) thinking that some excellence that one possesses is greater insofar as others do not have it.[75] Humility is the virtue that frees one from these illusions about oneself and disposes one to receive God's gifts *as* gifts, and as non-exclusive gifts.

---

71. *CD* 16.4.
72. *CD* 19.25.
73. Comte-Sponville, *A Short Treatise*, 142.
74. *ST* II-II 162.4.
75. Andrew Pinsent, "Humility," in Austin and Geivett (eds.), *Being Good*, 242–64.

Humility does not lower human excellence as such. Rather, it is acknowledging that one is what one can be and not what one cannot be: God. And even if one is sad about how one is, such decency of the humble is much better than the self-satisfied arrogance of the impudent. The greatness of the virtue of humility is that it can lift the one who lacks almost all or many virtues but shows humility above the one who possesses almost all the virtues but lacks humility. Humility follows the evangelical order of the first becoming the last and the last becoming the first. The greatness of humility is its love for the truth: "Humility is the effort through which the self attempts to free itself of its illusions about itself and—since these illusions are what constitute it—through which it dissolves."[76] It is gaining oneself by losing oneself.

In this sense, humility is the virtue which holds together one's excellence and one's frailty. Humility acknowledges that insofar one possesses the virtues, this is so because what one has acquired depends on what one is given, and that insofar as one does not possess the virtues, this is precisely what makes one humble. In the virtue of humility both the possession of virtue and the lack of virtue can be held together. Humility is the paradoxical virtuous way to acknowledge that one does not have the virtues, at least not in their fullness, that is, as being the realization of the highest good, the beatitude of unity with God. Humility is a joyful virtue, because it makes one open to receive this good and its final realization as a gift from God.

Conclusion

In this chapter I have argued that, from an Augustinian and Protestant perspective, it can be acknowledged that the moral life of most people exhibits virtues alongside moral flaws or even deep-seated vices, without the pursuit of a virtuous life being abandoned. As Paul Ramsey says, we all are "narrow specialists in virtue" and moral goodness "seems to travel in sections which never arrive at the same destination at the same time."[77] The courageous may not be temperate, the temperate person not fearless, and the wise may not be humble. It may even be possible that virtues transform into real vices. Combining a realistic account of sin, including the persistence of vices, with a gradualist notion of virtue that is identified with *caritas*, Augustine succeeds in maintaining the thesis of the interconnection of the virtues without ending up with the objectionable conclusion that all human persons lack all the virtues.

Furthermore, the merit of the Protestant ideas of the distinction between the *Totalaspekt* and the *Partialaspekt*, the *duplex gratia*, and the 'continuous renewal' is that they enable us to deal with the lack of congruence in our characters, that is, the coexistence of virtues and moral flaws in the lives of most of us. On the

---

76. Comte-Sponville, *A Short Treatise*, 147.
77. Ramsey, *Basic Christian Ethics*, 193.

one hand, participation in Christ opens up the possibilities of fostering a Christ-like character and cultivating pertinent virtues, to the extent that these virtues can really become part of our character. On the other hand, the human being is continuously in need of redemption since sin and moral flaws are still part of the human being's condition and profoundly affect even 'the most holy' and morally excellent persons. This does not discourage us in that we are completely abandoned to our own failures, but rather are we lifted up time and again by divine grace in continuous renewal, which puts us in the wide space of divine goodness that is present for us despite our failures and flaws. Humility is the paradoxical virtue by which this goodness is virtuously embraced.

Chapter 8

THE SANCTIFICATION OF ORDINARY LIFE

As we have seen in the previous chapters, sanctification is a proper locus for thinking about the cultivation of virtues in the Christian life, though concepts of character, narrative, and community are needed in addition. At the same time, the doctrine of sanctification also points in a direction that is less explored in recent theological accounts of virtue ethics, such as Hauerwas's, namely the sanctification of all domains of life. For the doctrine of sanctification (and justification), as it has particularly been developed within the Calvinistic tradition, not only has implications for the cultivation of character within the church as 'the communion of the saints,' as Hauerwas and others point out, but also emphasizes the sanctification of the ordinary, which extends to all domains of life and society as a whole. Therefore, in this chapter the perspective will be broadened in two related directions.

First, if the sanctification of life extends to all domains of (societal) life, as lived by ordinary people, these domains become instances where the Christian character can be shaped in a positive way. This indicates an openness to worldly domains and ordinary life. The sanctification of life concerns the formation of character in adherence to Christ that extends to the various spheres of (societal) life. What could it mean for the cultivation of virtues needed to live this life, especially in terms of emulating moral exemplars? For the sanctification of life in all its domains also affects the interpretation of moral exemplarity. Though the saints seem to be diminished in Protestantism, the emphasis on the ordinary offers new possibilities to reevaluate the meaning of exemplars, in particular exemplars in ordinary life. In principle everyone can become a moral exemplar. How and under which conditions may the virtues be learned from moral exemplars in ordinary life?

Secondly, from a Protestant perspective all the domains of life are not unreservedly embraced as places of the good life. These domains should be transformed and reformed. (Neo-)Calvinists have typically insisted that not only people's personal lives but also human society should be transformed. The social order must not merely be accepted without complaint, but "surveyed with the critical eye of an Old Testament prophet."[1] Transformation designates a commitment to social justice, including a prophetic role full of commitment to challenge and influence current and future social arrangements. How can this notion of social reform be related to exemplarity and character formation?

In this chapter, the Protestant idea of the affirmation of ordinary life as well as the need to transform this life will be taken up as a starting point to investigate the role of moral exemplarity in the cultivation of the virtues. Although the saints no longer play a pivotal role, their moral role is not completely diminished. More importantly, moral exemplarity is relocated in the sphere of ordinary life, including an increased awareness of the moral complexities and ambiguities that characterize their and our own lives. I will start with a short historical reconstruction of the Protestant turn to ordinary life as the locus of sanctification and transformation, followed by a section on the place and function of the virtues in this context. Gradually, the focus of this chapter will be more constructive. I will argue that from the Protestant affirmation of ordinary life moral exemplarity particularly can be understood as fully related to the complexities and ambiguities of ordinary life. As such this provides an important contribution to a virtue ethical understanding of exemplarity. In addition, I will distinguish between 'role exemplarity' and 'existential exemplarity' and argue that this distinction offers an opportunity to understand exemplarity as related to social practices, on the one hand, and to something that runs deeper, to the depth of our own subjectivity, on the other.

Sanctification and Transformation

The emphasis on ordinary life is deeply rooted in Protestantism. The Reformation is a major factor in the displacement of the locus of the good life from a special range of higher activities to 'life itself.'[2] Abandoning the traditional distinction between the *vita activa* and the *vita contemplativa* and the implied hierarchy between laity and clergy (and the latter's mediating role), the Reformers affirm ordinary life as the space where God is to be glorified for his grace in the face of human sinfulness, where Christ is to be followed and where the Christian life is to be lived as devoted to the common good and the needs of the neighbor. Since salvation solely rests on God's grace, clergy, monks, and saints no longer have a special role in the mediation between the believer and 'the sacred.' Each believer has to live his or her life *coram Deo* and all life spheres are to be sanctified as divinely given avenues through which all believers respond to God's call to serve him and the neighbor offering every aspect of life as their divine worship. In domestic, cultural, educational, economic, and political spheres the believers are called to act in accordance with the 'offices' of parent, spouse, teacher, farmer, or

---

1. Lee Hardy, *The Fabric of This World: Inquiries into Calling, Career Choice, and the Design of Human Work* (Grand Rapids: Eerdmans, 1990), 65.
2. Taylor, *Sources of the Self*, 213.

lawyer.³ It is one's task to live and work in one's ordinary station in life, renewed by the love of Christ and living a pattern of life marked by glorifying God and serving humankind in a prayerful discipleship. One should not remove oneself from the common fabric of life. Rather one should live, move, and have one's being in the common life in order to fill it and transform it with a new spirit from within.⁴

This idea of what Charles Taylor calls "the affirmation of ordinary life"⁵ found fertile ground in the new, technological complex modern world. The repudiation of the monastic ideal and the application of vocation to the laity working in many occupations inaugurated "a social and economic revolution."⁶ In their famous accounts of this historical process, Ernst Troeltsch and Max Weber point out how the Protestant understanding of the 'royal priesthood of all believers' transferred the classical notion of ascetic discipline from the monastery to the hearts of the believers and to the spheres of ordinary life in a so-called inner-worldly asceticism.⁷ Although these thinkers insufficiently emphasize the Reformers' view of vocation as primarily meaning to become a disciple of Christ in the community of faith, they rightly argue that the Protestant notion of vocation as a divine calling in everyday life contributed to the rise of industry and the promotion of a modern work ethic (Weber) and to democratic forms of polity and a new appreciation of marriage and family life (Troeltsch). Although 'the priesthood of all believers' may not have been fully implemented in the structure of the Reformation churches, it was adopted by lay believers and promoted directly and indirectly the disciplined ordering of everyday life.⁸

The relevant point here is that the turn to ordinary life has significant implications for understanding the good life and, as a consequence, the virtues. Whereas Aristotle distinguished the good life (εὖ ζῆν) from life (ζῆν) and regarded the latter as only conditional for the pursuit of the good life in terms of *eudaimonia*, the turn to ordinary life in modernity is a break with this tradition that continued in a modified form in medieval theology and that valued the *vita contemplativa* over the *vita activa*. Aristotle defined the good life as the life of contemplation and the life of the polis, marked by deliberation on the good life, contemplation of the order of things in politics, consideration of the common good, and deciding about the shaping and application of laws—activities that are all beyond the pursuit of

---

3. Douglas J. Schuurman, *Vocation: Discerning our Callings in Life* (Grand Rapids: Eerdmans, 2004), 4–6.

4. Max Stackhouse, "Vocation," in Gilbert Meilaender and William Werpehowski (eds.), *The Oxford Handbook of Theological Ethics* (Oxford: Oxford University Press, 2005), 198.

5. Taylor, *Sources of the Self*, 211.

6. Stackhouse, "Vocation," 197.

7. Ernst Troeltsch, *The Social Teachings of the Christian Churches* (New York: Harper, 1932); Max Weber, *The Protestant Ethic and the Spirit of Capitalism* (New York: Charles Scribner's Sons, 1958).

8. Stackhouse, "Vocation," 197–8.

bare life, the fate of slaves and animals.[9] Although not all ancient and medieval philosophers shared this Aristotelian conception, the hierarchy of ethical life in which the lives of contemplation and social and political participation were favored was dominant till modernity. The affirmation of ordinary life is a major transition, "which displaces the locus of the good life from some special range of higher activities and places it in 'life' itself."[10] Contemporary virtue ethics cannot be understood properly and developed adequately without taking into account this turn to ordinary life as rooted in the transition that got its main impetus from the Reformation.

Before I elaborate on this, it should be noted that the affirmation of ordinary life and the redefinition of the callings of every believer is not to be understood as static. In this respect Calvin's view is more promising than Luther's. Although Calvin's thought on vocation in ordinary life is continuous with the Lutheran view, it differs in some important respects. Luther's conception of the ordering of society as pre-structured by God-given orders of creation is less dynamic than Calvin's. Luther understands one's *Beruf* (profession) in terms of one's *Stand*, meaning one's social position (*Stellung*), trade (*Gewerbe*), or office (*Amt*) as part of the created order of things.[11] As we have seen in Chapter 3, Calvin agrees with Luther that our various callings in life commit us to duties fitted to our situation and possibilities assigned to us by God and that we should not transgress our limits so as not to "heedlessly wander about throughout life."[12] However, according to Calvin, true vocation as living, moving, and having one's redeemed being in the common life, also means to *transform* this life with a new spirit from within. One's status is not given by one's original location in a predetermined social order, and the ranks and orders of classes in society are not fixed. God's creative activity in history constantly brings about new possibilities in social life. This means that one should develop one's talents in the common life in order to become what one is not yet. For instance, someone who is born a craftsman may be called to become a scientist or a city council member. On the other hand, society can also be deformed by sinful desires and ungodly attempts that make it structurally unsound. Therefore, social life is always in need of critical assessment and continuous reform, in accordance with God's Word.[13]

Following this (Neo-)Calvinistic line of thought, it is possible to develop a view of the good life in which the need for continual transformation and social reform is emphasized. Since the orders of creation are affected by sin, social orders must

---

9. Aristotle, *Politica* 1280b.
10. Taylor, *Sources of the Self*, 213.
11. WA 34.2, 307.
12. *Inst.* 3.10.6.
13. See for a critical examination of contemporary Protestant views of work and societal structures Pieter Vos, "Celebrating God's Works: The Day of Worship and the Ethics of Work," in Pieter Vos (ed.), *Liturgy and Ethics: New Contributions from Reformed Perspectives* (Leiden and Boston: Brill, 2018), 246–65.

not be merely accepted, but be reformed. Calvin speaks of "a full reformation of all the parts," as an interpretation of Paul's saying, "Be transformed by the renewal of your minds" (Rom. 12:2). This transformation first of all concerns the redemption of all these parts of the soul (the traditional Platonic parts of the soul: the sensual, the intellectual, and the will) in their respective relations to God,[14] and secondly extends to the moral, social, political, and economic spheres as a result of the renewal of human beings' relations with God. This vision has three aspects that belong together as the facets of one insight: (1) the need for transformation, (2) the imperfections of human beings, and (3) the greatness of God. This is reflected in the opening sections of the *Institutes*, where Calvin holds together, in dynamic relationship, knowledge of God, self-knowledge, and the need to seek transformation.[15] As a consequence, *coram Deo* our condition is twofold: on the one hand, we are created and endowed with no mean gifts, and on the other hand, we should weigh our lack of abilities; we are both divine image bearers and sinners. We have the means and the calling to transform life in its full extent, but at the same time we should acknowledge that we are prone to grave distortions.[16] The importance of these emphases is not that they betray a pessimistic view, but rather that they call our attention to the continuous need for reform and self-critique before God. Self-critique should be at the heart of the sanctification of life, in order to prevent it from deteriorating into sectarianism, superiority, or perfectionism. This is especially important when it comes to the use of human power, since power corrupts, as Calvin repeatedly remarks.[17] This is also important to prevent us from seeking personal holiness that is no longer directed toward the good of the neighbor.

From this perspective, it was possible to develop a wide-ranging Christian view of life, which enables the application of these purposes in every sphere of life, as became manifest by the seventeenth century. The Puritan minister Thomas Case, for instance, addressed the English House of Commons in 1641 in the following way:

> Reformation must be universal. Reform all places, all persons, and callings; reform the benches of judgement, the inferior magistrates. . . . Reform the universities, reform the cities, reform the countries, reform the inferior schools

---

14. *Inst.* 2.1.9.
15. *Inst.* 1.1.1; cf. Taylor, *A Secular Age*, 77.
16. *Inst.* 2.1.3; Frank Sawyer, "Some Transformational Aspects in John Calvin's Thought and Influence," in Bram de Muynck, Johan Hegeman, and Pieter Vos (eds.), *Bridging the Gap: Connecting Christian Faith and Professional Practice* (Sioux Center: Dordt College Press, 2011), 205.
17. For example, John Calvin, *Commentary on the Catholic Epistles* (Grand Rapids: Baker, 1999), 304: ". . . the more power a person holds, the worse he will be, and the more roughly he will treat his neighbors."

of learning, reform the Sabbath, reform the ordinances, the worship of God . . . you have more work to do than I can speak.[18]

Another example is the Neo-Calvinism of Abraham Kuyper, Herman Bavinck, Herman Dooyeweerd, and others in the Netherlands. Kuyper, for instance, developed a theocentric life view that starts with God's sovereignty and is reflected in human sovereignty or 'sphere-responsibility' consisting of the different responsibilities of state, church, family, and employers, each serving God in their own areas of life and calling.[19] An example of how the transformative power could work out is the way Kuyper addressed the so-called social question, concerning the bad circumstances of workers and their families in late nineteenth-century industrialized capitalistic society. Because Scripture states that "the laborer deserves his wages" (1 Tim. 5:18, English Standard Version), Kuyper criticized capitalism for doing injustice toward the poor and using the worker as just an instrument serving the worship of Mammon. Such work conditions are contrary to what God calls us to do.[20]

In sum, historically the sanctification of ordinary life has a double effect. On the one hand, it has a leveling effect since the cleric is no holier than the laborer and the nun no holier than the mother. Everyone can have a part in the good life. On the other hand, it has the effect of ratcheting up expectations for lay people, since ordinary life itself is taken up and sanctified. Hence, the transition to the ordinary is at the same time an engine of social change, including new ideals of life, criticism of social and political hierarchies, and the need for continuous self-criticism. In some cases, the new faith of salvation from God alone even becomes "a tremendously potent motive force behind revolutionary change."[21] Ordinary life is seen as more than just profane, as itself to be hallowed and in no way second class. It should be sanctified and is in need of transformation toward the fulfillment of God's purposes. The concept of 'reform' can serve to correct a fixation on a particular identification of the Christian life and to underline the implications of sanctification for social justice.

The question is what this development in general and the intrinsic relation between the sanctification of all parts of life and transformation in particular imply for the valuation and interpretation of virtues and the meaning of exemplarity.

---

18. Thomas Case, *Two Sermons Lately Preached* (London, 1642), 2.13.16, quoted from Hardy, *Fabric*, 67.

19. Abraham Kuyper, *Lectures on Calvinism* (Grand Rapids: Eerdmans, [1898] 1931).

20. An important impetus for taking up this matter in terms of social and political responsibilities was Kuyper's lecture on "The Social Question and Christian Religion" (*Het sociale vraagstuk en de christelijke religie* (Amsterdam: Wormer, 1891)) at the first "Christian Social Convention" (*Christelijk Sociaal Congres*) in 1891. Note that in twentieth-century Neo-Calvinism this critical transformative potential did not always result in an actual critical stance of resistance against unjust circumstances.

21. Taylor, *Sources of the Self*, 216.

One interpretation, advocated by MacIntyre, Gregory, and others, as we have seen, is that the turn to ordinary life and the emphasis on personal commitment since the Reformation furthered the replacement of virtue ethics by a formal ethics of individual rights. A different interpretation, one that I defend in this book and will be completed in this chapter, is that the affirmation of the ordinary can also be seen as concurring with virtue ethics and as a potential contribution to its development. The turn to ordinary life results in a particular account of virtues and exemplarity which can be understood as an alternative within the broad and widely varying virtue ethical tradition. The affirmation of ordinary life is not necessarily to be understood as a breakdown of the virtue ethical tradition. Not only is a teleological view of life and the understanding of the good life in terms of attaining particular virtues still present in the Protestant view of a variety of authors, as has been demonstrated in Chapters 3 and 4, but also this view has some particular contributions to offer in understanding the virtuous life and the meaning of exemplars in attaining the virtues needed to live this life, as we have seen already in Chapter 6 with regard to the *imitatio Christi*. Character cultivation finds its proper locus in ordinary life, which in turn is seen as more than just profane, for the whole extent of mundane life must be sanctified.

One of the implications is that moral exemplarity is not primarily to be found in the exceptional lives of the sages or the saints who live in the distinct realm of the contemplative life, but can in principle be found in the lives of ordinary people who live their mundane lives in devotion to God in an exceptional way. This view of the potential exemplarity of ordinary people, which is part of contemporary understandings of virtue ethics, can only be grasped fully against the background of the affirmation of ordinary life in which Protestantism has been a main factor. For sure, the historical impetus of the Protestant turn to ordinary life does not mean at all that this turn is *exclusively* Protestant. For instance, a current Catholic view may well include the necessity of relating extraordinary exemplars to the fullness of ordinary life. The turn to the ordinary in Protestantism rather has a *general* impact.

A second implication is that this understanding of exemplarity as related to ordinary life changes the relation between the extraordinary and the ordinary. Ordinary life as seen in its full extent is not just a locus that should be transformed in accordance with some pre-given exceptional models, but exceptional exemplars and ordinary people are related in more complex ways, including the ambiguities and complexities in the lives of exemplars themselves. Before I elaborate on these issues, the meaning of the virtues in the ordering and transformation of ordinary life deserves more clarification.

Virtues Ordering and Transforming Life

One basic thought in the Protestant tradition is that the sanctification of life includes a love for the world in which, as it were, the things of the world should be passed through to God—a thought that reflects the Augustinian distinction between *uti* and *frui*. In a Protestant view, we should neither renounce the things of the world nor become absorbed by these things. From this perspective, Puritan thought, in which a love for the world is paradoxically related to a detestation of the world, articulates particular virtues that exemplify this ethos. According to the English Puritan John Cotton (1585–1652), diligence in the world is accompanied by the virtue of devotion to God:

> There is another combination of vertues strangely mixed in every lively holy Christian, And that is, Diligence in worldly businesses, and yet deadnesse to the world; such a mystery as none can read, but they that know it. For a man to [take] all opportunities to be doing something, early and late, and loseth no opportunity, go any way and bestir himselfe for profit, this will he doe most diligently in his calling: And yet bee a man dead-hearted to the world ... though hee labour most diligently in his calling, yet his heart is not set upon these things.[22]

Dedication to work was seen as spiritually earnest business as opposed to the vice of idleness. From these and other testimonies one could create an image of particular Protestant virtues such as frugality, charity, diligence, punctuality, honesty, modesty, and sobriety.[23] These virtues may be regarded as somewhat frugal and limited in scope. However, one should notice that the core of these virtues consists in *other-centered* virtue. Work done in the various callings is done with the specific purpose "to serve God *in the serving of men* in the works of our callings," as Joseph Hall (1574–1656) puts it.[24] Central to the understanding of one's calling is that it is to benefit one's neighbor. William Perkins (1558–1602) states that one's calling is to be seen as a certain kind of life *for the common good*.[25] Similarly, Calvin neither advocates an ascetic attitude to material life nor promotes the accumulation of capital in the sense assumed in Weber's thesis of inner-worldly asceticism that he attributes to some Puritans. Rather he condemns both as vices and emphasizes that the supreme purpose of the benefits God grants us is *to help the poor*. According to Calvin, the neighbor's needs are the touchstone for the whole of Christian ethics.[26] Frugality may be regarded as a Calvinist virtue, but it is only a virtue in regard of the purpose to serve the good; in other words, frugality is ordered from the theological virtue of charity, which is basically continuous with the broader Christian virtue ethical tradition, the difference being that the locus of charity is explicitly extended to the ordinary life of work and profession. Similarly,

---

22. John Cotton, quoted from Taylor, *Sources of the Self*, 223.
23. See the list of Calvinistic virtues described in the volume Louke van Wensveen and Harm Dane (eds.), *Zuinigheid met vlijt: Over calvinistische (on)deugden* [Frugality and diligence: On Calvinistic virtues/vices] (Zoetermeer: Boekencentrum, 2009).
24. Joseph Hall, quoted from Taylor, *Sources of the Self*, 225. Italics mine.
25. Quoted from Taylor, *Sources of the Self*, 225.
26. Biéler, *Calvin's Economic and Social Thought*, 190.

wealth can be regarded as a relative good but should be balanced throughout society and used for the common good. The virtues that spring from the new professional ethic that has developed from Calvin's understanding of the value of work acquire their meaning from the ultimate purpose of serving God and his Kingdom, including care of one's neighbor.[27]

Yet, part of the Calvinistic ethic was not just a moderation of life, but rather its transformation. The active drive to reorganize the orders of life, both in the church and in the world, shaped particular virtues or shaped some virtues in a particular way. "Calvinist movements aspired to build a new, proper order of things,"[28] correcting all kinds of personal and social disorder. On the one hand, the emphasis is on virtues that contribute to order, such as the virtue of discipline (which in an Aristotelian view would be no more than a pre-virtue), that is, the capability of controlling oneself and taking responsibility for one's life, as a basis for social order and in order to rectify the disorder in the world. On the other hand, the emphasis on transformation and reform is expressed in virtues that exemplify the concern for social reform, such as zeal for justice. Although Calvinists can be unfeeling and unmerciful to those who stand outside their circle, their identification as the people of God's law can also become a source of tremendous strength.[29] In its best form, the Calvinist zeal for justice results in a commitment to social justice, as for instance in the struggle against apartheid.[30] Initially, Reformed theology was a theology of the oppressed as the elect people distinguished from the oppressors, who were seen as the reprobate. In its worst forms, this order was reversed: the poor, the black, women, or native North American inhabitants were oppressed and the rich, the white, men, or the immigrant pioneers privileged. Yet, such aberrations do not necessarily result from Reformed theology and ethics. On the contrary, critical (self-)reflection has been part of the Reformed notion of reform or transformation. Therefore, if we take the notion of transformation as viable with regard to virtue ethics, it should always include a self-critical understanding, including a prophetic role full of commitment to challenge and influence current and future social arrangements.[31] The aspects of reform and social justice following the command to love one's neighbor as oneself should serve to prevent virtue ethics from lapsing into conventionalism.

The argument so far is that Protestantism contributes to a particular modern shape of virtue ethics. This argument can be extended in the sense that the affirmation of the ordinary as rooted in Protestantism also shows its influence in the way virtue ethics is rediscovered and developed in late modernity. It is arguable that the recent return of virtue ethics, as advocated by MacIntyre and

---

27. Ibid., 148, 275, 282–3, 438, referring to Calvin's commentaries.
28. Taylor, *Sources of the Self*, 228.
29. Ibid., 230.
30. Cf. Alan A. Boesak, *Black and Reformed: Apartheid, Liberation, and the Calvinist Tradition* (New York: Orbis Books, 1984).
31. Nolan, *Reformed Virtue After Barth*, viii, 8, pointing to the Barmen declaration.

others, is not just to be understood as a return to classical Aristotelianism and Thomism, but is also a continuation of the early modern Protestant turn to life in its full extent. It has often been stated that it is a Kantian ethics that could develop within the context of the Protestant turn to divine commandments and derived laws, rules, and obligations as the primary source of ethical precepts for living the moral life. However, this conceals a more nuanced and ambivalent picture. The way virtue ethics is readopted and developed recently cannot be understood fully without the turn to ordinary life. For, nowadays, virtue ethics is regarded as an alternative to deontological ethics or utilitarianism precisely because it provides a comprehensive picture of moral experience and in this sense is closer to issues of *ordinary life*. An ethics of virtue is understood as focusing on the development of people displaying virtuous character in the routines of everyday life. Rather than focusing on moral quandaries arising out of exceptional ethical dilemmas, virtue ethics is about a morality as it is experienced in real life. Therefore, recent virtue ethical research shows a turn to the "moral phenomenology of ordinary life," as Chappell observes.[32] In doing so, it is as modern as it is premodern in its approach, and the turn to ordinary life is not fully understandable without the historical impetus of the Protestant affirmation of the ordinary.

Protestant Exemplars

The Protestant turn to ordinary life also changes the perception of moral exemplarity and its meaning in the cultivation of the virtues. A focus on ordinary life presupposes that moral exemplars are not only—and perhaps not primarily—provided by exceptional characters and extraordinary stories of moral excellence, but also provided by those excellent characters who represent the dilemmas, stories, and struggles of everyday life. This presupposes an understanding of moral exemplarity that is close not only to the ordinary life most of us live, but also to the complexities and ambiguities we experience in this life.

The importance of ordinary exemplars is confirmed by empirical research in the field of moral psychology. Research of more than two decades ago already demonstrated that people identify a wide range of moral exemplars, including humanitarians, revolutionaries, social activists, religious leaders, and politicians. Yet, the most frequent categories mentioned are those who are most close in ordinary life: family members and friends.[33] Both historical, publicly visible,

---

32. Chappell, "Virtue Ethics in the Twentieth Century," 149–71. We see parallels in other fields of research. Sayer, *Why Things Matter to People*, for instance, criticizes the social sciences for neglecting ordinary life and advocates a turn to everyday concerns in order to do justice to the 'things that really matter to people.'

33. Lawrence J. Walker, Russell C. Pitts, Karl H. Hennig, and M. Kyle Matsuba, "Reasoning about Morality and Real-Life Moral Problems," in Melanie Killen and Daniel

and 'local,' personal exemplars may serve well as moral examples in character formation, if their lives are examined in their fullness, including the complexity of their personalities, the formative aspects of their experiences, and their weaknesses and struggles in daily life.[34] On the other hand, a focus on everyday morality does not exclude exceptionality, for ordinary life too can be lived in an exceptional way, and in this sense particular ordinary people may be recognized as morally exceptional and exemplary. Such an understanding of exemplarity in the realm of the daily complexity of life may come up against a problem given with the traditional concept of emulating exceptional exemplars. This problem is that no matter how exceptional the moral exemplar may be, his or her exemplarity is only meaningful if ordinary people, which most of us are, succeed in 'applying' the example in the daily complexity of their own lives.

My argument is that the Protestant turn to ordinary life—though not separated from other influences—has been an important impetus for a reinterpretation of moral exemplarity as it is traditionally understood. Exemplarity is no longer only conceived of as emulating morally exceptional persons like heroes and saints, but also conceived of as relating to exemplars that express the complexities and ambiguities of everyday life. To develop this argument, I must first clarify what happened to the saints and their exemplary role in Protestantism.

It should be noted that the teachings of the Reformers do not require an end to commemoration of the saints.[35] The *Augsburg Confession*, for instance, says: "the memory of saints may be set before us, that we may follow their faith and good works, according to our calling."[36] Rejected are particular uses of the saints, namely in their vicarious roles: "Scripture teaches not the invocation of saints or to ask help of saints, since it sets before us the one Christ as the Mediator, Propitiation, High Priest, and Intercessor."[37] Though the Reformers decry the role of saints as intermediaries, their role as moral exemplars is maintained. Melanchthon, for instance, encourages appropriate honor to the saints through imitation: "first, of faith, then of the other virtues, which every one should imitate according to his

---

Hart (eds.), *Morality in Everyday Life: Developmental Perspectives* (Cambridge: Cambridge University Press, 1995), 392. See also the groundbreaking work of Anne Colby and William Damon, *Some Do Care: Contemporary Lives of Moral Commitment* (New York: Free Press, 1992).

34. Lawrence J. Walker, "Moral Exemplarity," in William Damon (ed.), *Bringing in a New Era in Character Education* (Stanford: Hoover Institution Press, 2002), 65–84.

35. Michael Banner, "On What We Lost When (or If) We Lost the Saints," in Brian Brock and Michael Mawson (eds.), *The Freedom of a Christian Ethicist: The Future of a Reformation Legacy* (London: Bloomsbury T&T Clark, 2016), 175–90.

36. *Triglot Concordia: The Symbolical Books of the Evangelical Lutheran Church: German-Latin-English* (St. Louis: Concordia Publishing House, 1921), quoted from http://bookofconcord.org/augsburgconfession.php.

37. Ibid.

calling."³⁸ All this is in line with the patristic church's tradition of mentioning by name particular Christians and their lives in its worship, primarily for the praise of God, but in a secondary sense to provide an ethical *model* for other believers.³⁹ As Kierkegaard remarks, not only Christ is the example, but apostles and disciples as well as martyrs and saints are also exemplars, "derived exemplars."⁴⁰ Generally, in a Protestant valuation of the saints, the focus is not so much on these exemplars and their holiness, but on how God's grace works in their lives. The saints are saints because and insofar as they are truthful imitators of Christ.

Yet it must be said that in most Protestant churches and countries the remembrance of the saints as exemplars has not been sustained in practice, with the result that an important resource for moral teaching tends to be lost, namely the saints portrayed in hagiographic literature as examples to be followed. As Michael Banner states, since in the Christian faith human life is construed in relation to the life of Christ, the telling and retelling of the lives of saints is important too as a way to reflect upon human life. For the lives of saints are to be interpreted as commentaries on the life of Christ and therefore provide valuable examples to be followed.⁴¹

At the same time, it should be acknowledged that in the history up to the Reformation the saints generally did not provide examples that were *actually* followed by ordinary believers, as we already observed in Chapter 6. Robert Bartlett points out that in practice saints were more often seen as wonderworkers to be prayed to rather than exemplars to be emulated. "There is a big difference between the awestruck approach to a mighty source of supernatural aid and the attempt to model oneself on a virtuous man or woman."⁴² It is the exceptionality of their sanctity that distances the saints from everyday life and prevents them from becoming realistic models to be imitated. The problem is that the saints are not sufficiently understood as examples *for us*. What they do on behalf of us, in their vicarious role, is not what we can do too.

However, this image would be a little too simple. It presupposes that exemplars are only exemplary if ordinary people succeed in *copying* or imitating them very closely. But copying is not what the saints are about at all, as Banner remarks.⁴³

---

38. His *Apology* (Defense of the Augsburg Confession), 21.6, quoted from http://book ofconcord.org/defense_20_saints.php.

39. Bernd Wannenwetsch, *Political Worship*, trans. Margaret Kohl (Oxford: Oxford University Press, 2010), 201–2.

40. *JN* 8, 168 / *SKS* 24, 170 (NB22:128). However, "Instead of letting them remain as exemplars, they were transformed into intercessors who prayed for a person." In the margin of this journal entry Kierkegaard refers to Naander, *Chrysostomus* I, 51, where this view is described as a way of thinking that "Stützen der Unsittlichkeit statt Vorbilder des Sittlichkeit sucht" (*JN* 8, 168 / *SKS* 24, 170 (NB22:128a)).

41. Banner, "On What We Lost," 176 and 178.

42. Bartlett, *Why Can the Dead Do Such Great Things?*, 511.

43. Banner, "On What We Lost," 182.

Rather, exemplary figures are exemplary because of the values and virtues they embody. We develop our moral sensibilities by encountering the values and virtues that we find actually existing and experientially available in exemplary characters. The exemplary meaning of exemplars does not depend upon whether or not anyone sets out to be them, but "the fully worked example of a particular value holds that value in play even for those who do not themselves pursue that value fully or exclusively."[44] In this sense the saints are still relevant exemplars. As Alessandro Ferrara states:

> Examples—Achilles, Saint Francis, Jesus of Nazareth—become *exemplary*, i.e., capable of exerting an influence on us, who are not within their context of origin, by virtue of their ability to realize, within the horizon of an action or of a life course, an optimal congruity between the deed and a certain inspiring motive underlying it—a congruity that in turn resonates with us by tapping the same intuitions that works of art, for all the diversity of styles and intentions underlying them, are capable of tapping.[45]

What matters is whether and how the moral integrity of exemplars resonates with our own lives. From this perspective the turn to ordinary life is first of all promising in the sense that it makes us all the more aware of the singularity of *our own lives* in which the values and virtues as exemplified by exemplary people, including the saints, are to be cultivated and internalized. A Protestant contribution in reflecting on the exemplary meaning of saints and other exemplars consists especially in a sharpened awareness of the necessity of bringing these exemplars back into ordinary life. First, this concerns the way we as ordinary people can emulate exemplars, which is not by copying them but by imagining the values and cultivating the virtues as exemplified by these exemplars in *our own particular moral lives*. Secondly, such an understanding also changes the perception of the *lives of moral exemplars*. They are not seen as just ideals, that is, as perfect examples of what they exemplify, but as *persons* who show virtues and live out particular values in the midst of the moral complexity of their lives. Exemplars are seen as being fully part of life, including its moral complexity and ambiguity. This does not mean that the extraordinary is simply replaced by the ordinary. Rather, the ordinary and the extraordinary are dialectically related. The exemplar is extraordinary but not in such a way that it is set completely apart from the ordinary. Insofar as there was indeed a distance between the extraordinary saints and ordinary people,[46] the relocation of exemplars in ordinary life helps to *bridge* this gap.

---

44. Ibid., 184.
45. Alessandro Ferrara, *The Force of the Example: Explorations in the Paradigm of Judgement* (New York: Columbia University Press, 2006), 61.
46. Banner, "On What We Lost," 183, refers to several studies, for example, Aviad Kleinberg, *Flesh Made Word: Saints' Stories and the Western Imagination* (Cambridge: Belknap Press, 2008).

Generally speaking, in Protestantism it is indeed extraordinary people in the midst of ordinary life who become regarded as exemplars, rather than 'holy' people that are exceptions in the profane world. Since ordinary life is emphasized as the locus of sanctification, it is within the fullness of this life that people can show exceptionality and become exemplars. It is not just saints in the classical sense, but also people who participate in family life and work—the two loci Taylor identifies as the places where ordinary life takes place and one can fulfill one's vocation in the Protestant view—that are seen as exemplary: the baker who works with discipline, the mother who shows caring love, etc. These ordinary people are typically characterized not as having a full complement of moral virtues but rather as embodying a smaller subset and thereby expressing how they participate in the full complexity of moral life. They serve as exemplars not only because they are exemplary in their virtues, but also because their lives are present in their fullness, including the complexity of their personalities and their weaknesses and struggles in daily life.[47]

One instance that demonstrates the relocation of moral exemplarity in the complexities of ordinary life is how examples are present in early modern literature starting from the Renaissance. In this literature examples are less seen as exemplifications of general truths and more as complex narratives in which it is not immediately clear what they precisely exemplify. Writers took advantage of newly available scholarly means to study the actual lives of those who were seen as exemplary and employed new dramatic and narrative means to render human character more fully.[48] In his investigation into the rhetoric of the example in the works of the humanists of early modern France and Italy, John Lyons points to the transition from medieval ethical genres, like the novella, the fable, and the morality play, to more detailed literary representations of individual characters and situations in stories about their actual lives, especially in the works of modern essayists. Montaigne, for instance, often begins with examples, without knowing exactly what they exemplify, and invites readers to a critical examination. In his essays examples serve neither to become part of a system of abstract ideas, nor as a moralistic story, but rather as the representation of a unique life full of ambiguities that go beyond generalizations.[49] As Jeffrey Stout states: "The more attention the humanists gave to the narrative or dramatic details of putatively exemplary lives, the more trouble they had relating them

---

47. Cf. the psychological investigations into moral exemplarity by Walker et al., "Reasoning about Morality and Real-Life Moral Problems," 392; Walker, "Moral Exemplarity," 77.

48. See for these observations: Jeffrey Stout, *Democracy and Tradition* (Princeton: Princeton University Press, 2004), 169–70.

49. John D. Lyons, *Exemplum: The Rhetoric of Example in Early Modern France and Italy* (Princeton: Princeton University Press, 1989); Stout, *Democracy and Tradition*, 165, 169–70.

to the virtues and general truths the lives were supposed to exemplify."[50] The thicker the descriptions of characters are, the more ethically complicated and realistic their exemplarity becomes.

This emphasis on moral complexity is, I think, meaningful with regard to the development of a relevant account of moral exemplarity. Importantly, the enriched depiction of characters and their circumstances in essays, Shakespearian plays, and novels makes it harder to take them as just exemplifying 'something.' The exemplary significance of characters becomes less clear, since they become more like human beings living with the tensions of life rather than clear-cut figures carrying a didactic label. Rather than exemplifying a determinate moral, they appear to be mixtures of vice and virtue. As a consequence, the example is always excessive, because it will have characteristics that go beyond what can be covered by generalization.[51] Stories and characters presented in literature are not just illustrations of what could also be said in other forms, but themselves present and represent the complexity of moral life in a fuller sense than abstract generalizations can do.

In principle, this approach is in line with Neo-Aristotelian accounts of virtue ethics, in which the fullness of moral life as it is actually lived is acknowledged too. It is the abstraction of (deontological and utilitarian) ethical theory that is criticized by virtue ethicists like MacIntyre and Hauerwas. They propose to replace the thin descriptions of modern quandary ethics and their cases by thicker descriptions of real-life stories as, for instance, represented in novels. Yet, these authors basically present their argument as an *alternative* to modernity and modern ethical discourse as a whole, without acknowledging that in their plea they are praising precisely a *modern* feature that can only be understood well by taking into account the historical development from the tradition of modern essayists to modern literature. Hauerwas, for instance, considers the novel a 'school of virtue' and mines the ethical significance of modern novels,[52] but his dependence on this modern genre does not appear in his historical narrative in which modernity is primarily evaluated in terms of the decline of virtue ethics in favor of abstract ethical theory.[53] However, as Stout rightly argues, modern culture contains resources of its own for resisting the generalization and abstract nature of modern ethical theory: the narrative discourse of essayists, novelists, and dramatists.[54]

---

50. Stout, *Democracy and Tradition*, 169.

51. Lyons, *Exemplum*, 34; Stout, *Democracy and Tradition*, 169.

52. For example, Stanley Hauerwas, *Dispatches from the Front: Theological Engagements with the Secular* (Durham: Duke University Press, 1994), 31–57; Stanley Hauerwas, "Bearing Reality: A Christian Meditation," *Journal of the Society of Christian Ethics* 33/1 (2013), 3–20.

53. For example, Stanley Hauerwas, "How 'Christian Ethics' Came to Be," in *The Hauerwas Reader*, ed. John Berkman and Michael Cartwright (Durham: Duke University Press, 2001), 37–50.

54. Stout, *Democracy and Tradition*, 168–9, 172.

Emulation in the Complexities of Life

The emphasis on examples that exemplify moral complexity and ambiguity does not imply the end of modeling oneself on and emulating moral exemplarity. On the contrary, I think this view rather deepens our understanding of it. Though moral formation should not consist in modeling oneself on clear-cut characters, learning from moral exemplars remains a crucial element in our moral development. It still holds that we largely become who we are by responding to models, but we do not suppose that our moral formation requires us to become the docile disciple of a model as a straightforward exemplification of good character and virtue. In an understanding of exemplarity that locates the exemplar within the complexities of life, thin descriptions of exemplars are replaced by thick descriptions. Thin descriptions of character often serve to offer straightforward examples that keep the problem of excess under control in order to establish the desired relationship of exemplification.[55] Thick descriptions of character, as for instance provided in (modern) literature but also the exemplarity of Martin Luther King who appears to be a 'flawed saint,' point to the complexity of moral life and locate exemplarity within this complexity. This means that emulation of exemplary excellence is still indispensably part of becoming excellent in one's own person, but that the focus is not the imitation or copying of a clear-cut model, but rather the singularity of the way particular virtues of exemplars may be emulated in the particularities of one's own life.

A relevant element of a Protestant theological approach is that it puts the sanctity of exemplars into perspective. As Protestants would say, no exemplar is worth idolatry. This turns the focus from the life of the exemplar to our own lives. Similarly, the complexity of the characters of exemplars as present in modern literary narratives makes emulation a struggle that turns our attention to the complexity of our own lives. Rather than copying the character, the traits, or the particular deeds of exemplary people, we should seek to become moral characters in our own particular contexts and situations, as exemplary people are in their particular circumstances. This requires us not only to look behind particular exemplars to *what* they exemplify, but also to cultivate the virtue of self-trust. Since we should prevent ourselves from idolatry, we must not put our trust completely in exemplars, but rather emulate the excellence of self-trust as precisely exemplified by exemplars.[56]

It would be a mistake to presuppose that exemplars only function as exemplars if ordinary people succeed in imitating them literally. The aim is neither to react as the virtuous model does nor to acquire his or her virtuous qualities in order to behave as the model does. Rather is the aim to *emulate* exemplars, so that in a sense we

---

55. Ibid., 171–2. Stout considers this strategy to be standard in classical and Biblical accounts of exemplarity, but I think this is overstated, since in Greek tragedies and Biblical narratives characters, including Jesus, are often depicted in their complex struggles full of distress, fear and failure.

56. Ibid., 172–3.

try to embody the virtues even better than the exemplar does. This means that we understand that exemplars are not themselves the measure of moral virtue and vice but that they merely embody them and that the task is to embody them ourselves in our own particular way. In this sense we can do it better than the exemplar can do it, since the exemplar cannot do it in our place. There is a significant difference between 'becoming like the exemplar' and 'becoming like what the exemplar exemplifies.' Only in the second case does the question arise of what it means *for me* to have the exemplified virtuous quality myself in my own situation. This includes deliberation about what kind of person I currently am and how I can alter my character to become virtuous in my own way and in my particular context.[57]

In this interpretation, emulation of moral exemplars is not about literal imitation or copying—although copying can be an initial meaningful step, as for instance in early childhood. Emulation of exemplars demands that we do not imitate their personalities but that we deliberately emulate what they exemplify. Yet, this 'what' can only be perceived as and because it is *embodied* concretely by moral exemplars and cannot be substituted by some general truth.

Role Exemplarity and Existential Exemplarity

Now that the nature of our relationship to moral exemplars has been explained in general, the next step is to differentiate in how exemplarity functions. I would like to introduce a relevant distinction that differentiates in the way we understand exemplars, namely between what I propose to call 'role exemplarity,' on the one hand, and 'existential exemplarity,' on the other. This distinction helps to give more nuances to the way we relate to exemplars and is not identical with the distinction between extraordinary exemplars such as heroes, sages, and saints, on the one hand, and ordinary people, on the other. For both 'ordinary' and 'extraordinary' exemplars can become meaningful in two different ways, either as defined from their pre-given roles in social practices or as exemplifying something which is so innovative that it goes beyond what is already known from pre-given roles and is meaningful on a deep, existential level. This distinction helps to differentiate in how exemplarity may have transformative meaning in the moral life. Let me first clarify both types of exemplarity and then explain their transformative meaning.

Moral exemplarity in the sense of role exemplarity can be understood as being defined from the roles we play in particular social and professional practices, as parent, teacher, professional, neighbor, member of a society, or a congregation. In these social practices people can become exemplary through the way they embody the virtues needed to realize the internal goods of such practices. In these roles family members, friends, colleagues, teachers, and so on may get exemplary meaning, being those exemplars that are most frequently listed by people as actual important

---

57. Wouter Sanderse, "The Meaning of Role Modelling in Moral and Character Education," *Journal of Moral Education* 42/1 (2013), 28–42.

exemplars.[58] On the other hand, exceptional exemplars like humanitarians, social activists, and religious leaders can also be meaningful in their roles, but more often they will have exemplary meaning because they exceed these roles. They exemplify something that goes beyond what already exists and open up new perspectives. People like Ghandi, Bonhoeffer, King, Mandela, and Pope Francis are exemplary because they disclose new vistas on what exists and are inspiring because of their pure exemplarity and transformative strength. They are 'existential exemplars,' because they acquire meaning on a deeper, existential level, that is, with regard to what it means to be a human being and to be a human being with and for others. Less known people too, who are exceptional in being exemplary beyond their given roles, can have such existential meaning and become existential exemplars. This also means that role and existential exemplarity do not necessarily exclude each other. One and the same person can be an existential model while also being a role model and vice versa. My parent, colleague, or teacher can be exemplary as parent, colleague, or teacher, but at the same time be exemplary in a way that goes beyond these roles, showing me something about the meaning of human existence.

In what sense do these two distinct kinds of exemplarity have distinctive exemplary meaning for us? This concerns first of all the recognizability in our own lives. In role exemplarity the exemplar and what he or she exemplifies is immediately recognizable. As Alessandro Ferrara describes this kind of exemplarity:

> What is exemplary embeds and reflects a normativity of which we are fully aware: we already know of what the example is an example. Examples of virtuous conduct, of best practices in the professions, of statemanship in politics, of courage in combat or of parental care are often of this kind.[59]

It is the *role* within a particular social practice which determines the standards of excellence—to use MacIntyre's terms—by which such an exemplar is recognized as exemplary. In this kind of exemplarity, the exemplar indeed exemplifies 'something' that is not uniquely represented by one exceptional person but is a 'good' that is intrinsically part of given practices.

In the second kind of exemplarity, however, exemplariness and that which is exemplified are not immediately recognizable in this way. In the case of 'existential exemplarity' the exemplariness of the exemplar is innovative and goes beyond what is already given. We only vaguely sense it by drawing on analogies with past experiences and only subsequently do we succeed in identifying the normative moment that is reflected in the conduct at hand. As Ferrara states:

> Fully grasping exemplarity in this case requires that we formulate ad hoc the principle of which it constitutes an instantiation. Political revolutions, the founding of new religions, groundbreaking works of art are often of this kind:

---

58. See the empirical investigation of Walker et al., "Reasoning about Morality."
59. Ferrara, *Force of the Example*, 3.

with one and the same gesture they disclose new vistas on what exists *and* new dimensions of normativity.[60]

The appeal and force with which such exemplars inspire us morally rest on a pure exemplarity that goes beyond what is already given in existing social practices. They resonate on a deeper level of our subjectivity.

Both kinds of exemplarity are meaningful for learning from exemplars in ordinary life. In role exemplarity something is embodied which we already recognize as important. Part of our character is the various roles we perform as professional, parent, relative, citizen, and so on in the social practices in which we participate. We try to emulate in *our own* roles what makes these persons exemplary in *their* roles.

From 'existential' exemplars, on the other hand, we can learn something which can be fully expressed neither by given practices or pre-given understandings of virtues nor by moral principles. These exemplars have an authority and a claim on us, prior to and apart from the authority and claims of moral principles.[61] It is also a claim that points beyond our social roles and the social practices in which we participate. The force of such examples is that "they tap intuitions that run deeper [than abstract principles], in the constitution of our subjectivity."[62] This points to a form of emulation that is not just aimed at our formation in particular roles, but rather at the formation of character that addresses the singularity of our subjectivity. An 'existential' exemplar shows in an ideal way what it means to exist as human being. At the same time, in being existentially exemplary such an exemplar points to the ideal self of the one who relates to the exemplar. Therefore, what counts is not to copy the exemplar's particular actions, but to realize the existential meaning of the exemplar in my own life, by starting to exist *in the way* the exemplar exists. If I were to understand emulation as the literal imitation of an exemplar, then this would be a sign that I do not really want to 'become myself.' This would not do justice to the reality of my existence as being this concrete, singular individual and no other. In confrontation with the ideal outside myself as exemplified by the exemplar, it is my own ideal self that should become manifest in my actual existence, just as the exemplar strives to express his or her particular ideal self in his or her life. Therefore, emulating existential exemplars is in fact the realization of the task of 'becoming oneself' in the Kierkegaardian sense, that is, the call of each singular individual to strive for the ideal self in the complexities of his or her own particular existence.

Conclusion

From the Protestant view developed in this chapter, it follows that moral exemplarity has to do with both the shaping of an authentic moral self and the

---

60. Ibid.
61. Banner, "On What We Lost," 181.
62. Ferrara, *Force of the Example*, 61.

social responsibilities in ordinary life. It is within the spheres of life in its full extent, including all its ambiguities and complexities, that two kinds of exemplarity are relevant. Moral exemplarity in the sense of role exemplarity can be understood as defined from the roles we play in particular social and professional practices. Our moral sensibilities are formed through the encounter with the qualities, that is, the virtues, that are exemplified by these role exemplars. These virtues are experientially available in the exemplary persons and practices in our social surroundings and we are invited to practice them in our own roles within such practices. On the other hand, the exemplariness of existential exemplars points beyond given practices and roles. In such exemplariness moral exemplars like humanitarians, revolutionaries, social activists, and religious leaders are meaningful, not because they exemplify excellence in their social roles but rather because they go beyond their roles. Existential exemplars deepen our understanding of the particular virtues they exemplify, since they show them in unprecedented ways. What matters is not to copy or imitate literally what these exemplars do or how they are, but to emulate their values and virtues in our own particular existence. The task is not to become the exemplar, but to become oneself *in the way* exemplars exemplarily become themselves in their particular existence. The lives of exemplars are not to be perceived as ready-made models for our own. Examples rather provide us with holistic images that nevertheless remain concrete and are exemplary because and insofar as they appeal to our own life concerns.

Furthermore, these two distinct kinds of exemplarity fit into the double emphasis on the affirmation of the social structures of ordinary life and the need for continuous reform and transformation as particular Protestant—or Reformed—characteristics that I have distinguished as two aspects of the sanctification of life. This is what is at stake in the Neo-Calvinistic concept of 'normative practices,' in which both the recognition of social structures and the need for transformation are acknowledged, that is, the structural side of practices and the regulative side respectively, as we have seen in Chapter 3. On the one hand, in line with MacIntyre, these practices are understood as a coherent form of socially established human cooperative activity through which internal goods are realized, ordered by different types of principles, rules, or standards of excellence, and in which virtues are the qualities that enable the achievement of those goods and are extended by participation in this activity. In these social practices of ordinary life people can become exemplary through the way they embody the virtues needed to realize the internal goods of such practices. On the other hand, any performance of a practice is said to involve a specific interpretation of the rules and standards of excellence, which is derived from a broader interpretative framework on the meaning of the practice for human life and for society, that is, from a wider view on the *telos* of human life. As argued in Chapter 3, the specific contribution of this regulative aspect is to be found in its critical function, insofar as this wider view forms a reference point for a critical assessment of existing practices that may prevent practices from becoming conservative and self-referential.

We can now see that we need to take this one step further, since this 'worldview' or 'life view' approach may still turn out to be static, because these views are primarily pre-given in existing conceptions and convictions of particular (religious) traditions. It is, however, important to maintain a fundamental openness to criticism that is not yet included in these views. Here the second meaning of exemplarity comes into play: existential exemplarity. In the first kind of exemplarity, what is exemplary can be seen as part of social practices and also as part of the world and life views that function on the regulative side of these practices. Exemplary persons exemplify par excellence the standards of excellence of these practices or criticize these practices from their internal perspectives and in this sense are exponents, albeit exemplary exponents, of given social practices. The existential exemplar is different through the innovative force of what she or he (re)presents. Such exemplars are more like Old Testament prophets who criticize pre-given social structures and potential injustices. Here we find a core element of what Protestantism may contribute to a viable contemporary virtue ethics: life that is really the good life with and for others needs to be transformed and reformed continuously.

BIBLIOGRAPHY

Adams, Robert M. *Finite and Infinite Goods*. Oxford: Oxford University Press, 1999.
Agan, Jimmy. "Departing from—and Recovering—Tradition: John Calvin and the Imitation of Christ." *Journal of the Evangelical Theological Society* 56/4 (2013), 801–14.
Ames, William. *Conscience, with the Power and Cases Thereof*. London: Imprinted W. Christiaens, E. Griffin, J. Dawson, 1639.
Ames, William. *De conscientia et eius iure vel casibus libri quinque*. Amsterdam: Janssonium, 1630.
Ames, William. *Medulla theologiae*. London: Robertum Allottum, 1627.
Ames, William. *The Marrow of Theology*. Edited by John D. Eusden. Boston: Pilgrim Press, [1629] 1968.
Anderson, Raymond K. *Love and Order: The Life-Structuring Dynamics of Grace and Virtue in Calvin's Ethical Thought*. Chambersburg: Wilson College, 1973.
Annas, Julia. *The Morality of Happiness*. Oxford: Oxford University Press, 1993.
Anscombe, G. Elizabeth M. "Modern Moral Philosophy." *Philosophy* 33 (1958), 1–16.
Aquinas, Thomas. *Summa Theologica*. Translated by Fathers of the English Dominican Province. New York: Benziger Bros., 1947–1948.
Aristotle. *Art of Rhetoric* (Loeb Classical Library 193). Translated by J. H. Freese. Cambridge: Harvard University Press, 1926.
Aristotle. *Eudemian Ethics* (Loeb Classical Library 285). Translated by H. Rackham. Cambridge: Harvard University Press, [1935] 1982.
Aristotle. *Nicomachean Ethics* (Loeb Classical Library 73). Translated by H. Rackham. Cambridge: Harvard University Press, [1926] 1982.
Aristotle. *Nicomachean Ethics* (Cambridge Texts in the History of Philosophy). Translated by Roger Crisp. Cambridge: Cambridge University Press, 2000.
Aristotle. *Politics* (Loeb Classical Library 264). Translated by H. Rackham. Cambridge: Harvard University Press, [1932] 1989.
Augustine. *Confessions*. Translated by R. S. Pine-Coffin. London: Penguin Books, [1961] 1984.
Augustine. *Letters*, Vol. II/3: Letters 156–210 (The Works of Saint Augustine: A Translation for the 21st Century). Translated by Roland Teske and edited by Boniface Ramsey. New York: New City Press, 2004.
Augustine. *Political Writings*. Edited and translated by E. M. Atkins and Robert J. Dodaro. New York: Cambridge University Press, 2001.
Augustine. *The City of God against the Pagans*. Edited and translated by R. W. Dyson. Cambridge and New York: Cambridge University Press, 1998.
Augustine. *The Trinity* (The Works of Saint Augustine: A New Translation for the 21st Century). Translated by Edmund Hill. New York: New City Press, 1991.

Austin, Michael and R. Douglas Geivett (eds.). *Being Good: Christian Virtues for Everyday Life*. Grand Rapids: Eerdmans, 2012.

Bakker, Nelleke (ed.). *Tot burgerschap en deugd: Volksopvoeding in de negentiende eeuw* [For citizenship and virtue: People's education in the nineteenth century]. Hilversum: Verloren, 2006.

Banner, Michael. "On What We Lost When (or If) We Lost the Saints." In Brian Brock and Michael Mawson (eds.), *The Freedom of a Christian Ethicist: The Future of a Reformation Legacy*. London: Bloomsbury T&T Clark, 2016, 175–90.

Banner, Michael. *The Ethics of Everyday Life: Moral Theology, Social Anthropology, and the Imagination of the Human*. Oxford: Oxford University Press, 2014.

Barth, Karl. *Church Dogmatics*, Vol. II/2. Edited by G. W. Bromiley and T. F. Torrance. Edinburgh: T&T Clark, 1957.

Bartlett, Robert. *Why Can the Dead Do Such Great Things? Saints and Worshippers from the Martyrs to the Reformation*. Princeton: Princeton University Press, 2013.

Baschera, Luca. "Aristotle and Scholasticism." In Torrance Kirby, Emidio Campi, and Frank A. James III (eds.), *A Companion to Peter Martyr Vermigli*. Leiden and Boston: Brill, 2009, 133–59.

Baschera, Luca. "Ethics in Reformed Orthodoxy." In Herman J. Selderhuis (ed.), *A Companion to Reformed Orthodoxy*. Leiden: Brill, 2013, 519–52.

Baschera, Luca. *Tugend und Rechtfertigung: Peter Martyr Vermiglis Kommentar zur Nikomachischen Ethik im Spannungsfeld von Philosophie and Theologie*. Zurich: Theologische Verlag, 2008.

Bavinck, Herman. *Gereformeerde ethiek* [Reformed ethics]. Utrecht: Kok Boekencentrum, 2019.

Bayer, Oswald. *Freedom in Response: Lutheran Ethics: Sources and Controversies*. Translated by Jeffrey F. Cayzer. Oxford: Oxford University Press, 2007.

Berger, Peter. "On the Obsolescence of the Concept of Honor." In Stanley Hauerwas and Alasdair MacIntyre (eds.), *Revisions: Changing Perspectives in Moral Philosophy*. Notre Dame: University of Notre Dame Press, 1983, 172–81.

Berkouwer, Gerrit C. *De mens het beeld Gods* [The human being as image of God]. Kampen: Kok, 1957.

Biéler, André. *Calvin's Economic and Social Thought*. Translated by James Greig. Geneva: World Council of Churches, [1961] 2005.

Biermann, Joel D. *A Case for Character: Towards a Lutheran Virtue Ethics*. Minneapolis: Fortress Press, 2014.

Billings, J. Todd. *Calvin, Participation, and the Gift: The Activity of Believers in Union with Christ*. Oxford: Oxford University Press, 2007.

Boesak, Alan A. *Black and Reformed: Apartheid, Liberation, and the Calvinist Tradition*. New York: Orbis Books, 1984.

Bonhoeffer, Dietrich. *Discipleship* (Dietrich Bonhoeffer Works 4). Minneapolis: Fortress Press, 2001.

Bonhoeffer, Dietrich. *Ethics* (Dietrich Bonhoeffer Works 6). Minneapolis: Fortress Press, 2001.

Borgman, Erik. "Leven is een kunst [Life is an art]." In Hans Weigand (ed.), *Het volle leven: Levenskunst en levensloop in de moderne samenleving*. Zoetermeer: Boekencentrum, 2005, 9–19.

Bovendeert, Jasmijn. *Kardinale deugden gekerstend: De vier kardinale deugden vanaf Ambrosius tot het jaar 1000* [Cardinal virtues Christianized: The four cardinal virtues from Ambrose to the year 1000]. Nijmegen: Radboud University, 2007.

Braaten, Carl E. and Robert W. Jenson (eds.). *Union with Christ: The New Finnish Interpretation of Luther*. Grand Rapids: Eerdmans, 1998.
Brillenburg Wurth, Gerrit. *Eerherstel van de deugd* [Rehabilitation of virtue]. Kampen: Kok, 1958.
Bubmann, Peter and Bernhard Sill (eds.). *Christliche Lebenskunst*. Regensburg: Verlag Friedrich Pustet, 2008.
Burnaby, John. *Amor Dei: A Study of the Religion of St. Augustine. The Hulsean Lectures for 1938*. London: Hodder and Stoughton, 1938.
Bøgeskov, Benjamín Olivares. "Thomas Aquinas: Kierkegaard's View Based on Scattered and Uncertain Sources." In Jon Stewart (ed.), *Kierkegaard and the Patristic and Medieval Traditions* (Kierkegaard Research: Sources, Reception and Resources 4). Farnham and Burlington: Ashgate, 2008, 183–206.
Calvin, John. *Commentary on the Catholic Epistles*. Grand Rapids: Baker, 1999.
Calvin, John. *Institutes of the Christian Religion*, 2 vols. Translated by Ford Lewis Battles and edited by John T. McNeill. Louisville: Westminster John Knox Press, 1960.
Calvin, John. *Institutes of the Christian Religion*. Translated by Henry Beveridge. Peabody: Hendrickson, 2008.
Calvin, John. *The Gospel according to St. John 11–21 and the First Epistle of John* (Calvin's Commentaries 5). Grand Rapids: Eerdmans [1959] 1995.
Calvin, John. *The Second Epistle of Paul the Apostle to the Corinthians and the Epistles to Timothy, Titus and Philemon* (Calvin's Commentaries 10). Grand Rapids: Eerdmans, [1964] 1991.
Case, Thomas. *Two Sermons Lately Preached*. London: Raworth, 1642.
Chappell, Timothy. "Virtue Ethics in the Twentieth Century." In Daniel C. Russell (ed.), *The Cambridge Companion to Virtue Ethics*. Cambridge: Cambridge University Press, 2013, 149–71.
Cicero. *De officiis* (Loeb Classical Library 30). Edited and translated by Walter Miller. Cambridge: Harvard University Press, [1913] 1968.
Cicero. *De re publica* (Loeb Classical Library 213). Translated by Clinton Walker Keyes. Cambridge: Harvard University Press, 1977.
Clair, Joseph. "Wolterstorff on Love and Justice: An Augustinian Response." *Journal of Religious Ethics* 41/1 (2013), 138–67.
Cochran, Elizabeth Agnew. *Protestant Virtue and Stoic Ethics* (Enquiries in Theological Ethics). London: Bloomsbury T&T Clark, 2018.
Cochran, Elizabeth Agnew. *Receptive Human Virtues: A New Reading of Jonathan Edwards's Ethics*. University Park: Pennsylvania State University Press, 2011.
Colby, Anne and William Damon. *Some Do Care: Contemporary Lives of Moral Commitment*. New York: Free Press, 1992.
Compaijen, Rob. "Authenticity and Imitation: On the Role of Moral Exemplarity in Anti-Climacus' Ethics." In Heiko Schulz, Jon Stewart, and Karl Verstrynge (eds.), *Kierkegaard Studies Yearbook* 2011. Berlin: De Gruyter, 2011, 341–63.
Compaijen, Rob. *Kierkegaard, MacIntyre, Williams, and the Internal Point of View*. London: Palgrave MacMillan, 2018.
Compaijen, Rob. "'Ne Quid Nimis': Kierkegaard en de deugd van de matigheid [Kierkegaard and the virtue of temperance]." *Tijdschrift voor Filosofie* 75/3 (2013), 455–85.
Comte-Sponville, André. *A Short Treatise on the Great Virtues*. Translated by Catherine Temerson. London: Vintage, [1996] 2001.

Crisp, Roger. "Rights, Happiness and God: A Response to *Justice: Rights and Wrongs*." *Studies in Christian Ethics* 23/2 (2010), 156–62.

Crisp, Roger and Michael Slote (eds.). *Virtue Ethics*. Oxford: Oxford University Press, 2001.

Daneau, Lambert. *Ethices christianae libri tres*. Geneva: Eustathius Vignon, 1577.

Davenport, John J. "The Meaning of Kierkegaard's Choice between the Aesthetic and the Ethical: A Response to MacIntyre." In John J. Davenport and Anthony Rudd (eds.), *Kierkegaard after MacIntyre: Essays on Freedom, Narrative, and Virtue*. Chicago and La Salle: Open Court, 2001, 75–112.

Davenport, John J. and Anthony Rudd (eds.). *Kierkegaard after MacIntyre: Essays on Freedom, Narrative, and Virtue*. Chicago and La Salle: Open Court, 2001.

Deijl, Aarnoud van der, Alida Groeneveld, and Stephan de Jong (eds.). *Doornse levenskunst: Mooi, goed en waarachtig leven* [Art of living from Doorn: Beautiful, good and truthful life]. Utrecht: Kok, 2014.

De Lange, Frits. "Schipperen met het eigen leven: Zelfsturing als normatief ideaal [Giving and taking in one's own life: Self-direction as normative ideal]." In Theo Boer and Angela Roothaan (eds.), *Gegeven: Ethische essays over het leven als gave*. Zoetermeer: Boekencentrum, 2003, 59–77.

De Lange, Frits. "The Modern Life Course and the Ethics of the Art of Living." Guest Lecture University of Western Cape, South-Africa, July 27, 2004, www.fritsdelange.nl.

Der Einzelne und die Kirche: Über Luther und den Protestantismus. Berlin: Wolff, 1934.

Dohmen, Joep. "Aristoteles: De vader van de deugdethiek [Aristotle: The father of virtue ethics]." In Maarten van Buuren and Joep Dohmen, *Van oude en nieuwe deugden: Levenskunst van Aristoteles tot Nussbaum*. Amsterdam: Ambo, 2012, 42–73.

Dohmen, Joep. *Brief aan een middelmatige man: Pleidooi voor een nieuwe publieke moraal* [Letter to an ordinary man: A plea for a new public morality]. Amsterdam: Ambo, 2010.

Dohmen, Joep. "De rol van deugden in een humanistische ethiek [The role of virtues in a humanistic ethics]." *Algemeen Nederlands Tijdschrift voor Wijsbegeerte* 106/2 (2014), 139–44.

Dohmen, Joep. *Het leven als kunstwerk* [Life as a work of art]. Amsterdam: Ambo, 2011.

Dohmen, Joep. "Philosophers on 'the Art-of-Living.'" *Journal of Happiness Studies* 4/4 (2003), 351–71.

Dohmen, Joep. *Tegen de onverschilligheid: Pleidooi voor een moderne levenskunst* [Against indifference: A plea for a modern art of living]. Amsterdam: Ambo, 2007.

Dohmen, Joep and Frits de Lange. *Moderne levens lopen niet vanzelf* [Modern lives are not lived as a matter of course]. Amsterdam: SWP, 2006.

Dooyeweerd, Herman. *A New Critique of Theoretical Thought*, 4 vols. Translated by D. H. Freeman and W. S. Young. Amsterdam and Philadelphia: Paris/ The Presbyterian and Reformed Publishing Company, 1953–1958.

Douma, Jochem. *Grondslagen* [Foundations], Christelijke ethiek, Vol. 1. Kok: Kampen, 1999.

Epicurus. *Letter to Menoikos*. Translated by Peter Saint-Andre. http://monadnock.net/epicurus/letter.html, 2011.

Evans, C. Stephen. *Kierkegaard's Ethic of Love: Divine Commands and Moral Obligations*. Oxford: Oxford University Press, 2004.

Ferrara, Alessandro. *The Force of the Example: Explorations in the Paradigm of Judgement*. New York: Columbia University Press, 2006.

Foucault, Michel. *Breekbare vrijheid: Teksten en interviews* [Fragile freedom: Texts and interviews]. Amsterdam: Boom/Parrèsia, 1995.
Foucault, Michel. *Le souci du soi*. Paris: Gallimard, 1984.
Foucault, Michel. "L'étique du souci de soi comme pratique de liberté." Interview by Raúl Fornet-Betancourt, Helmut Becker and Alfredo Gomez-Müller (January 20, 1984). Translated in Michel Foucault, *Breekbare vrijheid: Teksten en interviews* [Fragile freedom: Texts and interviews]. Amsterdam: Boom/Parrèsia, 1995, 169-207.
Foucault, Michel. "On the Genealogy of Ethics: An Overview of Work in Progress." In Paul Rabinow (ed.), *The Foucault Reader: An Introduction to Foucault's Thought*. London: Penguin Books, 1991, 340-72.
Foucault, Michel. *The Care of the Self, The History of Sexuality*, Vol. 3. London: Penguin Books, [1984] 1990.
Frede, Dorothea. "The Historic Decline of Virtue Ethics." In Daniel C. Russell (ed.), *The Cambridge Companion to Virtue Ethics*. Cambridge: Cambridge University Press, 2013, 124-48.
Gibbs, Lee W. "The Puritan Natural Law Theory of William Ames." *Harvard Theological Review* 64 (1971), 37-57.
Gouwens, David J. *Kierkegaard as Religious Thinker*. Cambridge: Cambridge University Press, 1996.
Grabill, Stephen J. *Rediscovering the Natural Law in Reformed Theological Ethics*. Grand Rapids: Eerdmans, 2006.
Gregory, Brad. *The Unintended Reformation: How a Religious Revolution Secularized Society*. Cambridge and London: Belknap Press of Harvard University Press, 2012.
Gregory, Eric. *Politics and the Order of Love: An Augustinian Ethic of Democratic Citizenship*. Chicago: University of Chicago Press, 2008.
Gustafson, James. *Christ and the Moral Life*. Louisville: John Knox, [1968] 2009.
Haas, Guenther H. "Calvin's Ethics." In Donald K. McKim (ed.), *The Cambridge Companion to John Calvin*. Cambridge: Cambridge University Press, 2004, 93-105.
Hadot, Pierre. *Exercices spirituels et philosophie antique*. Paris: Études Augustiniennes, 1981.
Hadot, Pierre. *Philosophy as a Way of Life: Spiritual Exercises from Socrates to Foucault*. Oxford: Blackwell Publishers, 1995.
Hardy, Lee. *The Fabric of This World: Inquiries into Calling, Career Choice, and the Design of Human Work*. Grand Rapids: Eerdmans, 1990.
Hauerwas, Stanley. *A Community of Character: Toward a Constructive Christian Social Ethic*. Notre Dame: University of Notre Dame Press, 1981.
Hauerwas, Stanley. "Bearing Reality: A Christian Meditation." *Journal of the Society of Christian Ethics* 33/1 (2013), 3-20.
Hauerwas, Stanley. *Character and the Christian Life: A Study in Theological Ethics*. San Antonio: Trinity University Press, 1975.
Hauerwas, Stanley. *Dispatches from the Front: Theological Engagements with the Secular*. Durham: Duke University Press, 1994.
Hauerwas, Stanley. "How 'Christian Ethics' Came to Be." In John Berkman and Michael Cartwright (eds.), *The Hauerwas Reader*. Durham: Duke University Press, 2001, 37-50.
Hauerwas, Stanley. *Moral Character as a Problem for Theological Ethics*. New Haven: Yale University Press, 1968.
Hauerwas, Stanley. *The Peaceable Kingdom: A Primer in Christian Ethics*. Notre Dame: University of Notre Dame Press, [1983] 1986.

Hauerwas, Stanley and Charles Pinches. *Christians among the Virtues: Theological Conversations with Ancient and Modern Ethics*. Notre Dame: University of Notre Dame Press, [1997] 2009.

Helm, Paul. "Nature and Grace." In Manfred Svensson and David VanDrunen (eds.), *Aquinas among the Protestants*. Oxford: Wiley Blackwell, 2018, 229–48.

Herdt, Jennifer A. *Putting on Virtue: The Legacy of the Splendid Vices*. Chicago: The University of Chicago Press, 2008.

Herms, Eilert. "Virtue: A Neglected Concept in Protestant Ethics." In Eilert Herms, *Offenbarung und Glaube: Zur Bildung des christlichen Lebens*. Tübingen: Mohr, 1992, 124–37.

Hesselink, John. *Calvin's Concept of the Law*. Allison Park: Pickwick, 1992.

Hofheinz, Marco. *Ethik – reformiert! Studien zur reformierten Reformation und ihrer Rezeption im 20. Jahrhundert*. Göttingen: Vandenhoeck & Ruprecht, 2017.

Hollenbach, David. *The Common Good and Christian Ethics*. Cambridge: Cambridge University Press, 2002.

Horner, David and David Turner. "Zeal." In Michael W. Austin and R. Douglas Geivett (eds.), *Being Good: Christian Virtues for Everyday Life*. Grand Rapids: Eerdmans, 2012, 72–103.

Jochemsen, Henk and Gerrit Glas. *Verantwoord medisch handelen: Proeve van een christelijke medische ethiek* [Accountable medical practice: An account of Christian medical ethics]. Amsterdam: Buijten & Schipperheijn, 1997.

Jochemsen, Henk and Johan Hegeman. "Connecting Christian Faith and Professional Practice in a Pluralistic Society." In Bram de Muynck, Johan Hegeman, and Pieter Vos (eds.), *Bridging the Gap: Connecting Christian Faith and Professional Practice in a Pluralistic Society*. Sioux Center: Dordt College Press, 2011, 73–85.

Joest, Wilfried. *Gesetz und Freiheit: Das Problem des tertius usus legis bei Luther und die neutestamentische Parainese*. Göttingen: Vandenhoeck & Ruprecht, [1951] 1968.

Keckermann, Bartholomaeus. *Opera omnia*. Geneva: Aubert, 1614.

Keckermann, Bartholomaeus. *Systema ethicae tribus libris adornatum et publicis praelectionibus traditum in gymnasio Dantiscano*. Hanau: Antonius, 1607.

Kekes, John. *Moral Wisdom and Good Lives*. Ithaca and London: Cornell University Press, 1995.

Kekes, John. *The Art of Life*. Ithaca and London: Cornell University Press, 2002.

Kierkegaard, Søren. *Christian Discourses*. Edited and translated by Howard V. Hong and Edna H. Hong. Princeton: Princeton University Press, 1997.

Kierkegaard, Søren. *Concluding Unscientific Postscript*. Edited and translated by Howard V. Hong and Edna H. Hong. Princeton: Princeton University Press, 1992.

Kierkegaard, Søren. *Eighteen Upbuilding Discourses*. Edited and translated by Howard V. Hong and Edna H. Hong. Princeton: Princeton University Press, 1990.

Kierkegaard, Søren. *Either/Or II*. Edited and translated by Howard V. Hong and Edna H. Hong. Princeton: Princeton University Press, 1987.

Kierkegaard, Søren. *Journals and Papers*, Vol. 2. Bloomington: Indiana University Press, 1967.

Kierkegaard, Søren. *Philosophical Fragments*. Edited and translated by Howard V. Hong and Edna H. Hong. Princeton: Princeton University Press, 1985.

Kierkegaard, Søren. *Practice in Christianity*. Edited and translated by Howard V. Hong and Edna H. Hong. Princeton: Princeton University Press, 1991.

Kierkegaard, Søren. *The Book on Adler*. Edited and translated by Howard V. Hong and Edna H. Hong. Princeton: Princeton University Press, 1998.

Kierkegaard, Søren. *The Sickness unto Death*. Edited and translated by Howard V. Hong and Edna H. Hong. Princeton: Princeton University Press, 1980.
Kierkegaard, Søren. *Three Discourses on Imagined Occasions*. Edited and translated by Howard V. Hong and Edna H. Hong. Princeton: Princeton University Press, 1993.
Kierkegaard, Søren. *Two Ages*. Edited and translated by Howard V. Hong and Edna H. Hong. Princeton: Princeton University Press, 1978.
Kierkegaard, Søren. *Upbuilding Discourses in Various Spirits*. Edited and translated by Howard V. Hong and Edna H. Hong. Princeton: Princeton University Press, 1993.
Kierkegaard, Søren. *Works of Love*. Edited and translated by Howard V. Hong and Edna H. Hong. Princeton: Princeton University Press, 1995.
Kim, David Yoon-Jung. "Kierkegaard and the Question of the Law's Third Use." In Jon Stewart (ed.), *Kierkegaard and the Renaissance and Modern Traditions* (Kierkegaard Research: Sources, Reception and Resources 5.2). Farnham: Ashgate, 2009, 81–110.
Kinneging, Andreas. *Geografie van goed en kwaad: Filosofische Essays* [Geography of good and evil: Philosophical essays]. Utrecht: Spectrum, 2005.
Kirmmse, Bruce. "Possibilities for Dialogue." In John J. Davenport and Anthony Rudd (eds.), *Kierkegaard after MacIntyre: Essays on Freedom, Narrative, and Virtue*. Chicago and La Salle: Open Court, 2001, 191–210.
Kleinberg, Aviad. *Flesh Made Word: Saints' Stories and the Western Imagination*. Cambridge: Belknap Press, 2008.
Kuyper, Abraham. *Het sociale vraagstuk en de christelijke religie* [The social question and Christian religion]. Amsterdam: Wormer, 1891.
Kuyper, Abraham. *Lectures on Calvinism*. Grand Rapids: Eerdmans, [1898] 1931.
Langan, John P. "Augustine on the Unity and the Interconnection of the Virtues." *Harvard Theological Review* 72/1-2 (1979), 81–95.
Lillegard, Norman. "Thinking with Kierkegaard and MacIntyre about the Aesthetic, Virtue, and Narrative." In John J. Davenport and Anthony Rudd (eds.), *Kierkegaard after MacIntyre: Essays on Freedom, Narrative, and Virtue*. Chicago and La Salle: Open Court, 2001, 211–32.
Luther, Martin. "Large Catechism." In T. G. Tappert (ed.), *The Book of Concord*. Philadelphia: Fortress Press, 1959, 357–462.
Luther, Martin. *Studienausgabe*, Vol. 1. Berlin: Evangelische Verlangsanstalt, 1979.
Lyons, John D. *Exemplum: The Rhetoric of Example in Early Modern France and Italy*. Princeton: Princeton University Press, 1989.
Løkke, Håvard. "*Nicomachean Ethics*: Ignorance and Relationships." In Jon Stewart and Katalin Nun (eds.), *Kierkegaard and the Greek World: Aristotle and Other Greek Authors* (Kierkegaard Research: Sources, Reception and Resources 2.2). Farnham and Burlington: Ashgate, 2008, 46–58.
MacIntyre, Alasdair. *After Virtue: A Study in Moral Theory* (Third edition). Notre Dame: University of Notre Dame Press, [1981] 2007.
MacIntyre, Alasdair. *A Short History of Ethics: A History of Moral Philosophy from the Homeric Age to the Twentieth Century*. London: Routledge, 1974.
MacIntyre, Alasdair. *Ethics in Conflicts of Modernity: An Essay on Desire, Practical Reason, and Narrative*. Cambridge: Cambridge University Press, 2016.
MacIntyre, Alasdair. "Once More on Kierkegaard." In John J. Davenport and Anthony Rudd (eds.), *Kierkegaard after MacIntyre: Essays on Freedom, Narrative, and Virtue*. Chicago and La Salle: Open Court, 2001, 339–55.
MacIntyre, Alasdair. *Three Rival Versions of Moral Inquiry: Encyclopaedia, Genealogy, and Tradition*. Notre Dame: University of Notre Dame Press, 1990.

MacIntyre, Alasdair. *Whose Justice? Which Rationality?* Notre Dame: University of Notre Dame Press, 1988.

Mannermaa, Tuomo. *Christ Present in Faith: Luther's View of Justification.* Edited by Kirsi Stjerna. Minneapolis: Fortress, 2005.

Mannermaa, Tuomo. "Justification and *Theosis* in Lutheran-Orthodox Perspective." In Carl E. Braaten and Robert W. Jenson (eds.), *Union with Christ: The New Finnish Interpretation of Luther.* Grand Rapids: Eerdmans, 1998, 25–41.

Marino, Gordon D. "The Place of Reason in Kierkegaard's Ethics." In John J. Davenport and Anthony Rudd (eds.), *Kierkegaard after MacIntyre: Essays on Freedom, Narrative, and Virtue.* Chicago and La Salle: Open Court, 2001, 113–28.

Mehl, Peter J. "Kierkegaard and the Relativist Challenge to Practical Philosophy (with a New Postscript)." In John J. Davenport and Anthony Rudd (eds.), *Kierkegaard after MacIntyre: Essays on Freedom, Narrative, and Virtue.* Chicago and La Salle: Open Court, 2001, 2–38.

Meilaender, Gilbert C. "The Place of Ethics in the Theological Task." *Currents in Theology and Mission* 6 (1979), 190–205.

Meilaender, Gilbert C. *The Theory and Practice of Virtue.* Notre Dame: University of Notre Dame Press, 1984.

Melanchthon, Philipp. *The Elements of Ethical Doctrine: Book 1, Selections.* In Jill Kraye (ed.), *Cambridge Translations of Renaissance Philosophical Texts, Vol. 1: Moral Philosophy.* Cambridge: Cambridge University Press, 1997, 109–19.

Miller, Christian B. *The Character Gap: How Good Are We?* New York: Oxford University Press, 2017.

Miller, Christian B. "The Mixed Trait Model of Character Traits and the Moral Domains of Resource Distribution and Theft." In Christian B. Miller, R. Michael Furr, Angela Knobel, and William Fleeson (eds.), *Character: New Directions from Philosophy, Psychology, and Theology.* Oxford: Oxford University Press, 2015, 164–91.

Mooney, Edward F. "The Perils of Polarity: Kierkegaard and MacIntyre in Search of Moral Truth." In John J. Davenport and Anthony Rudd (eds.), *Kierkegaard after MacIntyre: Essays on Freedom, Narrative, and Virtue.* Chicago and La Salle: Open Court, 2001, 233–64.

Mouw, Richard J. *The God Who Commands: A Study in Divine Command Ethics.* Notre Dame: University of Notre Dame Press, 1990.

Muller, Richard A. *Post-Reformation Reformed Dogmatics*, 4 vols. Grand Rapids: Baker, 2003.

Muller, Richard A. "Reformation, Orthodoxy, 'Christian Aristotelianism,' and the Eclecticism of Early Modern Philosophy." *Nederlands archief voor kerkgeschiedenis / Dutch Review of Church History* 81/3 (2001), 306–25.

Murphy, Nancy, Brad J. Kallenberg, and Mark Thiessen Nation (eds.). *Virtues and Practices in the Christian Tradition: Christian Ethics after MacIntyre.* Notre Dame: University of Notre Dame Press, 1997.

Nietzsche, Friedrich. *Die fröhliche Wissenschaft.* In Friedrich Nietzsche, *Kritische Studienausgabe*, Bd. 3.2. Edited by Giorgio Colli and Mazzino Montinari. München: De Gruyter, 1999, 343–651.

Nolan, Kirk J. *Reformed Virtue after Barth: Developing Moral Virtue Ethics within the Reformed Theological Tradition.* Louisville: Westminster John Knox Press, 2014.

Nussbaum, Martha. *The Fragility of Goodness: Luck and Ethics in Greek Tragedy and Philosophy.* Cambridge: Cambridge University Press, 1986.

O'Donovan, Oliver. *Finding and Seeking, Ethics as Theology*, Vol. 2. Grand Rapids and Cambridge: Eerdmans, 2014.
O'Donovan, Oliver. *The Problem of Self-Love in St. Augustine*. New Haven: Yale University Press, 1980.
Outka, Gene. "Following at a Distance: Ethics and the Identity of Jesus." In Garrett Green (ed.), *Scriptural Authority and Narrative Interpretation*. Philadelphia: Fortress Press, 1987, 144–60.
Peura, Simo. "Christ as Favor and Gift." In Carl E. Braaten and Robert W. Jenson (eds.), *Union with Christ: The New Finnish Interpretation of Luther*. Grand Rapids: Eerdmans, 1998, 42–69.
Peura, Simo. "What God Gives Man Receives: Luther on Salvation." In Carl E. Braaten and Robert W. Jenson (eds.), *Union with Christ: The New Finnish Interpretation of Luther*. Grand Rapids: Eerdmans, 1998, 76–95.
Pinckaers, Servais. *The Sources of Christian Ethics*. Translated by Mary Thomas Noble. Edinburgh: T&T Clark, 1995.
Pinsent, Andrew. "Humility." In Michael Austin and R. Douglas Geivett (eds.), *Being Good: Christian Virtues for Everyday Life*. Grand Rapids: Eerdmans, 2012, 242–64.
Plato. *Laches, Protagoras, Meno, Euthydemus* (Loeb Classical Library 165). Translated by Jeffrey Henderson. Cambridge: Harvard University Press, 1924.
Plato. *Republic*, Vol. I: Books 1–5 (Loeb Classical Library 237). Edited and translated by Christopher Emlyn-Jones and William Preddy. Cambridge: Harvard University Press, 2013.
Porter, Jean. "Virtue and Sin: The Connection of the Virtues and the Case of the Flawed Saint." *The Journal of Religion* 75/4 (1995), 521–39.
Porter, Jean. "Virtue Ethics." In Robin Gill (ed.), *The Cambridge Companion to Christian Ethics*. Cambridge: Cambridge University Press, 2001, 96–111.
Porter, Jean. "Virtue Ethics in the Medieval Period." In Daniel C. Russell (ed.), *The Cambridge Companion to Virtue Ethics*. Cambridge: Cambridge University Press, 2013, 70–91.
Quartel, Jochem and Jan Hoogland. *Levenskunst voor iedereen* [The art of living for everyone]. Utrecht: Kok, 2014.
Ramsey, Paul. "A Theory of Virtue According to the Principles of the Reformation." *The Journal of Religion* 27/3 (1947), 178–96.
Ramsey, Paul. *Basic Christian Ethics*. Louisville: John Knox Press, [1950] 1993.
Roberts, Robert C. "Existence, Emotion, and Virtue: Classical Themes in Kierkegaard." In Alastair Hannay and Gordon D. Marino (eds.), *The Cambridge Companion to Kierkegaard*. Cambridge: Cambridge University Press, 1998, 177–206.
Roberts, Robert C. "Kierkegaard, Wittgenstein, and a Method of 'Virtue Ethics.'" In Martin J. Matuštík and Merold Westphal (eds.), *Kierkegaard in Post/Modernity*. Bloomington/Indianapolis: Indiana University Press, 1995, 142–66.
Rothuizen, Gerard Th. *Primus usus legis: Studie over het burgerlijk gebruik van de wet* [Primus usus legis: Study of the civil use of the law]. Kampen: Kok, 1962.
Rudd, Anthony. "Reason in Ethics: MacIntyre and Kierkegaard." In John J. Davenport and Anthony Rudd (eds.), *Kierkegaard after MacIntyre: Essays on Freedom, Narrative, and Virtue*. Chicago and La Salle: Open Court, 2001, 131–50.
Russell, Daniel C. (ed.). *The Cambridge Companion to Virtue Ethics*. Cambridge: Cambridge University Press, 2013.
Sanderse, Wouter. "The Meaning of Role Modelling in Moral and Character Education." *Journal of Moral Education* 42/1 (2013), 28–42.

Sawyer, Frank. "Some Transformational Aspects in John Calvin's Thought and Influence." In Bram de Muynck, Johan Hegeman, and Pieter Vos (eds.), *Bridging the Gap: Connecting Christian Faith and Professional Practice*. Sioux Center: Dordt College Press, 2011, 203–16.

Sayer, Andrew. *Why Things Matter to People: Social Science, Values and Ethical Life*. Cambridge: Cambridge University Press, 2011.

Scheible, Heinz. "Aristoteles und die Wittenberger Universitätsreform: Zum Quellenwert von Lutherbriefen." In Michael Bayer and Günther Wartenberg (eds.), *Humanismus und Wittenberger Reformation* (Fs. Helmar Junghans). Leipzig: Evangelische Verlagsanstalt, 1997, 125–51.

Scheler, Max. *Zur Rehabilitierung der Tugend*. In Max Scheler, *Abhandlungen und Aufsätze*, 2 Bdn. Leipzig: Verlag der weissen Bücher, 1915, Bd. 1, 1–38.

Schmid, Wilhelm. *Die Liebe neu erfinden: Von der Lebenskunst im Umgang mit Anderen*. Berlin: Suhrkamp, 2010.

Schmid, Wilhelm. *Filosofie van de levenskunst: Inleiding in het mooie leven* [Philosophy of the art of living: Introduction to the beautiful life]. Translated by Carola Kloos. Amsterdam: Ambo, 2001.

Schmid, Wilhelm. *Philosophie der Lebenskunst*. Frankfurt: Suhrkamp, 1998.

Schmid, Wilhelm. *Schönes Leben*. Frankfurt: Suhrkamp, 2000.

Schuurman, Douglas J. *Vocation: Discerning Our Callings in Life*. Grand Rapids: Eerdmans, 2004.

Sill, Bernhard and Peter Bubmann. *Schritte durch die Lebensmitte: Facetten christlicher Lebenskunst*. München: Gütersloher Verlagshaus, 2013.

Sinnema, Donald. "Aristotle and Early Reformed Orthodoxy: Moments of Accommodation and Antithesis." In Wendy Helleman (ed.), *Christianity and the Classics*. Lanham: University Press of America, 1990, 123–8.

Sinnema, Donald. "The Discipline of Ethics in Early Reformed Orthodoxy." *Calvin Theological Journal* 28/1 (1993), 10–44.

Smidt, Jochen. "Critical Virtue Ethics." *Religious Inquiries* 3/5 (2014), 35–47.

Speenivasan, Gobal. "The Situationist Critique of Virtue Ethics." In Daniel C. Russell (ed.), *The Cambridge Companion to Virtue Ethics*. Cambridge: Cambridge University Press, 2013, 290–314.

Stackhouse, Max. "Vocation." In Gilbert Meilaender and William Werpehowski (eds.), *The Oxford Handbook of Theological Ethics*. Oxford: Oxford University Press, 2005, 189–204.

Stout, Jeffrey. *Democracy and Tradition*. Princeton: Princeton University Press, 2004.

Strohm, Christoph. *Ethik im frühen Calvinismus: Humanistische Einflüsse, philosophische, juridische und theologische Argumentationen sowie mentalitätsgeschichtlichen Aspekte am Beispiel des Calvin-Schülers Lambertus Danaeus*. Berlin: De Gruyter, 1996.

Svensson, Manfred. "Aristotelian Practical Philosophy from Melanchthon to Eisenhart: Protestant Commentaries on the Nicomachean Ethics 1529–1682." *Reformation and Renaissance Review* 21/3 (2019), 218–38.

Svensson, Manfred and David VanDrunen (eds.). *Aquinas among the Protestants*. Oxford: Wiley Blackwell, 2018.

Swanton, Christine. "The Definition of Virtue Ethics." In Daniel C. Russell (ed.), *The Cambridge Companion to Virtue Ethics*. Cambridge: Cambridge University Press, 2013, 315–38.

Taylor, Charles. *A Secular Age*. Cambridge: Belknap Press of Harvard University Press, 2007.

Taylor, Charles. *Sources of the Self: The Making of the Modern Identity*. Cambridge: Harvard University Press, [1989] 2000.
Triglot Concordia: The Symbolical Books of the Evangelical Lutheran Church: German-Latin-English. St. Louis: Concordia Publishing House, 1921.
Troeltsch, Ernst. *The Social Teachings of the Christian Churches*. New York: Harper, 1932.
Van Asselt, Willem J., T. Theo J. Pleizier, Pieter L. Rouwendal, and Maarten Wisse. *Introduction to Reformed Scholasticism*. Translated by Albert Gootjes. Grand Rapids: Reformation Heritage Books, 2011.
Van den Bersselaar, Victor. *Bestaansethiek: Normatieve professionalisering en de ethiek van identiteits-, levens- en zingevingsvragen* [Existential ethics: Normative professionalisation and the ethics of questions of identity, life and meaning]. Amsterdam: SWP, 2009.
VanDrunen, David. *Natural Law and the Two Kingdoms: A Study in the Development of Reformed Social Thought*. Grand Rapids: Eerdmans, 2010.
Van Tongeren, Paul. *Deugdelijk leven: Een inleiding in de deugdethiek* [Virtuous life: An introduction to virtue ethics]. Amsterdam: Sun, [2003] 2004.
Van Tongeren, Paul. *Leven is een kunst: Over morele ervaring, deugdethiek en levenskunst*. Zoetermeer: Klement/Pelckmans, 2012. Translated in *The Art of Living Well: Moral Experience and Virtue Ethics*. London: Bloomsbury, forthcoming.
Van Wensveen, Louke and Harm Dane (eds.). *Zuinigheid met vlijt: Over calvinistische (on)deugden* [Frugality and diligence: On Calvinistic virtues/vices]. Zoetermeer: Boekencentrum, 2009.
Vermigli, Peter Martyr. *Commentary on Aristotle's Nicomachean Ethics* (The Peter Martyr Vermigli Library 9). Edited by Emidio Campi and Joseph C. McLelland. Kirksville: Truman State University Press, 2006.
Vermigli, Peter Martyr. *In primum, secundum, et initium tertii libri ethicorum Aristotelis ad Nicomachum commentarius*. Zurich: Froschauer, 1563.
Vos, Pieter. "Calvinists among the Virtues: Reformed Theological Contributions to Contemporary Virtue Ethics." *Studies in Christian Ethics* 28/2 (2015), 201–12.
Vos, Pieter. "Celebrating God's Works: The Day of Worship and the Ethics of Work." In Pieter Vos (ed.), *Liturgy and Ethics: New Contributions from Reformed Perspectives*. Leiden and Boston: Brill, 2018, 246–65.
Vos, Pieter. "Self." In Steven Emmanuel, William McDonald, and Jon Stewart (eds.), *Kierkegaard's Concepts* (Kierkegaard Research: Sources, Reception, and Resources 15.6). Aldershot: Ashgate, 2015, 23–8.
Vos, Pieter. "Setting Free and Bringing to Purpose: The Work of the Spirit in Cultivating the Virtues." In Gijsbert van den Brink, Eveline van Staalduine-Sulman, and Maarten Wisse (eds.), *The Spirit Is Moving: New Pathways in Pneumatology*. Leiden and Boston: Brill, 2019, 293–306.
Vos, Pieter. "The Irreducibility of Religious Faith: Kierkegaard on Civilization and the Aqedah." In Pieter Vos and Onno Zijlstra (eds.), *The Law of God: Exploring God and Civilization*. Leiden and Boston: Brill, 2014, 194–214.
Walaeus, Antonius. *A Compendium of Aristotelian Ethics Accommodated to the Standard of Christian Truth: Selections*. In Jill Kraye (ed.), *Cambridge Translations of Renaissance Philosophical Texts, Vol. 1: Moral Philosophy*. Cambridge: Cambridge University Press 1997, 121–9.
Walaeus, Antonius. *Compendium ethicae Aristotelicae ad normam veritatis christianae revocatum*. Leiden: Elzevir, 1620.

Walker, Lawrence J. "Moral Exemplarity." In William Damon (ed.), *Bringing in a New Era in Character Education*. Stanford: Hoover Institution Press, 2002, 65–84.

Walker, Lawrence J., Russell C. Pitts, Karl H. Hennig, and M. Kyle Matsuba. "Reasoning about Morality and Real-Life Moral Problems." In Melanie Killen and Daniel Hart (eds.), *Morality in Everyday Life: Developmental Perspectives*. Cambridge: Cambridge University Press, 1995, 371–407.

Walsh, Sylvia. *Kierkegaard and Religion: Personality, Character, and Virtue*. Cambridge: Cambridge University Press, 2018.

Wannenwetsch, Bernd. "But to *Do* Right… Why the Language of 'Rights' Does Not Do Justice to Justice." *Studies in Christian Ethics* 23/2 (2010), 138–46.

Wannenwetsch, Bernd. *Political Worship*. Translated by Margaret Kohl. Oxford: Oxford University Press, 2010.

Weber, Max. *The Protestant Ethic and the Spirit of Capitalism*. New York: Charles Scribner's Sons, 1958.

Werpehowski, William. *Karl Barth and Christian Ethics: Living in Truth*. Farnham: Ashgate, 2014.

Westberg, Daniel. "The Influence of Aquinas on Protestant Ethics." In Manfred Svensson and David VanDrunen (eds.), *Aquinas Among the Protestants*. Oxford: Wiley Blackwell, 2018, 267–85.

"Westminster Larger Catechism." In *The Constitution of the Presbyterian Church in the United States of America*. Philadelphia: Office of the General Assembly, 1954, 131–290.

Wetzel, James. *Augustine and the Limits of Virtue*. Cambridge: Cambridge University Press, 1992.

Whiting, Jennifer. "The Nicomachean Account of *Philia*." In Richard Kraut (ed.), *The Blackwell Guide to Aristotle's Nicomachean Ethics*. Malden and Oxford: Blackwell, 2006, 276–304.

Wilson, Stephen A. *Virtue Reformed: Rereading Jonathan Edwards's Ethics*. Leiden: Brill, 2005.

Wisse, Maarten. *Trinitarian Theology beyond Participation: Augustine's* De Trinitate *and Contemporary Theology* (T&T Clark Studies in Systematic Theology 11). London: Bloomsbury, 2011.

Witte, John. *The Reformation of Rights: Law, Religion, and Human Rights in Early Modern Calvinism*. Cambridge: Cambridge University Press, 2007.

Wittgenstein, Ludwig. *Philosophical Investigations*. London: Blackwell, [1953] 2001.

Wolf, Susan. "Moral Saints." *The Journal of Philosophy* 79/8 (1982), 419–39.

Wolterstorff, Nicholas. *Justice: Rights and Wrongs*. Princeton and Oxford: Princeton University Press, 2008.

Wolterstorff, Nicholas. *Justice in Love*. Grand Rapids and Cambridge: Eerdmans, 2011.

Wright, Tom. *Virtue Reborn*. London: Society for Promoting Christian Knowledge, 2010.

Young, Charles M. "Aristotle's Justice." In Richard Kraut (ed.), *The Blackwell Guide to Aristotle's Nicomachean Ethics*. Malden and Oxford: Blackwell, 2006, 179–97.

Zagzebski, Linda. *Exemplarist Moral Theory*. Oxford: Oxford University Press, 2017.

Zorgdrager, Heleen. "Mapping the Christian Character: Calvin and Schleiermacher on Virtue, Law and Sanctification." In Pieter Vos and Onno Zijlstra (eds.), *The Law of God: Exploring God and Civilization*. Leiden and Boston: Brill, 2014, 256–81.

INDEX

admiration 131 n.2, 144, 148
agent centeredness 41, 48–9, 56, 61
Ames, William 95, 100–1, 103–4, 106–8, 165–6
Antiquity 19, 115
  and Christianity 3–5, 32, 119, 166
Aquinas, Thomas 70–3, 86, 122 n. 73
  on pride 167
  and Protestantism 85, 100–1
  on unity of the virtues 155–7
Aristotle 44, 88, 151. *See also* Nicomachean Ethics
  on choice 117
  on common good 26, 46–7
  on community 46–7, 49, 51–2
  on *eudaimonia* 25–6, 28, 43–9, 61, 101–3, 173
  on external goods 16, 44–7, 151
  on God 47–8
  on good life 39, 45–6, 173–4
  on habituation 151
  on justice 49–52
  on *philia* 46–7
  on virtue(s) 77, 104–7, 118, 151, 155, 167
Aristotelian four causes (*causae*) 99, 103, 107
Aristotelianism 56, 88, 110
  medieval 3, 86–8
  Reformed 11, 87–8, 90–1
art of living 4, 19, 22–3, 28, 38
  Christian 20, 29–32, 39
  classical 22–3, 34
  modern 22–4, 30, 38–9
  philosophy of 4, 14–15, 19–28
  and virtue ethics 25–8
arts (*artes*) 90, 92–3
Augustine 15–16, 21, 74
  on common good 5, 56–7, 59
  on eternal life 34–6, 39, 72

  on *eudaimonia* 32–5, 42, 52–8, 61
  on good life 36–7, 42, 54, 61
  on grace 36–7, 60
  on justice 55, 59–60
  on love 52–8, 60–1, 159–60, 166–7
  on Stoa 35–6, 52–3, 56, 158
  on temporality 35–6
  on unity of the virtues 17, 154–5, 157–60
  on virtues 33–4, 36–8, 59, 86, 155
  on will 33–9, 55, 152

Barth, Karl 13, 67–8, 166
beautiful life 23–4, 27, 29
Bible 64, 95, 101, 186 n.55. *See also* Scripture
  Num. 12:3 167
  Ps. 11:5 57
  Ps. 143:2 159
  Eccl. 7:21 159
  Mt. 5:8 60
  Mt. 7:12 71
  Mt. 19:21 140
  Mt. 22:39 145
  Rom. 1:19 68
  Rom. 2:14-15 68, 80
  Rom. 7 152
  Rom. 12:2 67, 175
  Rom. 12:3 105
  Rom. 12:9-18 138
  2 Cor. 8:9 142
  Gal. 2:20 67
  Gal. 5:19-26 136
  Eph. 5:21–6:9 140
  Phil. 2:12 165
  Col. 3:18–4:1 140
  1 Tim. 5:18 176
  Jas 2:10 158–9
  2 Pet. 1:5-6 165
  1 Jn 2:6 139

Bonhoeffer, Dietrich 132, 139, 141–2, 149
breakdown of teleology 9, 63, 65, 83, 177

Calvin, John 8, 92, 128
   on God 66–7, 175
   on grace 70–4, 135, 138, 161
   on imitation of Christ 132, 134, 138–9, 142
   on law 16, 64, 66–7, 69–73, 75, 77, 83
   on moral life 11, 163–4
   on natural law 68–73
   on reason 67, 71–2
   on secular realm 64, 79–80
   on sin 71–3
   on societal life 78–9, 174–5, 178–9
   on virtue(s) 11, 73–7, 83, 135, 178
   on vocation 78, 174
Calvinism 7, 15, 65, 83, 87, 161, 171, 179. *See also* Neo-Calvinism
cardinal virtues 32–4, 37, 51 n.55, 59, 155–6, 165–6
care of the self 4, 19, 21–2, 24, 27
character 17, 37, 114–16, 124, 151, 153–4
   Christian 138, 160, 169, 171
   modern 180, 184–6
choice 23, 25, 28, 31, 64, 110, 117
Christ
   as exemplar/example 131–3, 139, 142, 144–5, 147, 149, 182
   as redeemer 139, 144
commandments 11, 64, 66–7, 75, 77, 108, 180. *See also* Ten Commandments
common good 5, 26, 46, 56–7, 59, 61, 125, 178–9
common grace 71, 73, 100
community 26–7, 49, 51, 59, 80, 161–2
conscience 70. *See also* synteresis
courage 33, 120, 123, 125, 155–6, 158. *See also* fortitude
covenant 66, 79
creational order 80, 174
criterionless choice 9, 16, 109–11
cultivation of virtue(s) 8, 25, 75, 105–7, 120, 138, 171, 183

Daneau, Lambert 93–4, 98–100, 103, 106
Decalogue 66, 69, 93, 97, 99–100, 106, 140. *See also* Ten Commandments
deconstruction 10–11
desire 33, 53, 151–2, 167
desires (*passiones*) 4, 35–6, 53, 104, 136, 153 n.10, 155–6
divine command ethics 7, 67–8, 113 n.18
Dooyeweerd, Herman 80–2, 176

Edwards, Jonathan 12, 106
emulation 131, 147, 181, 186–7, 189
eudaimonia 3, 25–6, 41–9, 51, 55, 60–1, 101–3, 118
   and external goods 28, 44–7
   as gift 47–8
eudaimonism 9–10, 16, 41–4, 48, 51–4, 56, 101–4
Euthyphro-dilemma 66
evil 33–4, 53, 151–2
   good and 71, 96, 99, 108
excellence, excellent 14, 46, 167–8, 186, 190
exemplarity 13–14, 131–3, 144, 149, 172, 177, 185–91
   role and existential exemplarity 187–91
exemplars 17–18, 131–2, 145, 148, 171, 177, 181–91
   exceptional 180–4, 188
   modern 184
   in ordinary life 13–14, 180–1, 183–4, 186
   and particularity 186–7
external goods 43–6, 53, 61, 102

Fall, the/fall into sin 60, 71–2, 96–7, 99, 108
flaws, moral 14, 152, 154, 157, 160, 164–6, 168–9
fortitude 165. *See also* courage
Foucault, Michel 4, 19, 20, 22, 24, 27
frugality 178

gift 47–8, 71, 73, 107, 135–6, 162–3, 167
Golden Rule 71, 100

good life 19, 23, 25, 36–9, 54, 103–4, 173
grace 36–7, 60, 71–3, 99–100, 108, 135, 138, 152, 163
grammar of virtue 2–3, 124–8
Gregory, Brad 9, 63–4, 85–6, 96, 107–8
growth, moral 17, 158, 160–4, 166

habituation 8, 105, 134, 142, 146–8, 151, 163 n.48
Hadot, Pierre 19, 24, 32 n.67
happiness 28, 34, 41, 54–5, 98, 101–3. *See also* eudaimonia
Hauerwas, Stanley 7–8, 47–8, 132, 160–2, 171, 185
Herdt, Jennifer 8, 132–5, 137, 146–7, 163 n.48
highest good 25, 34, 55–9, 101–3
Holy Spirit 67, 105–6, 136, 138
human agency 8, 107, 134–5, 137–8, 146–7
human nature 3, 17, 26, 60, 63, 77, 98–9, 113, 154
humility 143–4, 166–9

image of God (*imago Dei*) 60, 85, 96–7, 99, 108
imitation 132, 181–2, 186–7
imitation of Christ 17, 132–3, 139, 141–9

justice 10, 41–2, 49–52, 57, 59–60, 115
  social justice 15, 172, 176, 179
  as virtue 33, 49–51, 59–60, 105, 155, 165
justification, doctrine of 10, 74, 102, 105, 135, 146–7, 161

Keckermann, Bartholomaeus 94, 97, 102, 104–5
Kierkegaard, Søren 13, 109
  on aesthetic and ethical 111–13
  and Aristotle 110, 116–20
  on character formation 114–15, 124, 127
  on choice 111–12, 114, 117–18
  on human nature 121–2
  on imitation of Christ 132, 141–9, 182
  on self 112–14, 121, 147–9, 189
  on upbuilding/edification 120, 127
  on virtue(s) 118–21, 123–8
King, Martin Luther 152, 157, 160
knowledge of the good 3, 28, 96–101, 126, 152
Kuyper, Abraham 81, 176

law 14–15, 66–7, 71, 79–80, 82–3, 179, 180. *See also* commandments; natural law
  and gospel 7, 86, 91, 96, 162–3
  three uses of 69–70, 73
  and virtue 73–4, 77, 106
law-spheres 15, 80–1
love 60–1, 136
  of God 57–60, 125, 159
  of neighbor 53, 57–9, 71, 104–5, 136, 141–2, 145–6, 178–9
  order of (*ordo amoris*) 104, 125
  of self/self-love 57–8, 61 n.103, 145–6, 159
  as virtue 34 n.73, 75
love commandment 57–8, 70, 106, 145–6
lowliness 143–4, 167
Luther, Martin 8, 64, 90–1
  on Aristotle 90, 119
  on grace 135, 137–8, 162–3
  on imitation of Christ 132, 134, 139–41, 143
  on justification 135–6, 146, 162–3
  on virtue 135 n.18, 136, 137 n.27
  on vocation 174

MacIntyre, Alasdair 6–7, 63–5, 107
  and Aristotle 26–7
  and Kierkegaard 9, 16–17, 109–13, 116, 127
  and modernity 63–5, 179, 185
  on practice 14, 80–2, 188, 190
  on Protestantism 8–9, 16, 63–6, 72–3, 77, 79, 87, 177
magnanimity 50, 123, 148
meekness 125
Melanchthon, Philipp 86, 91–2, 96–7, 101–2, 104, 181
metaphysical biology 26
moderation 76–7
modern ethics 8–9, 63, 65 n.13, 109, 180

modernity 6, 22, 73, 78, 87, 132, 173–4, 185
modern literature 184–6

narrative 22, 65–6, 161–2, 184–6
natural law 59, 68–72, 83, 96–7, 99–100, 108, 135 n.20
Neo-Calvinism 9, 80–2, 171, 176, 190
Neo-Platonism 34 n.73, 56, 58
Nicomachean Ethics 16, 44, 50, 65, 131
  commentaries on 89–94, 97–8, 101–6
  Kierkegaard on 116–19
  Luther on 90–1, 135 n.18
Nietzsche, Friedrich 19, 77, 167
nominalism 41, 70, 88
normative practice 81–2, 190
Nussbaum, Martha 44–6, 50–1

obedience 64, 66–7, 76, 103, 140–1
ordinary life 5, 132–3, 139–41, 172–3
  affirmation of 173–4, 177, 190
  complexity of 183–4, 190
  sanctification of 176–7
  and virtue ethics 13–14, 180

participation in Christ 17, 136–9, 161, 163
patience 76, 123–5, 165
perfection 10, 35 n.77, 106, 121–2, 158, 164
pilgrim(age) 79, 162, 164
Plato 32–3, 117, 154
polis 26–7, 47, 49, 52
practice 14–15, 27, 65, 80–3, 187–91
pride 37, 166–7
prophetic 15, 172, 179, 191
Protestantism 1, 3, 6, 10, 12–13, 85, 131–2, 142–3, 179
Protestant universities 89–95, 107
prudence (practical wisdom) 33, 77, 83, 127, 154–6, 165
Puritanism 12, 89, 175–6, 178
purity of heart 60, 116

Ramsey, Paul 1, 168
Ramus, Peter 92, 94
reason 3, 35–6, 64, 67–8, 71–3, 101, 126–7, 151–2
reconstruction 11, 13

redemption 36, 133, 138, 175
reform 15, 166, 175–6, 179, 190
Reformation 11, 71, 90, 122, 172. *See also* Protestantism
  and Aristotelianism 3–5, 85–89
  and modern ethics 8–9, 64–5, 83, 85
Reformed ethics 87–8, 93–5
Reformed orthodoxy 87. *See also* Reformed scholasticism
Reformed scholasticism 11–12, 87, 89
  and Aristotelianism 88–9
  and *Ethica Nicomachea* 89–94, 97, 102
  on *eudaimonia* 101–4
  on the (highest) good 101–4
  on good life 103–4
  on natural law 96–7, 99–100
  on virtue(s) 104–7
renunciation 5, 76, 145–6
  critique of 20–1, 38–9
rights 9–10, 41, 51–2, 177
role 64, 77–9, 187–90

saints 131–2, 145, 171–2, 181–3
sanctification 8, 160–2, 164, 166
  of all domains 171–2, 175–6, 190
  and justification 71, 105, 138
Scripture 41, 75, 85, 87, 93, 98, 106, 181. *See also* Bible
secular 64, 79–80
self 21–2, 24, 29, 110, 132, 135, 161–2
  becoming oneself 112–14, 121, 129, 147–9
  first and deeper self 112–14, 116
  and other 56–7, 136, 145–6
  un-roled 64, 77–9
self-critique 175–6, 179
self-mastery 22–3, 27–8, 32
self-realization 25, 31, 42, 189
sin 14, 36, 69, 71–3, 100–1, 117, 154, 157, 159
  and grace 134–5, 154, 163
situationism 14, 153
social orders 77–8, 83, 87, 171, 174, 179
stability 116, 154
Stoa, Stoicism 5, 24, 28, 56, 158
  and *eudaimonia* 43
  influence of 28, 76
subjectivity 114, 128–9, 189

synteresis 99–101

Taylor, Charles 4–6, 173, 184
teleology 3, 9, 16, 63–6, 72, 83, 85, 111–13, 127–8
temperance 33, 35, 76, 154–6, 165
Ten Commandments 8, 11, 94, 99. *See also* Decalogue
theological virtues 38–9, 71, 75 n.63, 105, 125
transformation 122–3, 127
  of character 134, 161, 163, 165
  of Christian faith 30–1
  of orders 5–6, 15, 171–5, 179, 190–1

union with Christ 137–9, 161
unity of the virtues 17, 125, 154–60, 165–6, 168

Vermigli, Peter Martyr 11–12, 88, 91, 97–8, 102–3, 105, 164–5
vices 34–5, 106, 152–4, 157, 159–60, 164, 168
virtue, concept of 3, 9–10, 27, 104, 120
  as *habitus* 104–6, 119, 135
  as mean 104–5, 107, 118–19
virtue ethics

Aristotelian-Thomistic 17, 109–11
  contemporary 6, 13, 108, 174, 191
  definition of 2–3, 110–11
  medieval 70, 86–7
  Neo-Aristotelian 15–16, 26–7, 42, 82, 129, 185
  Reformed scholastic 86, 88–89, 95
virtues 104–7
  aquired and infused 71, 105, 156–7
  Christian and societal 8–9
  intellectual 25, 118
  other-centered, other-directed 5, 136, 178
  pagan 74, 98, 100
  Protestant 104–7, 178–9
vocation 78, 173–4, 184
vulnerability 29–31, 35, 45

Walaeus, Antonius 92–3, 98, 103, 105–6
will 33–9, 55, 67, 72, 85–6, 152
Wolterstorff, Nicholas 10, 16, 41, 61
  on Augustine 52–4, 56, 58–9
  on eudaimonism 41–6, 48–9
  on rights 41–3, 48, 51–2

Zagzebski, Linda 131

www.ingramcontent.com/pod-product-compliance
Lightning Source LLC
Chambersburg PA
CBHW072108010526
44111CB00037B/2096